BEYOND
LIBERAL
AND
CONSERVATIVE

BEYOND
LIBERAL
AND
CONSERVATIVE
REASSESSING THE
POLITICAL SPECTRUM

William S. Maddox and Stuart A. Lilie
Foreword by David Boaz

This book was made possible by a grant
from the Scaife Family Charitable Trusts.

CATO
INSTITUTE

Library of Congress Cataloging in Publication Data

Maddox, William S., 1949–
  Beyond liberal and conservative.

    Includes bibliographical references and index.
    1. Political science—United States. 2. Right
and left (Political science) I. Lilie, Stuart A.,
1941–   II. Title.
JA84.U5M374   1984   320.5   84-17027
ISBN 0-932790-47-X

Printed in the United States of America.

CATO INSTITUTE
224 Second Street SE
Washington, D.C. 20003

Contents

Foreword

Pollsters, journalists, and political practitioners seem to have an uncontrollable urge to put every politician and thinker into the liberal box or the conservative box. Increasingly, though, these terms fail to describe many Americans, and our understanding of politics has not caught up with reality. This may be at least partly because our outmoded political language continues to shape our thinking. As George Orwell wrote in "Politics and the English Language," "If thought corrupts language, language can also corrupt thought. A bad usage can spread by tradition and imitation, even among people who should and do know better." There may be no clearer example than the attempt to fit every American into the liberal-conservative straitjacket.

The difficulty of doing this, and the resistance to it by those whose views differ from liberal or conservative orthodoxy, is reflected in the proliferation of such terms as "neoconservative," "neoliberal," "progressive," "social conservative," and "New Right." (Perhaps it is a sign of surrender to label a politician as a "maverick.") All of these terms, however, are just variations on a theme, reflecting only nuances of difference. Surely a country with a political tradition as rich and diverse as our own contains many people whose political views are not adequately described by any of the current terms.

Indeed in the past few years we have seen a number of political figures, movements, and election results that defy traditional liberal-conservative analysis:

- In 1982 the voters of California soundly rejected a proposed gun-control initiative and approved several tax cuts—while simultaneously voting "yes" on a nuclear-freeze initiative.
- After 1968 such leading Democrats as Sen. Henry M. Jackson of Washington and Mayor Richard Daley of Chicago were often referred to as conservative Democrats. Yet they were enthusiastic supporters of the New Deal and subsequent social welfare legislation. Their "conservatism" consisted only of hawkish foreign policy views and a resistance to the lifestyle changes of the 1960s.

- Gov. George Wallace of Alabama was widely regarded as a right-wing presidential candidate in 1968. Yet his candidacy was rejected by most conservative leaders not just for its aura of racism but also for Wallace's reputation as a big-spending governor and his thoroughly interventionist positions on economic issues—such as a 60 percent increase in Social Security benefits, 100 percent parity for farm prices, and public works employment.

- In 1980 independent presidential candidate John Anderson attracted at times the support of as much as 25 percent of the public with his unusual combination of fiscal conservatism, social liberalism, and mildly dovish views on foreign policy. His support actually fell when his views began to seem more conventionally liberal. This decline may have been attributable to other causes, of course, but campaign aide Mark Bisnow in his book *Diary of a Dark Horse* suggests that Anderson lost much of his original support by moving away from his fiscal conservatism.

- Rep. Bill Green (R–N.Y.) and Rep. Ike Skelton (D–Mo.) received identical 50 percent ratings on their 1982 congressional votes from the liberal Americans for Democratic Action. As political analyst Alan Baron points out, though, they actually agreed on only five of nineteen issues, with Green voting liberal on social issues and Skelton voting liberal on economic issues.

- Currently, overwhelming majorities of the American public tell pollsters they support the nuclear freeze and the constitutional amendment to balance the federal budget. Clearly a significant number support both.

What is the common thread in all these phenomena? It is that these election results and political figures cannot be adequately described as liberal or conservative. The early John Anderson, with his fiscal conservatism and social liberalism, would seem the political opposite of George Wallace, with his New Deal economics and hostility to civil liberties and changing lifestyles. But which is the liberal and which the conservative? Or are they both, incongruously, moderates? When voters vote for both a nuclear freeze and tax cuts, are they being liberal or conservative? When California voters in 1978 voted against both a "liberal" anti-smoking initiative and a "conservative" anti-gay initiative, were they being conservative or liberal?

The problem is that our political language is not sufficient to describe political reality. The belief systems of Americans are more complex than the liberal-conservative dichotomy acknowledges. Perhaps the frustration that many Americans have in articulating their political views—the reluctance to describe themselves as either liberal or conservative, the apparently contradictory election and poll results—is a result of the inadequacy of our current political language. Political scientists, pollsters, and journalists offer only two labels to describe the beliefs of millions of Americans.

If these opinion leaders began to recognize the existence of more than two political perspectives in the United States—at least the four-way matrix provided by Professors Maddox and Lilie—our whole way of thinking about politics might change. People would begin to recognize that they have four possibilities to choose from in describing their own views. If the Gallup poll suddenly began asking people to describe themselves as "liberal, conservative, libertarian, or populist," it is likely that at first fewer people would choose "libertarian" or "populist" than actually hold those views, according to Maddox and Lilie. But as these terms gained currency, and their definitions came to be understood, people might come to describe themselves more accurately.

Building a winning coalition might then be seen as a more complex process. Instead of assuming that a moderate Republican would be more successful than a conservative, and a moderate Democrat more attractive than a liberal, because they are closer to the center of the liberal-conservative spectrum, journalists would see that a liberal Democrat and a conservative Republican would likely be fighting for the votes of libertarians and populists. The candidates' selection of issues would then be more complex than if their only goal was to move toward the center of a one-dimensional spectrum.

Given the obvious inadequacy of the terms "liberal" and "conservative," one is driven to ask why political observers continue to use them. Professors Maddox and Lilie offer several possibilities. One is that political scientists and others assume that political "elites" operate along liberal-conservative lines, and thus the dichotomy is relevant for the study of politics. A second possibility is that since the New Deal, divisions over the role of government in the economy have been the defining political issues in the United States and that these divisions fit neatly into the liberal-conservative spectrum. I am inclined toward their third suggestion: The liberal-conservative dichotomy is simple, and it is much easier to divide people into only two categories. Along with this methodological simplicity is a certain inertia. Having long discussed politics in liberal-conservative terms, one may find it easiest to continue in that vein. One hesitates to do further injustice to Thomas Kuhn's much-abused notion of scientific paradigms, but it is arguable that political scientists have constructed a paradigm of political interpretation—the liberal-conservative dichotomy—and are reluctant to give it up despite the evidence that it increasingly distorts our perceptions.

In this book Professors Maddox and Lilie have given us a better understanding of the political beliefs of Americans. The traditional premise of postwar political science is that Americans can be divided into liberals, conservatives, and "confused." The orthodox definition is that a liberal favors government involvement in the economy and protection of civil liberties, while a conservative is opposed to both economic intervention and the expansion of civil liberties. Anyone whose views do not fit those categories is explained away as "confused."

Maddox and Lilie ask a simple question: As there are two dimensions in this approach, each with two basic positions, should we not recognize four possible combinations of positions? Is it not possible to have a consistent political viewpoint that would lead one to both support economic regulation and oppose civil liberties, or vice versa? Indeed, perhaps going beyond Maddox and Lilie, I would argue that the two latter positions—either supporting government intervention in both economic and personal freedoms or opposing both—are more consistent than either the liberal or conservative viewpoint. Yet a person with either such view—designated "populist" and "libertarian" in this book—would have been defined by most political scientists as "confused" or "divided."

Of course it should be acknowledged that even a four-way matrix cannot adequately describe the political views of every American. Nor do the belief systems held by Americans, or described in this matrix, offer the rigor and consistency that political elites would prefer. Intellectual liberals, conservatives, and libertarians (and intellectual populists, if such exist) would certainly find their positions poorly presented in this matrix. The nature of polling, and of mass opinion, obviously requires us to talk about tendencies toward certain positions, not highly articulated ideologies. In addition some major issues—especially foreign and military policy—are left out of the two-dimensional approach. It is especially unfortunate that foreign policy is not integrated into the approach, but the polling data seem to be insufficient and foreign policy issues do not lend themselves to clear ideological divisions. Nevertheless, a two-dimensional approach seems a major advance over the one-dimensional approach.

When Maddox and Lilie went back to reexamine the data provided by the Center for Political Studies, they found, interestingly, that the libertarian and populist categories actually included more Americans in the 1970s than did the liberal and conservative categories. As many as 42 percent of those polled in 1980 would be "divided" in a traditional analysis, but are seen to be more or less consistently libertarian or populist in this study.

Professors Maddox and Lilie are not the only political observers to have noticed the inability of the traditional liberal-conservative dichotomy to adequately describe today's complex politics. In *The Almanac of American Politics 1982*, Michael Barone and Grant Ujifusa offered a similar four-part matrix of political beliefs. "Strictly on the basis of intuition," they suggest that 30 percent of the population can be described as liberal on economic issues and conservative on cultural issues (the Maddox-Lilie populists), and 25 percent may be conservative on economic issues and liberal on cultural issues (libertarians). Barone and Ujifusa seem most unfair to traditional liberals, assigning them only 10 percent of the population, whereas liberals averaged twice that proportion in the 1976 and 1980 calculations of Maddox and Lilie.

In 1982 *The Baron Report*, written by Alan Baron, and *National Journal*, under the direction of public opinion analyst William Schneider, began using a more sophisticated, three-dimensional analysis of members of Congress, recognizing that many members "are not liberal or conservative across the board." They chose about a dozen issues each from economic, social, and foreign policy and rated congressmen as liberal or conservative on each dimension.*A few (though only a few) congressmen had liberal ratings on economics and conservative scores on social issues, or vice versa, thus earning the designation "populist" or "libertarian" in *The Baron Report*.

In the 1983 edition of his *Dynamics of the Party System*, Brookings Institution political scientist James L. Sundquist goes beyond the

*A libertarian would quibble with this study's view of social issues. One could get a "liberal" score on social issues by voting for such interventionist measures as busing, automobile regulation, and food stamps.

two-dimensional, four-category approach of Maddox and Lilie to offer eight possible political viewpoints, based on whether a person is liberal or conservative on three sets of issues:

Issues	Groups							
Domestic economic and role-of-government issues	L	L	L	L	C	C	C	C
Social and moral issues	L	L	C	C	L	L	C	C
Foreign and military issues	L	C	L	C	L	C	L	C

Sundquist places a few political figures in his chart—President Reagan in Group CCC, Vice President Bush perhaps in CLC, Henry Jackson in LLC or LCC, Republican senators Bob Packwood and Lowell Weicker in CLL, and the populist elements of the New Right in LCC. However, he makes little attempt to assess the size of the various groups or their demographic makeup.

Professors Maddox and Lilie have provided the most comprehensive analysis of the demographics of ideological diversity in America. In chapter IV they look at the distribution of Americans among the four ideological categories—liberal, conservative, libertarian, and populist—over the past 30 years. Although the data are somewhat unreliable for the 1950s and 1960s, the figures for 1972, 1976, and 1980—when almost identical survey questions were asked— offer a fascinating new dimension to our understanding of current politics. The demographic analysis in chapter V adds to the picture with some decided differences between the ideological groups in age, education, and socioeconomic status. Chapter VI examines the voting behavior, ideological self-classifications, and attitude toward government of the four groups.

Some of the most interesting aspects of the entire Maddox-Lilie analysis can be seen in table 14 on voting behavior of ideological types. After nonvoters (overrepresented in 1980 among populists and, to a lesser extent, among liberals) are subtracted, there is a remarkable equality among the four categories in the voting booth. The 54 percent of all Americans who voted in 1980 can be broken down into 13 percent populists, 12 percent liberals, 12 percent libertarians, and 11 percent conservatives (with 6 percent being "divided" or "inattentive"). Reagan's "majority"—28% of the eligible voters—was largely built on conservatives and on libertarians, who apparently overlooked his views on social issues in their enthusiasm for his economic conservatism. President Carter's support was even more strongly concentrated among liberals and populists. Independent John Anderson and Libertarian Ed Clark drew almost all their support from libertarians and liberals.

What does the Maddox-Lilie analysis say about the future of American politics? Without repeating their own predictions in chapter VIII, let me suggest a few implications. If we assume that generally the Republican party offers a conservative candidate against a liberal Democratic candidate, then there are two large ideological groups whose views are not well represented by either candidate. During the 1970s the libertarians generally voted Republican and the populists Democratic, presumably because of the dominance of economic issues (though the populists apparently could not stomach George McGovern's views on "acid, amnesty, and abortion" and voted for President Nixon in 1972). This presumption is confirmed by the Dearborn study,* which found that economic issues outweighed law-and-order and morality issues for most people. However, should economic issues be superseded in an election year by civil liberties or lifestyle issues—during a long period of prosperity, perhaps, or if both major parties offered similar economic prescriptions, or if a major civil liberties issue such as the draft became important—then the libertarians and populists might find their partisan leanings shaken.

One of the most important aspects of this study is generational. Populists (and to a lesser extent conservatives) tend to be heavily concentrated in older generations, whereas libertarians and liberals tend to be younger. Liberals and libertarians particularly dominate the baby boom generation, those born between 1946 and 1964, who now constitute some 40 percent of the voting-age population. Although the baby boomers may never be a majority of the voters, their importance was pointed out several years ago by Democratic pollster Pat Caddell: "We have the largest bloc of people in history that are sitting outside the political process. It is, essentially, the baby boom that is not in the political process. . . . If they were all to enter the political system tomorrow and were willing to dispose one way or another—even the percentages of a 15–20 point differ-

*Frank Whelon Wayman and Ronald R. Stockton, "The Structure and Stability of Political Attitudes: Findings from the 1974–76 Dearborn Panel Study," paper prepared for the annual meeting of the American Political Science Association, 1980.

ential—they would totally turn the political system upside down. . . . He who finally gets these people around a program, the party that does that, will be the majority party for some time." Caddell said that the baby boomers were moderate to conservative on economics but "the liberal cutting edge of society" on cultural and social issues, much as the Maddox-Lilie analysis shows.

Perhaps the first outcroppings of political revolt by the baby boom generation—after the turmoil of the 1960s and the quiescence of the 1970s—came in 1980, when John Anderson displayed a strong appeal on college campuses and among young professionals. One national poll even showed Libertarian Ed Clark getting a remarkable 5 percent among voters in their thirties. Michael Barone has argued that even Eugene McCarthy in 1968 and Jerry Brown in 1976 were offering a program that was more conservative than Democratic orthodoxy on economics and more liberal on social and foreign policy issues. *Washington Post* columnist Mark Shields calls Jerry Brown "Gary Hart's John the Baptist," preparing the way for a candidate who would challenge traditional Democratic liberalism.

Hart's appeal to the "yuppies" (young urban professionals), in the words of some observers, by running to the left and the right of Mondale at the same time, fits this analysis well. Mondale's approach, basically New Deal politics with a few more interest groups added to the coalition, sits well with populist Democrats and many traditional liberals, and is especially popular with older voters. Hart's appeal was not just generational; it offered at least the appearance of ideological differences and appealed to liberals who leaned more toward social issues and to libertarians who liked Hart's attacks on outmoded economic programs and special-interest politics. In this context it is useful to note the large number of Hart voters who told exit pollsters they had voted for Reagan or Anderson in 1980—very likely libertarians in the Maddox-Lilie analysis.

Lee Atwater, deputy director of the Reagan-Bush '84 committee, thinks the baby boom generation—which he sees as "anti–establishment, anti–big government, anti–big institution and anti–big labor"—will have a major impact on the 1984 election. He believes the Reagan coalition of 1980 was a combination of conservatives and populists (though Maddox and Lilie's table 14 suggests that even then Reagan drew more support from libertarians than populists). In 1984, however, Atwater believes that the growing strength of baby boomers will mean that President Reagan must combine his conservative base with libertarian support. This means high-lighting the administration's economic policies and playing down its views on social issues. Reagan must "maintain the fact, as he always has, that he is tolerant," Atwater says.

Is the social liberalism of the baby boom generation a transitory phase? Will the baby boomers—or the yuppies—change their political views as they get older? It is often thought that people get more conservative as they age, especially on lifestyle issues. In general, though, I think that will not be the case here. The 1960s marked a watershed in Americans' thinking about moral and lifestyle issues; those who matured during or after that period are not likely to revert to pre-1960s thinking. As baby boom demographer Landon Y. Jones put it, citing Karl Mannheim, "The crucial question to ask regarding a person's politics—or a generation's—is not how old the person is but when the person was young."

What, then, is the final message of *Beyond Liberal and Conservative*? It is that American ideologies are too complex to be forced into the Procrustean bed of the liberal-conservative dichotomy, that a four-way analysis of ideologies can explain many aspects of current politics, that politicians will have to take into account this more complex ideological makeup in building their coalitions. Perhaps its most important message, though, is a challenge to political observers—to pollsters, journalists, political scientists, and others who analyze politics. These opinion molders have clung to the liberal-conservative dichotomy after it has long since ceased to explain. They have a responsibility to acknowledge that many Americans are not confused or inconsistent in their political views, but that they have a consistent viewpoint that orthodox analysis is not adequate to describe.

Professors Maddox and Lilie have laid down a foundation for further research and study. Political scientists will want to investigate whether the Maddox-Lilie four-way matrix of ideologies holds up in other studies and for different groups of people. Pollsters should begin to offer people the four ideological definitions and ask them to describe themselves as liberal, conservative, libertarian, or populist. Journalists will find the analysis useful in explaining why two "moderate" congressmen may disagree on almost everything, or why it seems likely that President Reagan won the 1980 election on the strength of his economic views and not his social policies—and why he will definitely have to win reelection that way.

The political world is a complex place; this book will make it a little more understandable.

DAVID D. BOAZ
Vice President
Cato Institute

Acknowledgments

The writing of a book, unlike the writing of shorter pieces, has required that we summon all of the resources, intellectual and otherwise, we have acquired over the years. Acknowledging the people who have contributed to the development of those resources is a difficult task, both because there are so many individuals and because many of them have contributed to our professional development and intellectual curiosity in very subtle ways. Those who have helped us both over the years will probably recognize the fruits of their efforts throughout this book, and we extend our appreciation to them.

Similarly professors cannot teach hundreds of students each year without incurring some debts to those who, by their reactions to lectures, questions raised, or involvement in informal conversations, stimulate the teachers' own interest. Indeed the enthusiastic response from students to whom we presented some of the ideas of this book has been a major reason we believed we had something to say about public opinion and ideology that made sense to others as well as to us.

As for this specific manuscript, we must thank Professor Joyce Lilie of Florida International University for her overall reading and critique of the evolving manuscript, and most especially for her ideas and comments in the discussions of Congress and the political parties. Her time and attention to those sections were invaluable benefits to us. Although she is not to be held responsible for all that we say about Congress and the parties, she does deserve the credit for anything that makes sense in those sections. We also thank the staff of the Cato Institute for their patience with us as we tried to complete this manuscript while maintaining full schedules in the academic world. Particularly, we thank David Boaz, who must have heard the phrase "As soon as this semester is over . . ." far more times than he cares to remember. The patient and speedy typing of the initial drafts by Sheila Call allowed us to see our scribbling turned into something readable and therefore something we could rewrite. Lee Anne Kirkpatrick typed the final manuscript under an end-of-the-year deadline and on short notice, a classy performance to say the least.

Finally, we thank the Inter-University Consortium for Political and Social Research for making available the data used in this book. Neither the original collectors of the data nor the consortium bears any responsibility for the analysis or interpretations presented here.

I. The Roots of Contemporary Ideologies

Almost everyone finds public opinion and ideology in the United States confusing in some way. All too often analysts explain this confusion by concluding that the public itself is confused. It is the central argument of this book that much of this confusion and misunderstanding stems from a simple fact: The liberal-conservative dichotomy (or even a liberal-moderate-conservative continuum) is inadequate to describe and understand the opinions and behavior of the American public.

The public's use of these labels often does appear to be confusing. People claim for themselves one ideological label, but then either express opinions that seem to contradict that label or vote in ways that appear incompatible with that ideological view. When asked by pollsters to define themselves, many call themselves moderate or middle of the road rather than use either label. In many surveys as many as a third of the people have refused to label themselves at all. We are offered two major parties defined as representing liberal and conservative views, and yet many voters complain that American elections present no real choices. Low voter turnout, split-ticket voting, disenchantment with the major political parties, and continuing alienation from politics and its leaders suggest serious problems between the public and its political system.

The class division on which ideological division historically has been based (the liberalism of the New Deal coalition versus Republican conservatism) no longer has the same meaning it once had and does not adequately explain the political behavior of the citizens. A person's economic standing is no longer a simple predictor of his ideology or voting behavior. As our economy changes from an industrial system to a service economy, the usual description of the occupational basis of ideological divisions between liberals and conservatives (blue collar versus white collar) no longer seems very useful. The accompanying increases in levels of educational attainment, mass media exposure to politics, and general affluence suggest that the class-based politics of liberal versus conservative, the "politics as usual" of the past, is not a very good description of what the public is thinking or doing ideologically.

Furthermore political candidates often do not fit neatly into either a liberal or conservative mold, and the term "moderate" does not provide a very clear way to describe them either. Candidates themselves often reject these labels, although rarely do they offer us more informative summaries of their overall point of view. The Democratic party has been ravaged by ideological disputes and seems not quite comfortable with itself whether it nominates traditional liberal candidates or less ideologically defined leaders. The latter can bring victory at the polls, but no sense of mission to the party. Republicans in recent years have avoided the bitter ideological battles that plagued them for much of the postwar period, but the party still includes major segments discontented with the purely conservative definition of the party in the 1980s. In the last decade voters have avoided presidential elections in ever-increasing numbers. Third parties face serious disadvantages in our system, but an independent candidate in 1980 drew 6 percent of the vote even though he offered little in the way of ideological clarity. New third parties, such as the Libertarian and Citizens parties, have emerged and acquired ballot access more quickly and easily than was possible in the past.

Political journalists, columnists, advisors, and consultants often note these trends, usually suggesting that a new coalition is about to appear or lamenting the lack of party leadership or the leadership's inability to communicate ideological viewpoints effectively. Professional political scientists note these trends as well, but tend to give them much less attention than they do to details of the current political behavior of the electorate. They chart the behavior of the public without doing much to explain these larger changes. They focus on questions of ideological consistency (holding a collection of opinions clearly definable as liberal or conservative) and the rise in "issue voting" (voting for a candidate because his or her position on major issues is similar to the voter's own).

Despite all this evidence and discussion of trends, awareness of the limitations of the terms "liberal" and "conservative" to describe the public's ideological points of view has not yet produced a systematic alternative or extension of our standard way of defining public belief systems. In this book we offer an alternative.

Existing analyses of ideology in the United States are not so much wrong as they are too narrow. As long as we operate within a framework in which liberal and conservative are the only identifiable or legitimate ideologies, we cannot make much sense of the public's ideological views or their behavior. We propose here a simple but crucial extension of the conceptions of ideology and provide both theoretical and empirical justifications for its use.

One recurring question in the analysis of public opinion and voting concerns the extent to which Americans are or are not ideological. In other words do Americans believe in a set of basic attitudes about politics (such as "government should do as much as possible") that gives them a consistent and interrelated set of opinions about political events and issues? The implication is that if this were true, American politics could be understood in terms of the continuing conflict between major ideologies. The usual assumption has been that two possible ideologies form the underlying basis for most conflicts, as well as for our dichotomized political party system. In the 1950s many observers declared the "end of ideology," as the level of American affluence rose and many economic issues seemed to be less crucial than they had in the New Deal era. In the 1960s, though, ideological commitment was resurrected to help explain the intensified political conflict of that decade. Then the internal battles of the Democrats in the early 1970s and of the Republicans in the mid-1970s were also explained in ideological terms. More recently political analysts have been concerned with a variety of "new" ideological phenomena, such as the New Right, the decay of liberalism, and the rise of neoconservatism, neoliberalism, and libertarianism.

Scholars, however, have generally reached one of two major conclusions regarding the ideological nature of the American public. One conclusion is that the public really is not very ideological at all, in that Americans are led by satisfaction, ignorance, apathy, or acquiescence to see political issues as fragmented or disconnected. The other conclusion is that most people can be categorized as ideological in the sense that they have an overall point of view about politics, but only fairly small numbers of people are truly liberal or conservative. The dominant ideology in the postwar era, according to this view, can be defined as "moderate," or middle of the road, on most issues, which makes the public appear to be nonideological.

Both of these conclusions are based on analysis that begins by assuming that American political attitudes can be understood only in terms of a liberal-conservative continuum. If Americans are ideological at all, the logic usually goes, they must be either liberal or conservative. If we find that they are not much of either of those, then the only ideological viewpoint that will describe them is something between those two extremes; in other words they are moderate.

It is the central thesis of this book that the single liberal-conservative dichotomy—and the resulting two-way analysis of American politics—is inadequate for understanding belief systems or ideologies in the United States. Rather we think that mass belief systems are better understood if they are analyzed in terms of two separate dimensions—thereby making possible a four-way description of American politics. One dimension is attitude toward government intervention in the economy, and the other is attitude toward the maintenance or expansion of personal freedoms.

Different positions on government involvement in the economy have generally been assumed to be the defining division between liberals and conservatives in contemporary America. However, the extent and nature of government regulation of personal behavior has also been an enduring conflict in American politics. We think that this conflict is both analytically and empirically distinct from conflict over the economic dimension. Other political scientists have recognized these two sets of issues and have surveyed public opinion on both dimensions; in doing so, though, they have still allowed for only two resulting ideological positions, liberal and conservative.

Our analysis uses these two issue dimensions—government economic intervention and expansion of personal freedoms—to define four rather than two ideological categories. We label these liberal, libertarian, populist, and conservative. Specifically the two dimensions combine as shown in figure 1. Liberals support government economic intervention and expansion of personal freedoms; conservatives oppose both. Libertarians support expanded individual freedom but oppose government economic intervention; populists oppose expansion of individual freedom but support government intervention in the economy. These four categories can be justified both theoretically and empirically. This book presents empirical evidence regarding these political attitudes of Americans. In this chapter we develop the theoretical and historical meaning of our four categories and show how they derive from the traditional political thought of the past few centuries.

4

Figure 1
ISSUE DIMENSIONS AND IDEOLOGICAL CATEGORIES

| | | Government Intervention in Economic Affairs | |
		For	Against
Expansion of Personal	For	Liberal	Libertarian
Freedoms	Against	Populist	Conservative

The Nature and Meaning of Ideology

There is much confusion about the meaning and content of such ideological terms as "liberalism" and "conservatism." There is even controversy over the meaning of the term "ideology" itself. Even a quick glance at the literature reveals dozens of different specifications of what constitutes an ideology. For our purposes, though, it is useful to think of ideology at two different levels, at the philosophical level and at the level of mass belief systems. At the philosophical level an ideology may be said to be a set of interrelated ideas that purport both to explain how the political and social world works and to prescribe how that world should operate. At this level an ideology includes three elements: (1) a more or less complex, systematic set of normative statements setting forth political and social values; (2) descriptive and analytical statements intended to elaborate on those political values and provide a guide for explaining and evaluating political events; and (3) prescriptions describing desired political, economic, or social conditions. Thus, when viewed at the philosophical level, an ideology involves the elaboration of a world view and of desired processes of political change to reach desired values or goals (Dolbeare and Dolbeare 1971). The purpose of an ideology may be to provide a guide to action, to persuade others, to give legitimacy to a set of social structures, to engender passive acceptance of a set of social-political arrangements, or some mix of these purposes. Ideology thus understood is generally, although by no means exclusively, the province of philosophers and intellectuals. The masses of ordinary citizens seldom articulate an ideology, if ideology is defined solely in these terms.

5

That ordinary citizens are not philosophers does not necessarily mean their political beliefs are totally devoid of ideology. An analogy to religion may help clarify this point. One does not expect the Christian layperson, for example, to deal with his religious world in the same kind of theoretical language as does the theologian. This does not mean that the layperson is not religious or that he holds no sectarian principles. In his classic work, *Political Ideology*, Robert Lane recognizes this difference by distinguishing between "the 'forensic' ideologies of the conscious ideologist and the 'latent' ideologies of the common man" (Lane 1962, p.16).

The ordinary citizen may be largely unaware of or inarticulate about the philosophical underpinnings of his political beliefs, but nonetheless he may have a set of political beliefs and issue positions that are interrelated in a consistent fashion. We do not mean to take this line of reasoning to the other extreme to argue that any set of political attitudes held by an individual is an ideology. While mass beliefs need not be as complex, subtle, and complete as forensic ideologies to be considered ideological, they must have certain characteristics. First, the beliefs must be shared. Although it is possible that a purely individual, idiosyncratic set of beliefs may be ideological, this is neither very interesting nor very important. We are interested in sets of beliefs that are shared by significant numbers of people—and thus have some potential for being relevant to political action or political events. Second, these beliefs must be related to each other in some coherent fashion. Of course this is the crux of the problem. What constitutes a set of beliefs that are coherent or consistent? The answer to this question is often taken as self-evident. The method we use for initially establishing categories of mass belief systems, and for evaluating the coherence of a set of political beliefs, is to draw from the established traditions of Western political thought and philosophy. We are not simply interested in attitudes, but in shared sets of consistent attitudes that, at least in a latent sense, relate to established traditions of political thought.

We do not argue that Americans are political philosophers or that the American public is highly ideological. Philosophical levels of ideology may be seen as highly refined and extended versions of what many ordinary citizens believe. Mass belief systems, on the other hand, can be understood as highly simplified (and sometimes more pragmatic) versions of complex philosophical views of politics. Analysis that begins by looking at two dimensions rather than one, and thereby uses four rather than two ideological categories,

6

shows that a surprisingly large percentage of Americans have opinions on political issues that cohere in a consistent fashion and that can be seen as related to established traditions of Western political thought. The four categories we use here, therefore, are supported both by empirical evidence and by their relationship to traditions of political thought.

The American Experience

It is important to emphasize that this is an analysis of mass belief systems in the United States, and that the study of ideology in the United States involves some unique difficulties. Most of our ideological labels and ideas originate in European thought and history, even though the American and European political experiences are quite different. The two most obvious differences are the absence of a feudal tradition and the presence of the great frontier in the United States. Because we lack a feudal tradition, a European conservatism based on tradition and class privilege did not develop here. Furthermore the great frontier with its seemingly unlimited resources of land and wealth made the classical liberal concept of the independent and self-sufficient individual seem more realistic in the United States than was possible in relatively more developed Europe.

In this setting what is called classical liberalism took root to such an extent that all major ideologies in the United States share liberal assumptions to some degree. As we shall soon discuss, only the libertarians retain these assumptions in their classical form. For the other ideologies classical liberal assumptions are the starting point though they are often modified and reinterpreted. Thus from a global perspective the most striking thing about American thought is the degree of consensus rather than conflict. This consensus is one of the reasons why Americans often think of themselves as nonideological. In the context of consensus, basic assumptions are rarely seriously challenged, so that these assumptions seem natural, not ideological. These assumptions have become so automatic, so given, that they are often taken as self-evident truths rather than as political assumptions. Given the importance of these assumptions, it is useful to examine the basic tenets of classical liberalism as background for our four ideological types. At this point in the discussion, we will use the term "liberalism" in its classic or historical sense. (Modern liberalism, associated with such symbols as the Democratic party or Franklin D. Roosevelt, while based on classical liberalism, is a significant modification of the classical position.)

Some elements of liberalism may be found in the entire Western tradition, but we can conveniently date the immediate origin of liberalism from 16th-century England and the thought of Thomas Hobbes (1588–1679) and John Locke (1632–1704). Although Hobbes is very important to the development of basic liberal assumptions, the authoritarian conclusions of his major work, *Leviathan* (1651), place him somewhat outside the later development of liberal thought. On the other hand the foundations of liberalism are more democratically stated (although not without ambiguity) in John Locke's major work, *Two Treatises of Government* (1689). It is not without justification that Locke is called the father of the U.S. Constitution.

The work of Hobbes and Locke was the outgrowth of the breakdown of the so-called "medieval consensus." During the height of the medieval period there was basic agreement on a wide range of religious, political, and moral issues. Of course there were often differences of opinion as to specifics, but there was agreement on the basic outlines of society. God had created an orderly universe, and the traditions of the religious and secular hierarchies were reflections of this order. However the humanism of the Italian Renaissance and the assault on the Roman church by Martin Luther (1483-1546) made it impossible to maintain consensus on these assumptions. In time it became obvious that there was a need to establish a political and social philosophy that could overcome the religious and philosophical divisions that had developed. Whatever else, this new philosophy could not be predicated on extensive agreement on questions of religion and morality. These questions would have to be left for the individual to decide—an idea that would have been shocking in the Middle Ages. Rather this new philosophy would have to rest on a minimal basic framework of rational rules within which people could pursue their own specific ends in such areas as religion, morality, economics, and culture.

The "social contract" was the device developed (although not originated) by Hobbes and Locke as the basis for such a philosophy of society and government. Their approach was to ask the question: What minimal rules could rational men of all beliefs agree on as the basis of government and society? These rules then would be the content of the social contract. The very idea that government could be based on rational assumptions rather than tradition and God's will was in itself revolutionary. Although the social contract was a hypothetical construct (later liberals dropped the concept altogether), it was a useful analytic device to establish the argument that government is created by individuals and must serve the interests of these individuals. The implications of viewing society as being based on social contract are far-reaching and important to understanding American thought. These implications include six basic assumptions, which are briefly reviewed below.

1. *Individualism.* Probably the major shift from the medieval to the modern view was to make the individual rather than the community the basis for society and government. This is the most fundamental and familiar assumption of liberalism. The individual is seen as relatively discrete and autonomous. The individual is prior to society. Society is the product of individuals rather than the individual being the product of society. Individualism is so fundamental to liberalism that in some contexts the two terms are virtually interchangeable.

Not only is the individual viewed as the basic unit of society from which all else is derived, but the individual is seen as having basic motivations best described as rational self-interest. From the very beginning and particularly with the rise of capitalism, the individual was seen as striving to maximize his self-interest.[1] Altruism and identification with the community were assumed to be absent or too tenuous to be the basis for society. In its capitalist form, though, this self-interest was seen to work for the common good through market devices. Each individual pursuing his own self-interest in a market economy ultimately benefits society by increasing overall productivity. Nevertheless self-interest should not be equated necessarily with a narrow selfishness. Although liberal thinkers vary considerably on the specifics of this point, they generally agree that man is rational enough to recognize that it is in his self-interest to support government and society, even though this support means

---

[1]The relationship between liberalism and capitalism is complex and the subject of much scholarly analysis and debate. For present purposes it should be noted that the early formulations of liberalism predate capitalism and modern industrialization. Liberalism's emphasis upon individualism and private property, however, were important foundations for capitalism, and Adam Smith was an important early influence on liberal thought. By the 19th century liberal thought and capitalist ideology had become almost indistinguishable.

his giving up the right to do whatever he wants whenever he wishes.

2. *Instrumental View of the State.* Closely tied to individualism is the view of the state as an instrument to serve individuals, not as an end or value in and of itself. The state is created for and by individuals. The state exists to serve individuals; individuals do not exist to serve the state. Of course individuals do have certain obligations to the state, and they may be punished for violating these obligations, but the obligations are incurred because as rational individuals people must agree to these obligations if the state is to exist at all. These obligations are generated by individual agreement, not by the prior claims of the state, and they primarily involve the agreement to respect the equal rights of others.

3. *Limited Government.* A related but distinct concept is the view that the state should play a relatively limited role in society. Its central role should be, as Locke says, the protection of "life, liberty and estate." This view of the role of the state has also been called the "judicial state." These terms imply a state that protects individual rights and ensures the smooth running of society, while the initiative and energy for that society come from individuals.

It is a mistake to ascribe fully developed ideas of laissez-faire economics to early liberals, but as capitalism and industrialism developed, the liberal view of the minimal state was more and more identified with capitalism and the market economy. In the 19th century this view had developed to what Herbert Spencer called the nightwatchman theory of the state. The state should enforce contracts, provide defense and police protection, and do nothing more. This view can be contrasted with what was often called "mercantilism" in Europe. From the mercantilist point of view, the state not only controlled the individual's personal freedoms and religious practices but also directed the economy in every way so as to strengthen the nation as a whole.

4. *Individual Rights.* A key concept in liberal thought is that each individual possesses certain fundamental rights that should not be violated by government or other individuals. The exact nature and extent of these rights has been an important issue in the development of liberal thought. Locke's phrase "life, liberty and estate" and Jefferson's derivative in the Declaration of Independence, "life, liberty, and the pursuit of happiness," generally reflect the thrust

10

of liberal thought. The right to own and dispose of property as one wishes has been central to liberal thought from the beginning. Nevertheless rights have also included the right to free expression and behavior. Perhaps the ultimate statement of the liberal view of freedom is John Stuart Mill's *On Liberty* (1859), in which he argues that society has no right to suppress ideas no matter how distasteful and that individuals should be allowed to do as they wish (even self-destructive acts) so long as they do no substantial harm to others.

5. *Equality Under the Law.* Equality is also a central concept in liberal thought, but one that is often misunderstood. Equality is best considered as a legal equality in which all individual claims to rights and legal standing are to be the same. There are to be no special privileges attached to classes or castes based on heredity. In more modern times this idea of equal standing developed into the ideal of "equality of opportunity." This implied that birth should place no one at disadvantage not only in a relatively narrow sense of legal standing but in the larger sense of economic, educational, and other opportunities for development. Historically, however, equality has not meant equality of property or substance. In fact the major thrust of liberalism has been that the abolition of hereditary privileges and inequalities means that whatever inequalities develop in liberal society are the result of effort and ability and therefore are natural. Not only are these differences justified but it is a major task of government to protect them. As James Madison says in *The Federalist*, no. 10:

> The diversity in the faculties of men, from which the rights of property originate, is not less an insuperable obstacle to a uniformity of interests. The protection of these faculties is the first object of government. From the protection of different and unequal faculties of acquiring property, the possession of different degrees and kinds of property immediately results; and from the influence of these on the sentiments and views of the respective proprietors, ensues a division of the society into different interests and parties [pp. 17–18].

6. *Representative Government.* It may seem strange initially that representative government has not been treated more centrally in a discussion of liberal thought, but this relationship is in fact quite problematic. The two concepts are analytically and historically dis-

tinct, in that one can have a liberal system without representative institutions or vice versa. Most but not all early liberals favored some type of representative government. Early liberals, however, did not favor full adult suffrage. They assumed that universal suffrage would be a threat to property and other rights. In time it became increasingly difficult for liberals to support the idea of equality and at the same time resist pressures for extension of the franchise. By the end of the 19th century most liberals supported adult male suffrage, although the franchise was not achieved by women until well into the 20th century and effectively even later by blacks. Over time, then, liberalism came to include at least some degree of acceptance of institutions, such as a Congress or House of Commons, that allowed most citizens to express their views through government, although most liberals still demanded limits on how much influence the masses could have.

These then are the central assumptions of classical liberalism, which have provided the basis and context for most political thought and public opinion in the United States. At both the philosophical and mass levels, there has been a consensus on most of these assumptions. One consequence of this agreement is that ideological differences in the United States fall within a relatively narrow range. Rarely are these basic assumptions totally rejected by a political movement or leader. This is in contrast to many other Western nations where basic liberal assumptions are often rejected, for example by socialists who wish to give greater precedence to community or by conservatives who wish to return to a society based on rank and privilege. From a European perspective, American ideological disputes seem relatively confined. Nonetheless within the American consensus there have been important disagreements as to the proper emphasis, interpretation, and application to be given to these liberal principles. Two general areas of disagreement have in fact been central to modern American politics. One area is the extent to which government should or should not intervene in economic affairs, and the other is the extent to which government should or should not regulate individual behavior in matters of morality and conscience. These are the issue dimensions that underlie our four ideological categories. We will now briefly examine each of these categories.[2]

[2]The standard discussion of the role of liberal thought in America is Hartz (1955). For a good general discussion of American political ideas, see Minar (1964). An

12

Modern Liberalism

Modern liberalism differs from its classical ancestor basically on the question of the proper relationship between government and the economy. The development of modern liberalism is in large part a response to the effects of industrialization in the 19th and 20th centuries. (Throughout the rest of this volume, "liberalism" will refer to modern liberalism.) Industrialization, while considered progressive by liberals, was associated with a great deal of change and dislocation. Increasing numbers of people lived in cities with the concomitant problems of congested housing and poor sanitation, and increasing numbers worked as wage laborers instead of as independent farmers or craftsmen. To many liberals the results seemed far removed from the autonomous, independent individual envisioned in the liberal ideal. Many reformers, such as the later John Stuart Mill and T. H. Green, began to reexamine the liberal argument that the state should not intervene in economic affairs. Green argued that there are circumstances in which government intervention, particularly in the economic realm, might actually promote rather than hinder individual development. These 19th-century thinkers began to support wage and hour laws and compulsory education, although other liberals viewed such regulations as unacceptable violations of the right of the individual to choose to work for whom and for whatever wage he wanted and the right of parents to educate their children as they saw fit.

Attempts to regulate the business cycle were another source of modification of classical liberalism. While the first modification had been aimed more at individual welfare, this second one was an attempt to overcome the boom-and-bust business cycle, which reached its lowest point in the Great Depression of the 1930s. Liberals began to argue that government should attempt to slow expansion in boom periods and stimulate growth during recessions to even out the business cycle. The liberal theorist most associated with this view, of course, is John Maynard Keynes.

Modern liberals, while still valuing private property and the market, are willing to support government intervention to promote individual welfare and to regulate the economy. At the same time liberals argue fairly consistently that in terms of one's personal

---

excellent introduction to Western political thought more generally is Nelson (1982), and a good source of liberal writings and documents is Bramsted and Melhuish (1978).

activity outside the economic realm, the individual should remain free of governmental restriction.

Modern liberalism in America has been closely associated with the dominant wing of the Democratic party. From the Great Depression era and the presidency of Franklin Roosevelt to the 1960s, such Democratic party leaders as Harry Truman, Adlai Stevenson, and John F. Kennedy made the basic principles of liberalism a cornerstone of most political debates. Since the Vietnam era, spokesmen such as Hubert Humphrey, George McGovern, and Edward Kennedy have carried on the liberal tradition but have often been divided over foreign policy issues (a point discussed in detail in chapter VII). Today the principles of liberalism still are expressed primarily through Democratic party leaders and, on some issues, through spokesmen for civil rights groups or labor unions. Frustration with the results of liberal policies in the 1960s and 1970s has left liberalism an ideology on the defensive, often blamed for both economic dislocations and breakdowns in the moral order of our society. Although some liberals respond with what may be new variations or simply different labels, such as "progressive" or "neoliberal," their commitment to civil liberties and government intervention in the economy remains intact.

Libertarianism

Libertarian thought represents a highly individualistic extension of classical liberalism into the 20th century. Libertarians explicitly embrace most of the assumptions of classical liberalism. Consequently most of the discussion of classical liberalism applies to libertarians as well. Until fairly recently people holding the belief that government should play a minimal role in both the economic realm and the realm of personal liberties have been called Manchester liberals, classical liberals, or libertarian conservatives. The establishment of the Libertarian party and its associated publicity, however, make "libertarian" a less confusing term than these.[3]

---

[3]The Libertarian party's presidential candidate received 0.2 percent of the popular vote in 1976. Two years later the party elected an Alaska legislator and garnered 5.5 percent of the gubernatorial vote in the bellwether state of California. In the 1980 election the Libertarian party received 1.1 percent of the presidential popular vote nationally, with a state high of 12 percent in Alaska, thereby making it the largest national third party. Libertarian ideas have been increasingly debated within academic circles since the publication of Harvard philosopher Robert Nozick's *Anarchy, State and Utopia* (1974).

14

Libertarians emphasize very strongly the autonomy of the individual and the minimal role required of government. A recent statement of libertarian philosophy says that "we hold that all individuals are unique . . . [and] we also believe that each individual human being is morally autonomous. . . ." (Hart n.d.). Given that the rights of the individual are superior to all other political values, libertarians think that the individual should be free of government restraint in both economic and noneconomic spheres.

Property rights are central to individual rights; security and freedom in property transactions are prerequisites to individual development. Private property is seen as a liberating force, protecting the individual from arbitrary government intrusion. Libertarian thought opposes the economic interference of liberals on a variety of grounds. An unfettered market is more efficient than a regulated economy and therefore meets a greater variety of human needs. The truly needy can have their needs better met through private, voluntary action than through governmental programs. Further, need does not itself create a just claim to the property and wealth of others.

Property rights are necessary for human actualization, but it is also essential that the individual remain free of coercion in matters of religion, morality, conscience, and other purely private matters. Libertarians differ from their conservative colleagues in their rejection of government censorship and regulation of drugs and alcohol. Tolerance of individual differences is a crucial point in libertarian thought. Libertarians think that maximum individual choice in both economic and noneconomic realms can be achieved only if the individual is free from government interference.

In times of major economic crisis (the Great Depression, for example) or international problems (World War II or the East-West tensions that followed), the libertarian concern with issues of personal freedom has not been articulated in American politics. Several factors have changed this in recent years: a more politically conscious citizenry exposed to more education and mass media, increased affluence of a large middle class, the polarization of the two major parties into "liberal" Democrats versus "conservative" Republicans, and the inability of either ideology to deal with some continuing political problems. Thus we have begun to see some expression of libertarian views recently through individual leadership, the Libertarian party, and what has been erroneously called the "liberal" wing of the Republican party. Even such mainstream political

15

figures as Jerry Brown, Barber Conable, John Anderson, and Gary Hart have described themselves or have been described as fiscally conservative and socially liberal—which is roughly our definition of libertarianism, albeit in a very mild form. (In later chapters we demonstrate that support for nonintervention in both realms of economic activity and personal freedoms is increasingly present both among the public and, to a lesser extent, within our political institutions, such as Congress and the political parties.)

Conservatism

Conservatism is perhaps the most confusing of our four ideological categories. One source of confusion is the frequent use of the term as a defense of the status quo, especially as a rationalization for a particular set of property arrangements. Another source is that those contemporary Americans who call themselves conservative have also often been strident nationalists, thus bringing into American conservatism points of view not entirely consistent with the term's historical meaning. Popular perceptions and use of the term are also confusing. Conservatism has been associated with support for all basic American values, attachment to big business, religious approaches to politics, and general closed-mindedness, as well as with what we describe below as populism.

Traditional Burkean or "organic" conservatism developed out of the European feudal tradition and has not been a prevalent philosophy in the United States. Elements of this philosophy, though, do underlie much of American conservatism. Organic conservatism takes society, not the individual, as the fundamental entity to be protected and enhanced. Conservatives view the "autonomous individual" as a fiction. The individual can exist only in society, and is defined by society.

This kind of conservatism takes a pessimistic view of human nature, believing that humans, marred by original sin, are prone to be selfish and in need of moral guidance. Left to his own devices, man is dangerous. Human action needs to be restrained, guided in accordance with correct principles. Religion, natural law, right reason, and tradition are important sources of such principles. Government's function is to interpret and enforce these correct principles through law, thus ensuring justice and civility through the use of authority.

As societies evolve slowly, a given society represents centuries of accumulated wisdom, which is embodied in the society's tradi-

16

tional norms and institutional arrangements. Conservatives stress authority, seeing true freedom as possible only within an ordered society that guides and limits the baser human instincts. Without authority, the human individual is confused, alone, and likely to rebel and destroy his heritage of complex social and political institutions. Because they see inherited social and political institutions and established social patterns as so very important, and because they distrust human nature, conservatives believe that governmental power must be used to regulate individual choices in many areas that the liberal or libertarian would leave unfettered. What political observer Kevin Phillips calls "post-conservatism" (1982) is the contemporary manifestation of the basic conservative claim that a commitment to traditional values, such as religion and economic freedom, together with limits on personal behavior, is necessary to preserve society and therefore the individual.

Conservatives are highly skeptical of people's ability to correctly analyze the complexity of historically developed society, and thus are highly skeptical of people's capacity for correctly planning for or bringing about desirable economic conditions. Attempts to impose "rational" plans on an organically evolved society are almost certainly doomed to failure, or at least to produce unforeseen, undesirable consequences. Because they see human capacity as limited, conservatives oppose the use of government power to regulate economic affairs. European conservatives have not been as trusting of a free market, or of business, as their American counterparts, but conservatives generally see economic inequality as the natural consequence of inequality of human ability and energy. Attempts to counteract this natural inequality lead to the loss of initiative and excellence, which many conservatives see as having occurred in the United States. For these reasons conservatives see a need to use government power to guide and limit human behavior in the realm of individual morals, but at the same time oppose the use of government to restrict human behavior in the economic realm.

From the defeat of Herbert Hoover in 1932 to the election of Ronald Reagan in 1980, these conservative ideas functioned primarily as the "loyal opposition" to liberalism in the United States. An occasional spokesman, such as Robert Taft, Everett Dirksen, or Barry Goldwater, stood out, but conservative views rarely caught the public's attention at the national level or even dominated one major political party. The association of conservatism with big business or the rich probably had much to do with this, as did the tendency for the public to talk as conservatives at the abstract level ("government is too big") but act like liberals when they wanted a particular benefit from government. Furthermore the advancement of conservative thought in contemporary politics has been hindered by a tendency toward ideological infighting among its supporters. The 1980 Republican presidential nomination race, for example, often centered around which potential candidate was the most "pure"conservative.

Some of President Reagan's harshest critics have been conservatives displeased by his shifts from ideological purity. Two situations probably explain much of this displeasure. First, the immense size of government activity, increasing dependence on government, and such "uncontrollable" budget items as Social Security mean that conservatism's ideal of minimal economic activity cannot be achieved without drastic changes in the national economy and all citizens' lives. Therefore conservatives must compromise one of their basic tenets; how much and what to compromise is then a matter of intense debate. Second, the commitment to nonintervention in the economy is also confused by the capitalist system's connection with government. Conservatives see capitalism as essential for social stability, but modern capitalism is inextricably linked with and benefits from government action—tax loopholes, government contracts, price supports, and protection from foreign competition, for example. Thus the conservatives' belief in nonintervention often is not compatible with their support of business in today's mixed economy. It is this type of dilemma that leads a conservative such as Karl Hess (1975) to abandon that point of view and move toward libertarianism.

Populism

This fourth ideological category is in some ways the most difficult to identify in that "populism" is a term with a varied and largely historical meaning. Populism has been associated more with political protest and political action then with theoretical writings. Indeed, populists have often mistrusted intellectuals and their elaborate theories, so that the literature associated with populism is relatively small compared to that on the other ideologies discussed here.

Populists favor government intervention in the economy to benefit the "average man" or "little guy." Populists are not anticapitalist; they accept most of the assumptions of liberalism, especially emphasizing individualism, equality of opportunity, and property rights. Their protest is that the liberal, capitalist system has not provided these values for a large enough number of people. The system has been perverted or misused, and government must act to correct these abuses. Large corporations, especially railroads, banks and other financial institutions (and more recently multinational corporations), and the politicians who collaborate with them must be regulated so that the market economy can function properly. With an appropriate level of economic regulation, directed by an appropriate set of politicians who respond to the needs of ordinary people, a free-market economy will function properly to provide a wider distribution of private property. Populists are thus reformers more than economic radicals, and they are not antimarket or opposed to private property. While many populists today live in cities, they still retain an identification with a simpler, less urban society. Their ideal remains the independent, landowning farmer (in this they draw from Thomas Jefferson and Andrew Jackson), the small businessman, and perhaps the wage earner—people living in small towns or rural areas.

The populist political movement that culminated in the People's Party of the 1890s had its greatest support in the rural areas of the Midwest and South (many of today's self-proclaimed populists, such as Fred Harris, Barry Commoner, and George Wallace are also from these areas). Populism is the most explicitly mass-based of the ideological categories discussed here. Distrusting bigness and centralization, populists also tend to distrust the social and moral changes they see as a manifestation of bigness and centralization. They look backward to a time when life was simpler. This desire for a return to the simplicity of an imagined past is the basis for the moralism and at times ethnocentrism—and racism—of populism. In their search for an explanation as to why a liberal, capitalist system has not lived up to its promise, populists have sometimes blamed "foreigners," "Catholics," "pointy-headed bureaucrats," or "humanists," as well as giant corporations. Traditional social and moral values are an important part of the lost past, and populists are willing, sometimes eager, to use governmental power to establish or reestablish the traditional values of rural American life.

> For all the Southern Populists, financial reformers and antimonopoly greenbackers alike, the proper society bore a great resemblance to the rural, agricultural communities in which most of them lived or had grown up. . . . While individual economic com-

19

petition and the market system for the most part went unchallenged, personal relationships and moral and religious precepts more importantly than Adam Smith's invisible hand and the local police force appeared to delineate and guide the social and economic life of the community [Palmer 1980, p.199].

Thus populists support government regulation of the economy to prevent concentrations of wealth and to ensure a more equal distribution of private property—but not to destroy private property or capitalism. At the same time they support the use of governmental power to regulate individual behavior so that it conforms to traditional moral and social values.

The expression of populist views in American politics was probably clearest almost a century ago with the third-party movements of the late 19th century. Since then the dominance of economic issues has led many populists to support such liberal leaders as Franklin D. Roosevelt. (We discuss the peculiar difficulties of populism as a movement in later chapters.) The populist point of view has been most evident in national politics with the emergence of a particularly colorful spokesman, a George Wallace or Huey Long for example. It is difficult to define a modern populist movement when the populist name is claimed by politicians ranging from Fred Harris and Barry Commoner to George Wallace and Richard Viguerie. Perhaps, though, it could be argued that these apparently diverse figures ultimately have much in common: hostility to established interests, a desire to use government to enforce their own moral and economic beliefs, and a greater distrust of classical liberal values than is found among either liberals or conservatives. The moralist emphasis of the New Right sometimes seems to reflect populist assumptions. In the daily workings of politics, however, populism seems to be a guiding philosophy for quite a few congressmen (see chapter VI). An ideology that is difficult to simplify or identify, populism is also difficult to use as a basis for leadership or organized movements, despite its preeminence as a belief system for many Americans.

Conclusion

We have described four major ideological categories, in terms of their philosophical views and how they relate to questions of governmental economic intervention and the expansion of personal freedoms. In later chapters we examine the issue positions of individual Americans based on survey research to see how they may be classified in terms of these ideological categories. We do not maintain that the segments of the public we classify as libertarian, liberal, conservative, and populist do in fact hold these complex philosophical positions. Nonetheless we can say that their positions are consistent with these well-established systems of thought and therefore should not be considered nonideological or inconsistent. Before undertaking this analysis, however, it is useful to examine in the next chapter some of the more technical questions and controversies that have emerged within political science and opinion research about the nature and extent of ideology among the American people.

II. The Empirical Study of Ideology and Mass Belief Systems

The study of political ideology—a major topic within the discipline of political science—is obviously important for understanding political behavior. For centuries political observers and practitioners have speculated and argued about the exact nature of ideology. The academic study of politics began to emerge at the beginning of the 20th century, and it purported to observe, analyze, and explain politics rather than simply speculate or prescribe. Although the academic study of politics has always been concerned with the underlying theories and implications of ideology, not until the so-called behavioral movement of the 1940s was there any systematic empirical investigation of the public's ideological thinking. Analysis of voting patterns and the use of scientific survey research techniques has enabled political scientists to reach important conclusions about the American public's ideological leanings. These findings, however, have accumulated into a fuzzy and often conflicting total picture.

To help understand this confusing picture, we first review the emergence of three mythical and conflicting portraits of the American citizen, which provide different conclusions about what the public thinks. We then identify a common thread running through these various studies of ideology, suggesting that this confusion reflects an often-ignored view of the topic: That the ideological viewpoints of Americans are more complex and diverse than normally recognized. Finally we look at some reasons why this alternative view has not been given the consideration it deserves and how a two-dimensional approach to studying ideology, rather than the usual one-dimensional approach, allows us better to understand public attitudes. Scholars, it should be noted, often seem at least as confused as the public about the question of public ideology.

The Myth of the Textbook Citizen

In their book *Subliminal Politics* (1980), political scientists Dan Nimmo and James Combs point out that their discipline has developed through several stages, each with its own view or myth about the nature and study of politics. Each view dominated the discipline until it was challenged by a new approach, which often then became the dominant view, or the new way of "doing political science." None of the old myths has withered away completely, however; political science in the 1980s has become a collection of competing paradigms and methodologies (see Nimmo and Combs, chapter 7). In a similar way, the study of mass belief systems has developed three major myths purporting to explain the beliefs of Americans. These myths also leave us with a muddle of competing points of view, methods, and interpretations of findings.

The first view that political scientists developed saw the American citizen as being what democratic theory ideally expected citizens to be: attentive, informed, and rational in his political decision making. Under this view we have what may be called the textbook citizen. This implied, of course, that most citizens held at least some rudimentary ideology and used that ideology as a basis for casting votes and for other forms of political participation. Political scientists could then use this assumption to interpret historical trends and patterns in voting. After all, the splintered voting of 1860 reflected the basic conflicts over the nature of the political system that then led into the Civil War. Capitalists and unionist voters kept the Republican party in power for decades after the Civil War, only to be challenged in turn by "radical" or leftist movements of various extremity, from the populists of the late 19th century to the progressive and socialist movements of the early 20th century. This turn to the left and the clear left-right divisions among citizens culminated in the New Deal era and a sustained period of Democratic dominance. Despite a continued suspicion that many voters were not really all that ideological or rational, the assumption that people were at least an approximation of the textbook citizen made interpretations of political events and trends much easier. The commitment of political scientists to the goal of voter education has continually reinforced what Nimmo and Combs call "the democratic myth of the Alert and Informed Citizenry" (1980, p. 204).

Although the naive early view of the textbook citizen is almost impossible to defend in the face of contemporary empirical research, several political scientists have argued that there are general ideological clashes among the public even if the textbook citizen cannot quite be revived. The late Harvard political scientist V. O. Key, as well as James Sundquist and Walter Dean Burnham more recently, developed a theory of party realignment that argues that the basic divisions between the two parties, and the coalitions of voters supporting the parties, develop in periods of intense political confict. These divisions then endure over several decades. In time, however, an issue or set of related issues emerges that crosscuts and undermines the existing alignment of groups supporting each party. When a realignment occurs, major blocks of voters shift their party allegiance in response to changes in the kinds of issues that distinguish the parties. These shifts in voter allegiance may require several elections to solidify, but usually there is one critical election (1932, for example) in which the balance of power clearly shifts from one party to the other. The new balance is again maintained for several decades, even though a popular presidential candidate from the minority party (such as Dwight Eisenhower in the 1950s) may occasionally win election without changing the basic loyalties of the electorate. This theory of realignment suggests that critical elections are periods in which the textbook citizen myth becomes reality and elections turn on and greatly influence public policy, even though during noncritical periods the voters may be quite far removed from the textbook citizen model.

The Myth of the Nonideological Citizen

The myth of the textbook citizen was largely demolished by the findings of modern political science only to be replaced by a new myth of the "nonideological citizen." Nearly all the early studies of voters that used survey techniques contributed to this very pessimistic view of the American citizen's competence and, implicitly, to the view that Americans are not ideological (see Lazarsfeld et al. 1944; Berelson et al. 1954; Campbell et al. 1954; and Campbell et al. 1960). Analyzing both local and national surveys, researchers looked for evidence that American citizens perceived issues and cast votes as they "should." In the process these analysts tried to discover if the average citizen in fact was using any kind of ideological framework to make voting decisions or was even aware of ideological viewpoints in politics. Again and again, using various approaches to measuring ideology or belief systems, political scientists failed to find evidence of a textbook citizen.

The most influential work defining the myth of the nonideological citizen—what Pomper (1975) called the "dependent voter"—is surely that of Philip Converse (1964), who looked for evidence of ideological thinking in national surveys taken before and after the 1956 and

1960 presidential elections. Combing through responses to open-ended questions about what citizens liked or disliked about presidential candidates and parties, Converse found that no more than about 15 percent of the public could be defined as using ideological concepts or categories in their perceptions of politics. Although other scholars later modifed Converse's findings, the new portrait of the American citizen and his belief systems was now clearly stated: Except for political elites and a tiny proportion of the public at large, the typical democratic citizen has only a rough awareness of ideological terms, uses them rarely if at all, and casts his vote primarily as a reflection of a basically nonideological attachment to one of the political parties. An individual's issue positions are for the most part not organized or interrelated in any systematic way.

This last point, about issue positions, became crucial for the further study of political ideology, in that Converse defined a mass belief system primarily in terms of "constraint," or how well a person's attitude on one issue can be predicted if his position is known on some other issue. With this approach, consistency became the criterion for identifying ideological thinking. In other words, if a person is consistently liberal or consistently conservative across a set of issues, then that person is ideological. Of course what constituted consistency was defined in terms of post–New Deal meanings of liberalism and conservatism; that is, favoring or opposing a larger economic role for government.

After Converse's important work, many researchers tried a wide variety of methods to measure ideology, but most of them found that many citizens were not "consistent" in their issue positions and therefore they concluded that the public is not ideological. (Such studies include Pierre 1970; Robinson 1978; Kritzer 1978; Miller and Miller 1975; Miller 1978; LeBlanc and Merrin 1977; Levitan and Miller 1979; and Conover and Feldman 1981). The general point of view emerging from this approach was that most Americans are not ideological, and that voters' responses to ideological labels at best have a largely symbolic, partisan, or nonissue character. Nevertheless we can discern still a third view of the ideological character of the American public, as described below.

The Revisionist View: The Issue Voter

As if to revive the textbook citizen, or at least update the view, some political scientists responded to the characterization of the nonideological citizen with theoretical and methodological criticisms, using new data that poured out of the periodic national surveys of political beliefs and voting behavior. Although the methods and specific conclusions vary, in general a new myth emerged during the 1960s and 1970s: the myth of the "issue voter," or "responsive voter," as Pomper (1975) called him. The issue voter responds to political events and choices presented by elites, is concerned with at least some issues, and votes with an awareness of issues. The typical citizen may not be ideological in the philosophical sense discussed in the previous chapter, but many citizens do demonstrate some consistent use of issues in their perceptions of and responses to politics. Thus Americans do not quite meet the ideal of democratic citizenship, but they come as close to that ideal as can be reasonably expected. The issue voter portrait emerged out of four major objections to analysis of voting and elections during the 1950s and early 1960s.

First, some researchers have objected to the earlier conclusions on the basis of the methods used to detect ideological thinking. Open-ended questions that require the respondent to volunteer ideological terms in order to be classified as ideological mean that only the articulate will be considered ideological. Citizens may have an ideological point of view but simply be unable to communicate that view in response to the questions that happen to be asked. Perhaps citizens simply use language in a different way or at a different level than academics. Second, researchers of voting behavior in the late 1960s and 1970s have found evidence of a more issue-oriented and somewhat more ideological public than in the 1950s, when the nonideological citizen was "discovered" (see Field and Anderson 1969; Pierce 1970; Pomper 1972 and 1975; Nie and Anderson 1974; and Nie, Verba, and Petrocik 1976).

Third, some scholars have argued that to look at all issues that happen to be asked about in a survey does not do justice to the citizen's rationality. Citizens simply and quite reasonably are more interested in some issues than others, and they are likely to base their vote on the issues that are more important to them. This statement does not imply that every citizen has an ideological framework, but it does stress that voters are not devoid of the ability to differentiate between issues and to use them as a basis for electoral choice. Studies that examine opinions on issues that citizens say are important generally find that people do vote in a manner consistent with their positions on those issues they deem important

27

(Repass 1971; Natchez and Bupp 1977; and Kirkpatrick and Jones 1974).

Fourth, there are researchers who have raised a more general objection to the notion that most Americans are not ideological. Previous studies, they state, were focusing much too narrowly on responses to survey questions without paying sufficient attention to the larger political realities that surround citizen behavior. In *The Responsible Electorate*, V. O. Key presented "the perverse and unorthodox argument . . . that voters are not fools" (1966, p. 7). Key argued that if one looks at the behavior of voters in several elections, rather than in a single election, one finds that voters change or maintain their voting patterns on the basis of their positions on issues. This alone, according to Key, is sufficient to indicate that the public is in large part composed of issue voters, not mindless, nonideological sheep. Furthermore, Key argues (p. 7), "the electorate behaves about as rationally as we should expect, given the clarity of the alternatives presented to it and the character of the information available," a point also used to describe the political behavior of the electorate in more recent years by Benjamin Page (1978). In other words, if one looks at the voters and the political situations they face, one finds that the public is often presented with ambiguous policy positions by candidates and varying quality of political information on which to base decisions. Within that less-than-favorable set of circumstances, issue voters do the best job they can to behave rationally and express some set of policy preferences through the voting process. Again the public may not be composed of philosophers or ideologues, but citizens in the United States do in fact have points of view about politics that are important to them.

Moving Beyond the Myths

What is to be made of this confusion that political science has created in the study of mass political belief systems? Is there some underlying theme that unites these three views of the American public? If we look closely at the way in which ideology has been studied, we find that all these studies share a common approach: A single liberal-conservative dimension is the primary tool for evaluating the presence and direction of ideological thinking among the public. None of these studies seriously considers the possibility that the public's belief systems may be organized in more diverse or complex ways. Citizens whose attitudes do not fit the accepted liberal-conservative definition are categorized as nonideological or inconsistent. This approach assumes that liberal and conservative are the most meaningful and logical positions to take. The thrust of this book, however, is that mass belief systems are more complex in nature than a liberal-conservative dichotomy implies.

Why has the use of the liberal-conservative continuum been so remarkably persistent? There are several reasons. One is the assumption that elites in the American system rely on a single liberal-conservative dimension for their definitions of political issues, and that because elites largely determine the context of policy, they, in a sense, define the relevant ideological continuum. The exact formulation of this argument is often confusing because when scholars attempt to analyze the actual behavior of elites, they often must modify or discard the liberal-conservative continuum. Nonetheless in a noncritical way there is the loose assumption that elites think and operate in a liberal-conservative world.

A second reason for continued reliance on the continuum may be found in the argument that, since the New Deal, liberalism versus conservatism has been the "primary axis of ideological or policy conflict in the U.S." (Ladd and Hadley 1978, p. 89). In this view, policy conflicts since the 1930s have been largely an extension or maturation of the basic New Deal divisions over government regulation of the economy and elite responsibility for mass welfare. The socioeconomic base of party identification, the core of the party's electoral coalitions, and fundamental party divisions in Congress, for example, all have root in those New Deal divisions and have not been fundamentally disturbed by temporary crosscurrents. Thus *The Changing American Voter* examines mass opinions on issues of civil liberties, rights of dissent, crime, urban unrest, and drug use, and argues that these fit into a "generalized liberal-conservative ideology" (Nie, Verba, and Petrocik 1976, p. 138). In this view newly developing issues either fit into the old patterns or disturb them only temporarily. Even Ladd and Hadley (1978), who recognize dramatic shifts away from the New Deal alignments and from traditional meanings of the terms "liberal" and "conservative," still use the liberal-conservative continuum as their fundamental explanatory device. The continued use of such a device as the liberal-conservative continuum primarily because it allows scholars to interpret past, present, and future without changing their basic perspective sounds suspiciously like the myths that Nimmo and Combs discussed as guiding political science. In other words, scholars have held to their belief in a continuum regardless of changing events or contradictory findings; it is a belief with which they are comfortable.

A final reason for the continued use of the liberal-conservative continuum may be nothing more than its methodological simplicity. Conceptualization, question and scale construction, statistical analysis, and even graphic representation of data are all simplified when working with a single dimension. Describing complexity adds difficulty to each step of research. If this argument is correct, it would not be the first time that methodological convenience has blurred conceptual clarity in the social sciences. Nor would it be the first time that empirical analysis of politics has proceeded with only a glance over the shoulder at the theoretical notions that have developed over the centuries. In short, political science research into mass belief systems has often ignored the theoretical meaning and development of the ideological terms as discussed in the first chapter of this book and has focused on what is more easily conceptualized and measured.

The Complexity of American Belief Systems

As the previous chapter outlined, we believe that existing theoretical definitions of ideological points of view suggest the existence of complexity in mass belief systems. There are more than liberals and conservatives in the American political world; there are populists and libertarians and possibly others. Political science research has typically not moved beyond the liberal-conservative dimension to consider such complexity. Yet the findings of the past few decades offer ample evidence for going beyond a one-dimensional approach to measuring mass belief systems.

One indication that we should go beyond the simple liberal-conservative continuum to analyze mass belief systems is the nature of the findings over the past three decades of research. As we have seen, political scientists have generated three distinct views of the ideological nature of citizens, none of which is completely or even widely accepted. We could of course say that, as Walter Lippman (1965) pointed out, there are many publics, not one; some citizens are textbook citizens, some are nonideological, and others are issue-oriented. That truth, though, redefines the whole question of ideology and would describe the complexity of the public in terms of the people's orientation toward ideology rather than the actual directions in which their attitudes lean. Not only are there different

30

interpretations of research findings but there are a great many methodological disputes that undermine the acceptability of any of the three myths about the mass public. All of those disputes ultimately center around one basic question: How do we accurately measure liberalism-conservatism? Hence the research in this area has really focused on the study of constraint or consistency (i.e., consistency with the single dimension) rather than belief systems themselves.

Another important aspect of the findings on ideology is the research that has dealt specifically with ideological self-identification. When people are asked to label themselves on a liberal-conservative continuum, usually about one-third of them refuse to do so; they respond by either saying they "don't know" or simply refusing to answer the question altogether. Does this reflect the existence of an ignorant and apathetic public? In part, perhaps, but it also could reflect the fact that many citizens have ideological viewpoints that simply do not meet the definitions of either of the two major ideologies. Furthermore the evidence that the use of ideological labels reflects something other than positions on specific issues (see Conover and Feldman 1981) tells us that the labels do not measure belief systems. The evidence does *not* tell us, however, that the public has no belief system.

There is also substantial direct evidence of complexity within belief systems in the United States. Among public opinion researchers, as David Knoke notes, there is "an observation of great vintage: the content of mass political policy preferences is multidimensional . . ." (1979, p. 722). A major source of this recognition is the work done in the 1950s by Samuel Stouffer (1955) and Seymour Martin Lipset (1959), which showed that working-class individuals are more "liberal" on economic issues but less "liberal" with respect to civil liberties issues. Since then the nature of these dimensions and their relationship to social and economic status has been amplified and refined by many writers (Ladd and Hadley 1978; and Knoke 1979, for example). Questions about the oversimplified approach of the single continuum also emerge in studies using more in-depth interview or measurement techniques, usually with small groups of people, rather than large-scale surveys (see, for example, Lane 1962; Sennet and Cobb 1972; Lipsitz 1970; and Brown 1970).

Everett Ladd, Jr., argues that the liberalism of the New Deal is now channeled through two groups. These are the "new liberals," who support governmental economic intervention despite their upper-middle-class status but who are more concerned with self-fulfillment than with traditional economic issues, and the "new conservatives," who are working-class supporters of government economic intervention but also support traditional lifestyles and values. Conservatism of the classic kind, on the other hand, now includes both "moderate conservatives," who see the economic activities of big government as necessary and useful for big business, and "orthodox conservatives," who would prefer to minimize or dismantle the current level of economic intervention. Moderate conservatives apparently oppose challenges to traditional social values, but it is not clear where orthodox conservatives stand on this dimension (Ladd 1978 and 1978a).

Further it is not entirely correct to say that elites in fact are constrained by the liberal-conservative continuum. In his important analysis of Supreme Court decision making, for example, Glendon Schubert (1956) divides liberalism into two basic dimensions, which he calls economic and political liberalism. He defines political liberalism as relating to "personal (as distinguished from property) rights and freedoms" (p. 101) and economic liberalism as relating to "conflicts of interest between economically affluent and the economically underprivileged" (p. 128). Schubert's analysis of the components of ideology is more sophisticated than we use here, but his work does demonstrate the inadequacy of unidimensional analysis of liberalism and conservatism as applied to elites and suggests that the basic dimensions of U.S. ideologies deal with economic issues and the questions of personal liberties.

Another often-studied political elite is the U.S. Congress. Analysis of congressional roll-call votes has shown that political party is a strong predictive variable, suggesting that congressional elites do perceive some of their decisions in terms of Democrats versus Republicans. One recent study, however, casts some doubt on the extent to which party identification really reflects a liberal-conservative dichotomy (*The Baron Report*, May 10, 1982, and May 5, 1983). Moreover other dimensions are useful in explaining divisions in legislative votes: regions, majority-minority status, and state party delegation, for example (Turner 1951; MacRae 1958; and Truman 1959). Recent studies have concluded that several policy domains or issue sets (farm, labor, urban, civil liberties, social welfare, and international involvement) are more useful in explaining congressional voting and that "different alignments form as the policy content changes. . . . Liberal and conservative ideologies do not provide the bases for many, many policy decisions" (Clausen 1973, p. 31; see also Mayhew 1966).

Thus analysis of two significant segments of the political elite—the Supreme Court and Congress—calls into serious question the assumption that elites rely on the liberal-conservative continuum in their decision making and political conceptualization. A similar analysis of lawyers, a larger nonelected category that could be considered a political elite as well, reaches a similar conclusion: The liberal-conservative continuum does not adequately describe the multidimensional belief systems of political elites (Herzon 1980).

There is one more major reason for going beyond a one-dimensional approach to describing political ideologies in the United States. Although they may discuss ideology in unidimensional terms, most studies of public opinion in the United States either assume or empirically demonstrate that most domestic political issues center around one or two types of issues or dimensions. These types are economic intervention by government and government activity that affects personal freedoms (the latter sometimes referred to as social issues or lifestyle issues).

Studies using factor analysis to determine if citizens see various issues as grouped together in any way inevitably discover an economic dimension and a social dimension as prominent types of issues. (See, for example, Miller and Miller 1975; Stimson 1975; and Pomper 1975.) Other studies, such as the work with ideological self-identification by Conover and Feldman (1981), simply define economic and social issues (along with racial issues in this instance) as the "major domains of domestic policy" (p. 627). Or, as David Knoke has put it, "Economic and social politial orientations form distinctive dimensions, as a literature stretching back several decades leads us to believe" (1979, p. 788).

In short we have the following situation: Most observers of public opinion recognize that economic and social (or personal freedom) issues are two distinct dimensions, and, as we discussed earlier, people differ on them quite frequently—that is they are "liberal" on one and "conservative" on the other. Here, we believe, previous researchers have made a fundamental, consistent error: They have ascribed the terms "liberal" and "conservative" to the individual's place on the issue dimension, which leads them simultaneously to remain with the single-continuum definition of belief systems and to find that people are inconsistent. The two terms, however, refer to belief systems; that is, what a person thinks about several types of issues. The terms, as applied to positions on any one continuum (economic or individual liberties), in fact are nothing more than convenient (and misleading) labels to categorize support or opposition to whatever basic question defines the continuum. For example the economic continuum simply reflects degrees of support or opposition in regard to the proposition that government should actively intervene in the economic affairs of its citizens. To say one is liberal on the economic continuum does not mean that that person is a liberal; it simply means that he supports the idea of governmental economic intervention. We could replace the labels "liberal" and "conservative" here with the terms "pro" and "con" and we would still be saying the same thing. One does not have a "liberal" position on any one issue, such as government health insurance, for example; one simply supports that policy to some degree. The terms "liberal" and "conservative," therefore, should be used to refer only to a total belief system, not a position on any one issue or even a cluster of issues.

Summary

We have reviewed the evolution and definition of major ideological viewpoints that have been thought to exist within the American political culture: liberal, conservative, populist, and libertarian. We then looked at research by academic political scientists that attempted to measure ideological thinking in the public. There we saw that several views of the public's ideological tendencies have emerged, all of which rely basically on the terms "liberal" and "conservative" without regard to other possibilities. The recognition of two dimensions of domestic policy issues—economic intervention and personal freedoms—makes it possible, however, to unite the theoretical approach to ideology with the tools of modern survey research to analyze in more detail what the public actually thinks in terms of ideological preferences. Before turning to that task, however, we must describe and analyze trends in public opinion in recent years. In other words we must look more closely at the nature of the two issue dimensions, what issues constitute them, how those issues have changed over the years, and how public opinion has varied in regard to those issues.

III. Issues in American Politics: 1952–80

Public opinion about U.S. domestic politics centers around two major issue dimensions, economic intervention and personal freedoms, which also form the basis for describing four major ideological groupings in our society. We can now begin to look directly at the evidence provided by three decades of public opinion polling regarding these points. In this chapter we first briefly survey trends since the 1950s in the public's positions on economic issues and then on issues of personal freedoms. Having presented that evidence, we can combine the results on the two dimensions to estimate the proportion of supporters for each of the four ideological groupings. In other words we can offer a new analysis of the ideological thinking of the American public, more detailed than has been available before.

We rely on two major sources of survey data, which are nationally recognized by both scholars and practitioners as being among the most reputable and useful records of recent trends in public opinion. The Center for Political Studies (formerly the Survey Research Center) at the University of Michigan is the source of data on public opinion most widely used in the field of political science. Using the most sophisticated cluster-sampling techniques, the CPS has been conducting regular nationwide samples of from 1,400 to about 2,700 voting-age adults since 1952. The major emphasis of the CPS studies has been voting behavior, and therefore most of the questions asked on those surveys have been election-specific. Questions about general political issues and, in recent years, ideological viewpoints, have also been included, as well as detailed information about each respondent's background, social characteristics, and general involvement in politics. Unfortunately issue questions are not always repeated from one survey to the next. This reflects both the changing nature of political issues in the past years and the experimentation of the CPS staff with various questions over the years. The CPS studies, despite their limitations, do offer the best historical description of the American public and its political and social characteristics available to students of public opinion (nearly all of the studies cited in chapter II of this book rely on this source of data).

As a secondary source of information, we include some evidence from the National Opinion Research Center studies during the 1970s. These are also nationwide samples, usually of about 1,500 respondents of voting age, based on the use of advanced survey and sampling techniques. Although these surveys cover only the 1970s, many of the same questions were asked in several annual surveys, which allows us to chart opinion changes from one year to the next. The NORC studies are less oriented toward elections and generally include a greater variety of questions about contemporary economic, social, and political issues than do the CPS studies. Again, however, not every issue question is included in each year's survey, for both methodological and substantive reasons. Only in recent years have political scientists had access to the NORC data, but these surveys have provided an excellent alternative and additional source of information on public opinion trends.

In this chapter we present findings about public opinion change and ideological thinking with a minimum of discussion about methodological concerns or survey analysis. This approach is intended to enable the general reader to understand our findings without being overwhelmed by technical information and to enable the specialist familiar with the data and survey techniques to follow our arguments without being concerned about our simplicity of presentation (more details about question wording, sample sizes, and our analysis are presented in the methodological appendix). It should be kept in mind that when evidence about an issue is not presented in any particular year, that simply means that in neither source of survey data was that particular question asked. Also each year's survey represents a separate sample; the same people are not being reinterviewed each year.[4]

The basic patterns in public opinion about the issues under consideration form the context for understanding the ideological categories. The conventional wisdom of political columnists, campaign experts, and other commentators is that public opinion in the United States was quiescent, even complacent, in the 1950s and that the

---

[4]The CPS, however, has twice conducted modified "panel" studies, in which respondents from a previous survey were reinterviewed. Thus some of the respondents in the 1950 sample had been interviewed in 1956 and some of those in the 1976 sample had been interviewed in 1972.

country moved left in the 1960s, as the public became more divided and intense in its opinions about public issues. In the 1970s, according to this conventional wisdom, Americans looked inward to personal concerns, with the "me decade" culminating in a clear public move to the right. We have been offered various characterizations of the public mood as involving the "end of ideology," a "New Left," a "Silent Majority," an "emerging Republican majority," a "New Right," a "new moralism," and recently a "postindustrial conservatism." The political landscape has been seen as divided between "Sunbelt" and "Snowbelt," with both the public and political leaders divided between "Cowboys" and "Yankees." Many of these characterizations indeed involve an element of correctness, but they often conceal and confuse as much as they elucidate. The evident need to coin new terms is itself revealing of the inadequacies of traditional language for analyzing public opinion.

We also offer new language, concepts we think capture some of the complexity of public opinion. As our concepts relate to government intervention in the economy and to government regulation of personal freedom, it is necessary first to cut through the conventional wisdom and catchy phrases to examine the general patterns of public opinion about these two issue dimensions over the last three decades. During this time government action in each of these dimensions has been debated, praised, and condemned, often with much intensity. The specific issue questions involved change with time, but public opinion in these two dimensions falls into discernible patterns. When these patterns have been described, we can turn to analysis of how the opinions of Americans have been organized in fact into identifiable ideological categories.

Issues of Economic Intervention

In observing public opinion on the question of governmental economic intervention, it is important to remember that this analysis spans a time period in which this question underwent many variations, as did the general climate of political opinion in this country. Having moved massively into the economic realm during the New Deal, government by the 1950s was heavily involved in dealing with the economic needs of citizens. In the 1940s and 1950s the national leaders of both political parties generally accepted the fundamental economic premises of the New Deal, differing on methods rather than purposes and disagreeing about which set of leaders could carry out economic policy most efficiently and effectively. Those leaders also debated the extent to which initiatives begun earlier should be extended, including minimum-wage coverage, regulation of union activity, and aid to specific groups. By the 1960s debate had shifted to a more complicated level, as proponents of economic intervention urged even more expansion of government activity, including some form of support for health care and a government guarantee of a job or a standard of living for every citizen. Although the economic difficulties of the 1970s dampened enthusiasm for new areas of intervention, most of those same proposals were still evident during that decade.

An early view of opinion on economic intervention is evident in figure 2, which shows public opinion on the acceptability of government intervening to make utility and housing costs less burdensome for its citizens. Government involvement in guaranteeing this basic necessity was opposed by a plurality throughout the 1950s and into the 1960s. It is also evident, however, that conflict on this issue reflects the disagreement over economic issues that has con-

Figure 2

PUBLIC OPINION ON WHETHER GOVERNMENT SHOULD BE INVOLVED IN UTILITIES AND HOUSING

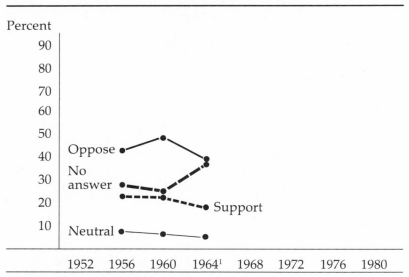

SOURCE: CPS.   [1]Utilities only.

38

tinued throughout U.S. history. There is some support for government involvement and a substantial amount of undecided responses on this question. Thus, beginning in the early 1950s, one can see economic issues leading to distinct divisions within the American public. On the issue of federal involvement in local education (figure 3), it is evident that there is a shift from overwhelming public support in the 1950s to a more evenly divided public in 1968. What was almost a consensus of support for governmental involvement in one decade became a pattern of division and conflict in the next decade, with more Americans opposing such involvement than supporting it.

Two major issues debated in various forms during the 1950s through the 1970s were government aid in the area of health care and in providing or finding jobs for citizens. These two issues also are among the issues that distinguish most clearly between self-identified liberals and conservatives in the CPS surveys (Robinson and Holm 1980, p. 58). Fortunately there is evidence on these issues

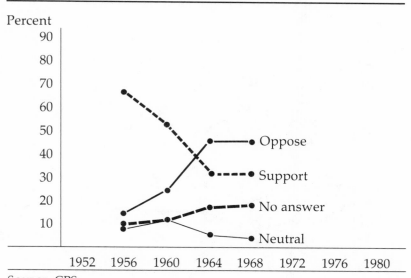

Figure 3

PUBLIC OPINION ON WHETHER THE FEDERAL GOVERNMENT
SHOULD AID LOCAL EDUCATION

SOURCE: CPS.

across all three decades. The question of health care has been part of the national political debate for many decades, although specific proposals for government action have varied from a minimum involvement through Social Security to comprehensive national health insurance and occasionally even to a national health care system approaching "socialized medicine." Figure 4 suggests that although support for such activity has been slowly declining over the years to the point where the most recent survey shows slightly more people in opposition than in support, this is an issue on which the American public has remained divided. After clear support for government involvement in health care for two decades, the 1970s show supporters and opponents each accounting for a little over one-third of the public, with an increasing proportion of citizens not sure about whether or not government should be involved here.

A similar pattern emerges from the survey data on the other major economic issue, the provision or guarantee of jobs òr a standard of living (figure 5). It appears that the optimism of the 1950s

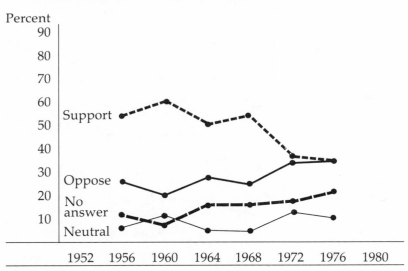

Figure 4

PUBLIC OPINION ON WHETHER GOVERNMENT SHOULD AID HEALTH COSTS/HEALTH INSURANCE

SOURCE: CPS.

40

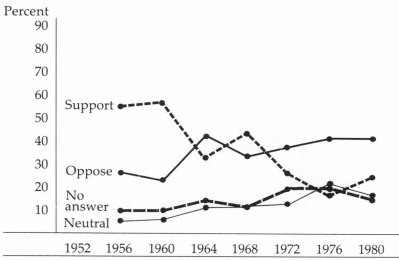

Figure 5

PUBLIC OPINION ON WHETHER GOVERNMENT SHOULD HELP
PEOPLE GET JOBS (GUARANTEE JOBS)

SOURCE: CPS.

allowed a majority of Americans to believe that government should and could provide jobs for its citizens. By the 1960s, however, when job guarantees began to take on economic (and possibly racial) connotations, public opinion became more divided on this issue. The 1970s then see an increase in the numbers of people who oppose job guarantees, although a significant minority still supports government activity in this area. The same patterns of conflict appear in figure 6, which measures support for the progressive taxation system in the 1970s. In both 1972 and 1976 almost equal numbers support and oppose the idea of government taxation being used as a way to redistribute wealth from the rich to the poor; in both cases significant minorities also either refuse to answer or take a neutral position on the issue.

Thus the issues of economic intervention are by no means a settled debate in American politics. There are clear differences in public reaction to such proposals in different decades: more support in the 1950s, more evenly divided conflict in the turbulent 1960s,

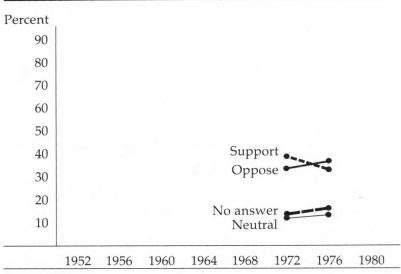

Figure 6

PUBLIC OPINION ON SUPPORT FOR PROGRESSIVE
TAXATION SYSTEM

Percent

90
80
70
60
50
40   Support
30   Oppose
20
10   No answer
        Neutral

1952   1956   1960   1964   1968   1972   1976   1980

SOURCE: CPS.

and a shift toward opposition to economic intervention in the 1970s. This pattern is also borne out by the data in figure 7, which presents responses to the question of whether or not the federal government is getting too powerful. Although not specifically economic in nature, this question certainly taps the public's response to taxes, regulation, government spending, and other economic issues. The trend here is definitely toward distrust of the federal government, part of what is often referred to as the "shift to the right" in recent American politics. One must be very cautious, however, about this kind of interpretation. As discussed in the previous chapter, opposition to some kinds of government intervention in the economic area does not necessarily indicate a shift to a general conservative ideology; it may be only a tendency to suspect one kind of government activity. This trend must be considered in light of public opinion change on other dimensions before we can make any ideological conclusions. At this point the simplest summary of Americans' views on government economic intervention is that they are

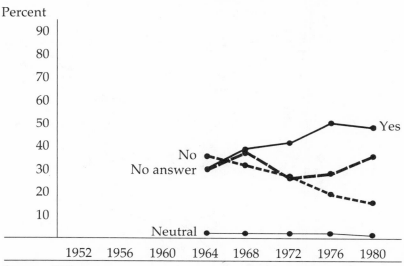

Figure 7
Public Opinion on Whether Federal Government Is Getting Too Powerful

Percent

SOURCE: CPS.

divided and have been becoming more divided over the past three decades.

The NORC surveys do not ask direct economic intervention questions over time, but they do contain a series of questions asking whether government spending is "too little," "about right," or "too much," in eleven issue areas. A useful way of tabulating change and levels of support for these questions has been suggested by James A. Davis (1980). He subtracts the percentage responding "too much" from the percentage responding "too little." On this scale a positive score of 1.00 would indicate that everyone responded "too little"; −1.00 would indicate everyone responded "too much"; and 0.00 would indicate equal proportions of people responding "too little" and "too much."

Figure 8 indicates the results of these calculations for eleven issue areas from 1973 to 1980. On the whole these figures show no dramatic shift in overall attitude toward government spending. Furthermore, with one exception (arms), no issue crossed from

Figure 8

SUPPORT SCORES FOR GOVERNMENT SPENDING ON NATIONAL ISSUES, 1973–80

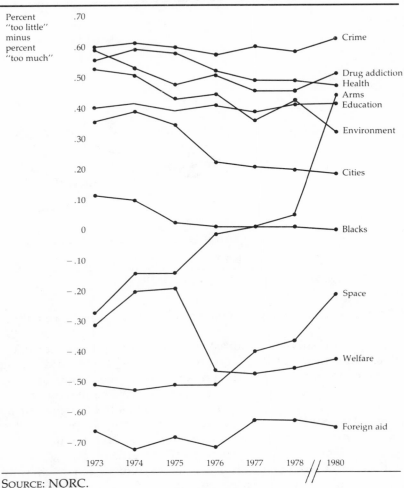

SOURCE: NORC.

NOTE: No survey was made in 1979. This figure presents the result of subtracting the percentage who say "too much" is spent by government from the percentage who say "too little" is spent. A positive score reflects support for more spending, a negative score indicates opposition to more spending, and a score near zero reflects absence of public agreement on the question.

44

negative to positive levels of support or vice versa. The figure indicates relatively high and consistent levels of support for increased spending on crime, health, drug control, and education. With the possible exception of health, these are areas of traditional government activity and do not seem to raise so much a philosophical question of government participation as they do questions of effective levels of funding. The two areas that show increased levels of support, arms and space, are also issue areas that do not so much raise questions of the legitimacy of government activity as they do questions about appropriate funding levels. Those areas where the question involves the proper role of government itself and not just levels of funding (environment, cities, blacks, and welfare) show signs of decreasing support, although even here only with welfare do a majority of respondents say that too much is being spent. Thus while there is some definite deterioration of support in the more controversial areas through 1980, there is not a predominant shift toward opposition to government spending. Of course some critics point out that such questions offer the respondent basically a yes/no choice on whether a particular problem should be alleviated. Respondents may well be saying only that they perceive a need for "better" crime prevention, health care, or environmental amenities, without having thought carefully about whether more government spending or some other government program would be best.

Personal Freedom Issues

The debate over governmental economic intervention, although a source of continuing severe conflict, is basically a simple one, in the sense that different issues in different time periods simply reflect variations in the proposed degree of government activity. National health insurance is different from Medicare, for example, in the degree of government involvement suggested. Personal freedom issues, however, differ in the substantive focus from one time period to the next and are often difficult to compare across time. Early in this century the debates about personal freedom centered around women's suffrage, the right to belong to a union, and an occasional "Red scare." In the early 1950s some political leaders claimed to see a continuing communist menace in government, but there was little indication that much of the public took this issue very seriously (only about a fifth of the public in 1956 believed that a suspected communist should be fired from government service, for example). The major public question regarding personal freedom for much of the 1950s and 1960s was that of civil rights for blacks; few other individual liberties questions were included in the public debate or were discussed by political leaders. Figures 9, 10, and 11 trace public opinion on civil rights issues between 1952 and 1980.

Government initiative in the area of desegregation was of course the basic divisive issue. As figure 9 indicates, equal proportions of Americans supported and opposed this idea across three decades, with a slight shift toward more support in the later years. Considering the civil rights issues that imply a major economic commitment, however, the issue becomes more confused and civil rights support declines. Government aid for blacks in seeking jobs and housing (figure 10) received majority public support in 1952 but was the source of definite public disagreement twenty years later, with an obvious turning point in the tide of opinion in about 1964. A more general question, whether government should help minority groups socially and economically (figure 11), provides evidence of the continuation of this trend up to 1980, when about a two-to-

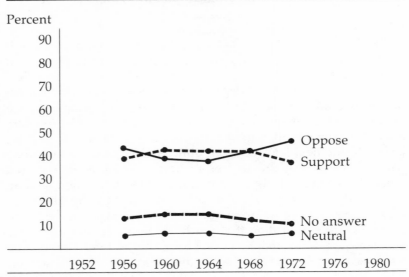

Figure 9

PUBLIC OPINION ON WHETHER GOVERNMENT SHOULD
AID DESEGREGATION

SOURCE: CPS.

46

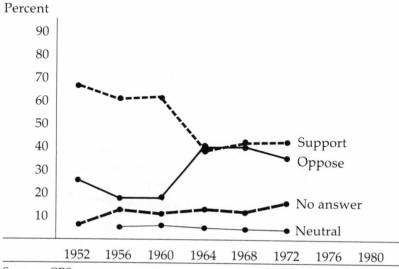

Figure 10

PUBLIC OPINION ON WHETHER GOVERNMENT SHOULD AID
BLACKS WITH JOBS AND HOUSING

Percent

SOURCE: CPS.

one ratio of Americans oppose this idea. Thus when civil rights issues include an economic component, the trend of public response on the issues parallels the trends evident on other kinds of economic issues.

Although civil rights issues were the only type of political issues included in the surveys used here that touched upon basic personal freedom controversies during the 1950s and 1960s, they are really not clear-cut individual liberties questions for many Americans. One reason they are not is that proposals for dealing with denial of black liberties usually called for economic action, therefore muddying the nature of the issue. One might be supportive of efforts to secure rights for blacks but reject the use of public funds for jobs and housing. A second reason is that the racial connotations of civil rights issues distinguish them from classic freedom issues. The question of race in American politics does not blend well with other basic types of political issues; it does not and never has fit neatly into any ideological framework for Americans. A classic example

47

259175

Figure 11

PUBLIC OPINION ON WHETHER GOVERNMENT SHOULD AID
MINORITY GROUPS SOCIALLY AND ECONOMICALLY

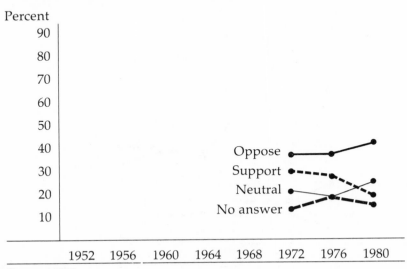

SOURCE: CPS.

would be the stereotype of the southern white who opposes growth of big government as an intrusion into individual freedoms but supports limitations on black civil rights, even through the use of government power to maintain such practices as segregation and miscegenation laws. A third reason is that the commitment of government activity to expand the rights of blacks is sometimes difficult to reconcile with a commitment to maximized personal freedom as an ideal, even when economic costs are not included. A libertarian, for example, would support the rights of individuals of any race to share in the benefits of the system, yet might be quite uncomfortable with the idea that massive government activity (possibly infringing upon other freedoms) was required to achieve this goal.

In recent decades, therefore, other types of issues are best used to chart public opinion about the personal freedom dimension. Because of the general lack of discussion of these types of issues in the 1950s, there is also little in the way of survey evidence here until the 1960s and 1970s. The emergence then of what were often

48

called the "social issues" provides a contemporary measure of this basic dimension of political conflict. The political agenda of the 1960s focused public attention on a new set of issues relating to personal freedoms, including the right to abortion, the legalization of marijuana, women's rights, new protections for the rights of defendants, and the debate over whether school prayers should be prohibited or required.

Supreme Court decisions touched off national controversies on more than one occasion during the era of the Warren court, but few were more explosive than the issue of prayer in the schools. Figure 12 indicates that from 1964 to 1980 a large majority of the public supported school prayer. A small minority, however, questioned the notion of whether religious training or exercises should be placed in the school instead of being left with the church and the family. It should be noted that opposition on this issue does not necessarily indicate opposition to prayer or religion itself; rather it may reflect the belief that religion is a private matter that should be

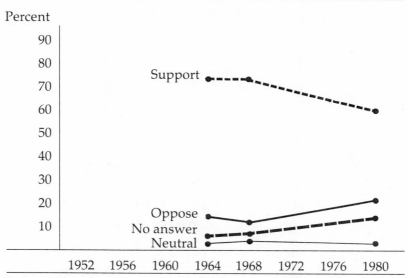

Figure 12

PUBLIC OPINION ON ISSUE OF PRAYER IN SCHOOLS

SOURCE: CPS.

49

separated from any sort of "public" sphere, including public schools. This is the purest form of support for private or individual liberties as opposed to government involvement in private affairs.

Figure 13 charts the public's response to another Court-initiated furor, whether defendants—those accused of crimes—should be protected from intrusion into their rights. Here one finds more of a picture of conflict, with a plurality believing that the prevention and control of crime is more important than protection of civil liberties, but with a substantial number of people either supporting the liberties of the individual or at least refusing to take a strong position. Similarly the highly emotional issue of abortion (figure 14) sharply divides the American public. Here the survey question is not phrased in terms of support or opposition, but in terms of four alternative views on abortion, which makes it more complicated to compare responses on this question to other questions of personal freedom. The most consistent support is for the availability of abortion for health reasons, although the "moderate" response

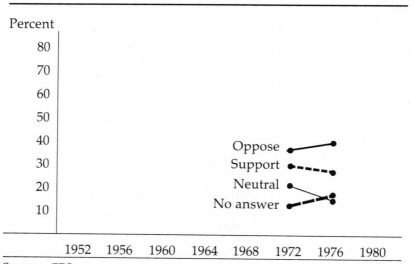

Figure 13

PUBLIC OPINION ON PROTECTION OF RIGHTS OF PEOPLE ACCUSED OF CRIMES

SOURCE: CPS.

50

Figure 14
PUBLIC VIEWS ON ABORTION

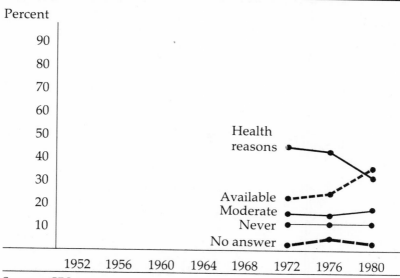

SOURCE: CPS.

(that a woman should be permitted an abortion if she does not feel capable of caring for the child) attracts a significant group of supporters. The more extreme options show opposing trends: Those who believe abortions should be available to any woman who wants one are a growing minority (and the largest group in 1980), while the position that abortion should never be allowed continues to attract a significant share of public support.

On the larger question of an equal role for women in society (as opposed to the more traditional role of wife and mother at home), there is a distinct trend toward support for expanding the rights of women (figure 15). Although obviously not reflected in public policy on such questions as the Equal Rights Amendment (ERA), the public has come to accept this expansion of personal freedom at least in principle. It should be noted, however, that this issue is far from one of consensus; a little over half of the public supports an equal role for women, leaving almost half who either oppose it or refuse to choose either extreme position. Thus this issue is still one

Figure 15
PUBLIC OPINION ON EQUAL ROLE FOR WOMEN

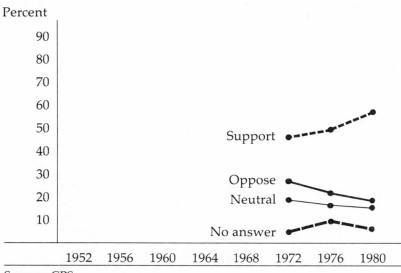

SOURCE: CPS.

that divides the public along the basic issue of the expansion of personal freedom. (Note also that this question is presented in the abstract and makes no mention of the ERA, government activity, or spending programs.)

Finally the issue of legalization of marijuana also provides some slight evidence that the public is becoming more supportive of expanded individual choices (figure 16). Opposition to the legalization of marijuana drops significantly from 1972 to 1976, although that is not translated into a groundswell of support for the position. Those people who are either neutral or do not express an opinion grew in numbers during the four-year period. The 1980 CPS study did not include this question, but the NORC surveys suggest that support for legalization peaked in 1978 and weakened slightly in 1980.

When then are the overall patterns of recent public opinion on personal freedom issues? First, it is useful to note the context and circumstance of the types of issues discussed here. These are all

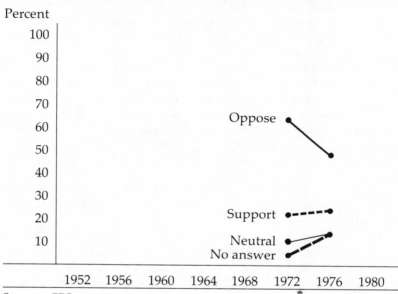

Figure 16

PUBLIC OPINION ON LEGALIZATION OF MARIJUANA

Percent

100	
90	
80	
70	
60	Oppose
50	
40	
30	
20	Support
10	Neutral No answer

1952   1956   1960   1964   1968   1972   1976   1980

SOURCE: CPS.

very emotional issues, often either evoking basic American symbols, traditions, and myths (such as the homemaker, motherhood,
and the morning school prayer) or implying support for people
widely perceived as lawbreakers (criminal defendants and marijuana users). It must be remembered that in American politics
personal freedoms are rarely discussed in the abstract and are never
free from other kinds of connotations. It is noteworthy, perhaps
even surprising, that despite the emotional and traditionalist character of these issues, significant minorities of the public have supported the pure liberties position in every case over the last two
decades. Furthermore, although the distributions for these issues
are somewhat more stable than those for economic issues, the small
changes in public opinion over the decades are in the direction of
increasing support for individual choice. We cannot say that the
American public is becoming dramatically more tolerant of individual lifestyle choices, but we can say that it does not appear to be

becoming any less tolerant, despite the conspicuous and highly publicized moralistic debates of the last five to ten years.

This conclusion is also supported by the NORC surveys, which enable us to look directly at less ambiguous issues of individual liberties. As can be seen from figure 17, there is consistent majority support for allowing unpopular speakers (homosexuals, communists, and those who oppose religion) to speak in one's community. If we combine those who want no restriction on pornography and those who want restrictions only for people under 18 years of age, we also find a majority (58 percent in 1980) who support no restriction on pornography for adults. The support for legalization of marijuana shows less consistency (ranging from 18.3 percent support in 1973 to a high of 19 percent in 1978) and obviously less than majority support. There has been a general trend toward greater support for legalization through 1978, with a small drop-off of 5 percent in 1980. This drop-off, however, is not paralleled in other issues of personal freedom where levels of support are remarkably consistent.

The recent past has seen highly publicized, often bitter debates on the personal freedom issues analyzed here. Much attention has been given to the "New Right" and the presumed electoral impact of the Moral Majority, the National Conservative Political Action Committee, Stop ERA, and anti-abortion groups. These organizations often claim or imply that they speak for a previously inactive, politically inarticulate mass of people who make up the majority of Americans. Whatever the successes of these "New Right" groups in raising money, attracting media coverage, or influencing elections, their support for imposing restrictions on personal freedoms is not shared by a wide majority of Americans. Nor is the flurry of activity by these groups (and the media attention to this activity), which peaked in the late 1970s and early 1980s, reflected in changes in public opinion. The distributions of public opinion regarding personal freedoms are remarkably consistent over the years. The small shifts that have occurred have generally been in the direction of more, not less, support for freedom of personal choices.

Issues and Ideology

Why is the liberal-conservative division inadequate as an explanation of ideological differences in the public? The trends described in this chapter suggest an obvious explanation. Public opinion in America has centered around two issue dimensions, rather than

54

Figure 17

PUBLIC SUPPORT FOR SELECTED ISSUES OF INDIVIDUAL LIBERTIES

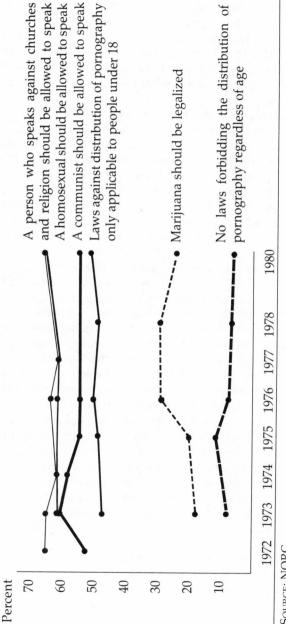

SOURCE: NORC.
NOTE: No survey was made in 1979.

55

just one. Although the economic dimension has dominated political debate, analysis of political trends, and public attention during much of U.S. history, another basic conflict has always been present in our political world in varying (and often subdued) form: To what extent should government help extend and maintain the personal freedoms implied in the Constitution but not specified for a modern mass society?

The usual assumption of political scientists who acknowledge the existence of these two issue dimensions has been that they are closely correlated; that is, that a voter who is "conservative" on economics will also be "conservative" on personal freedom. Thus there is no real need to distinguish between the two dimensions. A study of voters in Dearborn, Michigan, however, confirms our contention that the two scales may not be closely related. Frank W. Wayman and Ronald R. Stockton of the University of Michigan–Dearborn (1980) have found that there is no correlation between a voter's views on "social welfare liberalism" and his views on "law and order" or "the new morality." (Views on the latter two groups of issues are closely correlated.) In other words "liberalism" or "conservatism" on issues of personal freedom is essentially unconnected to "liberalism" or "conservatism" on economic issues.

A dichotomy of liberalism versus conservatism or any single-continuum approach of liberal-moderate-conservative, therefore, cannot possibly explain citizens' belief systems across two very different types of questions, such as economic intervention and personal freedom. A political world such as that in the United States allows us to dispute the proper course on each issue dimension even though we agree on the fundamental aspects of the political system and the underlying assumptions of classical liberalism, as discussed in chapter I. What we see in the past three decades is that both issue dimensions remain the source of major conflict. Economic issues continue to plague society or raise new questions about the options possible in an affluent society; citizens are as deeply divided over those kinds of issues as ever, despite the antigovernment spending rhetoric of recent years. (It must be remembered that for each well-publicized spending or taxing cutback that is approved by voters, there is usually another being defeated somewhere else in the same election.)

The dimension of personal freedom was crucial in many of the political battles of the 19th century, especially in state and local elections (Kleppner 1970; Kleppner 1978, p. 51). Aside from the overriding issue of slavery, the Democratic party was often called the "party of personal liberty" for its positions on such issues as prohibition, blue laws, and parochial schools. After the triumph of the pietistic Bryan wing of the Democratic party in 1896, issues of personal freedom were largely deemphasized in American politics until the civil rights revolution after World War II.

With the advent of the 1960s, with proposals for changing laws and roles for many groups in society, and with the political debates generated by Supreme Court decisions, it is evident that issues of personal freedom were demanding more attention from political leaders and were becoming more divisive among citizens. The simplistic liberal-conservative approach to describing public ideologies was probably always misleading. In a time of deep conflict over both dimensions at once, the usefulness of this approach is clearly limited. We must move beyond that approach, examine the dimensions of economic intervention and personal freedoms at the same time, and present a more complex but realistic description of the belief systems of ideological views of the American public.

IV. The Distribution of Ideology in America

We now turn to the central purpose of this work: To describe the ideological thinking of, or the presence of mass belief systems among, Americans over a period of time covering three decades. Ideally we would combine a wide range of issue questions reflecting each issue dimension in each year since 1952 and use that as the basis for discovering how many people fall into each of the four ideological types (liberal, populist, conservative, and libertarian) in each year. As we have suggested, however, severe methodological limitations prevent our pursuing this ideal approach. One limitation is that during the 1950s clear-cut individual liberties issues were not included in major surveys; those surveys included only questions on civil rights that would not clearly differentiate between groups. Another limitation is that surveys in many years have included only a handful of issues and in some years only one issue that reflects one of our basic issue dimensions. Only in the CPS studies since 1972 is there a large enough number of issues for each of the two dimensions to enable us to define precisely the four ideological types. Thus for the earlier years we can provide only some general estimates of the size of various ideological groups. For the 1970s, though, we can detail the major changes in ideological distribution.

It is useful to review our basic definitions of the four different mass belief systems. A person who supports government intervention in the economy and the expansion of personal freedoms is a liberal. One who opposes government intervention in the economy but supports government restrictions on personal freedoms is a conservative. A person who opposes government intervention both in the economic sector and in the private lives of citizens is a libertarian. One who supports government activity in the economy and opposes the expansion of personal freedoms is a populist.

Not all of the public can be classified according to these four categories, however. Individuals who did not answer at least four of six questions are people we label as "inattentive." Finally there are a variety of combinations that do not fit any of these categories. For example a person could support economic intervention but not answer or take a neutral position on all issues of individual liberties. Although most researchers would call such a person inconsistent, we prefer the term "divided," which indicates that the person's particular pattern of responses does not match any of the four ideological types but may reflect some other underlying beliefs. In the estimates of ideological distributions in the 1950s and 1960s, we omit this latter group because we are only roughly gauging the size of the major categories.

A brief discussion of our methodology is necessary at this point (details are given in the appendix). At each stage of our analysis, we attempted to create the most accurate and wide-ranging measures of opinion on each of the two issue dimensions. The economic intervention dimension is the one for which the most complete and comparable measures exist across the entire three-decade period. Therefore, with the exception of 1952, this dimension is measured by a three-question scale for each year. The three questions vary somewhat from year to year, but in most years they include both government involvement in health care and government aid for citizens who need jobs. Other questions used when necessary include the general extent of government power, government involvement in the power and housing industries, the progressive taxation system, and whether government services in general should be curtailed. As discussed in the previous chapter, economic issues demonstrate the most continuity over time in terms of the topics dealt with, and the questions asked in the CPS surveys reflect this fact.

The personal freedoms dimension is more difficult to deal with. It reflects the greater variability in the types of liberties issues discussed from one decade to the next and also variations in terms of which questions are included in the CPS surveys. For the 1950s we look at civil rights questions as a rough measure of this dimension, although we have to make some debatable inferences as to the positions that different ideological groupings would take on those issues. For the 1960s we again use some of the civil rights questions but also use the one measure of the emerging social issues (school prayer) that allows us to estimate what the public response was to this newer type of personal freedom issue. For the last three studies used (1972, 1976, and 1980), we are on much firmer ground in measuring this dimension. In the first two studies for the 1970s, we have three comparable questions: legalization of marijuana, women's rights, and abortion. For 1980, unfortunately, the marijuana question is no longer present and we had to replace it with a question on school prayer. We believe, however, that this one minor variation is not crucial, as the findings we present for this period will indicate.

In each case where a scale is used to measure a dimension, a simple principle is used to classify a survey respondent as either supportive or not supportive with regard to the government action in question. To be classified as supporting government intervention in the economy, a person must express pro-interventionist opinions on at least two of the three questions asked. To be classified as supportive of expanded personal freedoms, the person also must respond in a pro-liberties direction on at least two of the three questions used for that scale. Furthermore, to be classified as falling under any ideological heading, the respondent must express an opinion (that is, he does not respond with "don't know," "no answer," or a middle-of-the-road response) on at least four of the six issues used for the two scales. Thus the people we do classify as liberals, conservatives, populists, or libertarians are those who actually express definite preferences on both dimensions and on nearly all the issues used to measure those dimensions.

The Optimism of the 1950s

The decade of the 1950s has been labeled so often by various political and social observers that it has almost become stereotyped as a period of calm, passivity, and lack of ideological thinking. As we saw in our analysis of issue trends, the decade was characterized by an initial optimism regarding government action to solve problems, but this optimism began to taper off toward the end of the decade, especially with regard to commitment of resources to civil rights goals.

For the purposes of our analysis, we treat the studies from 1952, 1956, and 1960 as representative of this period; 1960 seems to represent the end point of that period more than the beginning of the next. Unfortunately our sources of information regarding these years are somewhat uneven. We do have questions that tap attitudes toward economic activity in all three years (a three-issue scale in the latter two years and a straightforward question in 1952 regarding government aid to citizens for housing purposes). For the other dimension we have only one clear-cut individual liberties issue: In

61

1956 the people surveyed were asked if a suspected communist should be fired from a government job. Clearly those supportive of individual liberties would oppose such a move and, in fact, most Americans did oppose it. In the other years, however, only questions that reflect civil rights activism were included in the CPS surveys. To provide an estimate of ideological divisions, though, we use those questions as follows. Support for desegregation (even though it implies government activity) was treated as support for personal freedom, whereas opposition to desegregation was treated as lack of support.[5]

The estimates in table 1 suggest the general outline of ideological ordering in the 1950s. Because we are able to use only one issue during this period to measure the personal freedom dimension, we are unable to measure the divided category in a way comparable to the later years. The term "divided" as used in our later analysis refers to individuals who do not fit directly into one of our four ideological types because of mixed responses on one or both dimensions. The comparison of the two issue dimensions lends more support to the notion of the 1950s as being an era of optimism about government activity; liberals are a majority of the sample in our 1952 estimate and a significant 20–25 percent of the samples in later years as well. In 1956 liberalism is just as high regardless of whether desegregation or communist rights is used to measure the second dimension. The other ideological position that favors government economic activity, that of the populist, is also fairly stable across time and, in fact, seems to increase across the decade when we use civil rights as a measure. The dominance of these two groups—the liberals and the populists—in the electorate helps explain the Democratic party's dominance in Congress during most of the 1950s, as well as the success of Eisenhower as a Republican president, whose ideological views on economic matters were never clearly anti-government.

[5]This classification certainly does justice to the positions of liberals, conservatives, and populists. The populists of course would definitely oppose the use of government to change social values or norms, but would support intervention to preserve those values. For libertarians the issue is not as simple. Libertarians would support the equal rights of blacks, yet some might doubt the wisdom of using government activity to support or create such rights. For our purposes of estimation, however, we could not classify the libertarian position as being supportive of racism or continued segregation. Thus the estimates of support for libertarians in the 1950s are more problematic than those for other groups.

Table 1

ESTIMATES OF IDEOLOGICAL DISTRIBUTIONS IN THE 1950s, BY PERCENT

Ideological Category	1952 Measured by Government Aid to Housing and Government Aid to Blacks	1956 Measured by Economic Issues Scale and Desegregation	1956 Measured by Economic Issues Scale and Accused Communist Rights	1960 Measured by Economic Issues Scale and Desegregation
Liberal	52.0	20.8	24.9	24.5
Populist	15.3	21.6	14.6	19.7
Conservative	7.2	24.3	11.6	23.6
Libertarian	11.8	15.1	28.3	14.9
Inattentive	13.7	18.1	20.5	17.4
Total Percent[1]	100.0	99.9	99.9	100.0

[1]Totals vary slightly because of rounding.
SOURCE FOR ALL TABLES: CPS, except as noted.

When we look at conservatism during this period, however, we see that there was always a core of conservative presence, one that appears to be the precursor of the skepticism and conflict over government activity that emerges in the 1960s. Not all of this conservatism, though, is a reflection of negativism toward the rights of individuals. When the rights of an accused communist are used as a measure in 1956, the number of people classified as conservative is cut in half. Clearly these are only rough estimates of the public's position on individual liberties; otherwise there would be less variation between the numbers of conservatives depending on which question was used.

Although our use of the term "libertarian" in this section of our analysis is somewhat limited (as discussed above), there does seem to be a core of people, somewhere between 10 and 15 percent, who opposed government economic intervention but supported the expansion of personal freedom during the 1950s. The most obvious intrusion of government into the rights of an individual, the rights of someone accused of unpopular beliefs, in fact creates the impression of a large proportion of libertarians in the 1956 sample. To say that 28 percent of the public was libertarian in 1956 would be an exaggeration, however. Remember that relatively few Americans were willing to take such a drastic step as to deny rights of employment to someone simply on the basis of accusations; the McCarthyism of this era never was supported by most Americans. If data were available from the 1950s on the individual liberties questions that were asked in the 1970s, we would probably find few if any libertarians in the earlier period, a suspicion corroborated by our age breakdowns in chapter V.

Finally the conventional wisdom that has always labeled the 1950s as a nonideological time receives some support from our findings regarding the inattentives, those who responded to too few questions to be classified. The proportion of inattentives found here ranges from about 14 to 20 percent, a figure much higher than that for the 1970s. In summary the 1950s period described here was dominated by the supporters of government economic intervention (the liberals and populists) and by people inattentive to most major political issues. A core of conservatives and a potentially significant minority of libertarians did exist, suggesting the conflicts to emerge in later years.

The Uncertain 1960s

The decade of the 1960s of course is often described as a period of turmoil, marked by assassinations, domestic unrest, bitter civil rights battles, foreign policy crises, and, toward the end of the period, economic uncertainty. With regard to domestic issue conflicts, the decade also marks the emergence of a new set of concerns regarding government involvement in the personal lives of citizens; Supreme Court decisions triggered political debates regarding prayer in school and the rights of people accused of crimes. Segments of the population began to challenge government's right to control personal behavior in such areas as drugs and abortion.

Here again we can only estimate the ideological manifestations of these events. In both 1964 and 1968 we have several economic issues that we combine into a scale of economic interventionism. For the personal freedoms dimension, we have only slight evidence: A continuation of the civil rights questions asked during the 1950s and a question on school prayer that is an initial measure of attitudes on the new kinds of liberties issues. Both of these measures present problems, though. The civil rights issue, represented by the desegregation issue in table 2, do not clearly distinguish libertarian viewpoints (as discussed in the previous section). The school prayer issue was one on which only a small minority of Americans in either 1964 or 1968 took a purely pro-liberties stand (keeping religion out of the public domain—that is, the schools). It also contains come degree of ambiguity: A person supportive of individual rights could argue that the right to school prayer should be supported, or he could argue that any government support of religious activity was a violation of individual rights. For purposes of this analysis, however, we use the latter definition.

Looking first at our estimates using the desegregation question, we find a pattern for the 1960s that is comparable to the findings from the previous decade. The range of support for liberalism and populism seems to decline somewhat but remains a dominant, if shrinking, force in public opinion. We do see increases in our estimates of support for both conservatives and libertarians. This of course is a reflection in part of the general trend described in chapter III: Support for government intervention in the economy began to decline in the 1960s.

Using the school prayer issue as a measure of the personal freedoms dimension presents a slightly different picture. There is little support for pure liberalism; what appears to be liberal support for the policies of Democratic leaders was probably the support of populists, who believed that many government initiatives for economic well-being were still necessary, but did not accept the notion of changing social values. The shift away from the Democratic party

65

Table 2

ESTIMATES OF IDEOLOGICAL DISTRIBUTIONS IN THE 1960s, BY PERCENT

Ideological Category	1964 Measured by Economic Issues Scale and School Prayer	1964 Measured by Economic Issues Scale and Desegregation	1968 Measured by Economic Issues Scale and School Prayer	1968 Measured by Economic Issues Scale and Desegregation
Liberal	4.1	14.8	5.7	24.4
Populist	23.3	10.9	28.7	10.6
Conservative	43.6	28.8	39.3	32.7
Libertarian	8.7	21.4	5.5	14.0
Inattentive	20.4	24.1	20.8	18.3
Total Percent[1]	100.1	100.0	100.0	100.0

[1]Totals vary slightly because of rounding.

in the latter part of this decade probably reflects this. Democratic leaders acted as if their support came from liberals when in fact most of it came from populists. Using an issue that is nearly consensual, such as support for school prayer, artificially boosts the conservative numbers in table 2 to a dominant position and minimizes the proportion of liberals and libertarians. What is consistent with the earlier findings is the large proportion of inattentives, although this also may be inflated somewhat because of the limited types of questions available for these years.

This portrait of ideological ordering in the 1960s is nothing more than an estimate. Clearly there are wide variations in our estimates, depending upon whether we focus on the old civil rights issues or the new social issues as a reflection of the personal freedoms dimension. The best we can do is suggest the ranges of support for different ideological groups. Liberals appear to be declining in number from their earlier dominance, while their opposites, the conservatives, clearly are gaining adherents as new issues enter the political scene and support for the ideals of an activist government declines. A populist viewpoint also became more common in the 1960s, reflecting a continuing group of supporters of economic intervention who were hostile to the expanding personal freedoms of the period. Again we can make the least reliable estimates of support for libertarians, suggesting only that a significant minority of them existed throughout this period and that their views (the elimination or minimization of government intrusion into both economic and personal realms) were not being discussed by most political leaders or groups. It is essential here to recall that these are only estimates of the size of various groups in the 1960s, offered as a preface to our discussion of ideological groupings in recent years. For the 1970s, though, we can make clearer statements about the size of each group, basing our findings on detailed measures of attitudes toward both economic intervention and personal freedoms.

Contemporary Ideological Divisions in the 1970s

Table 3 presents the distribution of ideological types in 1972, 1976, and 1980, based in each year upon a three-issue scale for both the personal freedom and economic dimensions. Thus we are able to specify the proportion of citizens who express fairly complex ideological positions as we have defined them and also to take note of those people who do not fall into any one of the categories, either

Table 3

DISTRIBUTION OF IDEOLOGICAL TYPES IN THE 1970s, BY PERCENT

Ideological Category	1972	1976	1980
Liberal	17.3	16.4	24.4
Populist	30.0	23.7	26.3
Conservative	18.3	18.0	16.5
Libertarian	9.4	13.0	17.7
Inattentive	5.7	9.6	4.6
Divided	19.2	19.2	10.6
Total Percent[1]	99.9	99.9	100.1
	(n = 1176)	(n = 2403)	(n = 1408)

[1]Totals vary slightly because of rounding off.

because they fail to respond to enough of the major issues investigated (the inattentives) or because they express some combination of attitudes that does not fit one of the four categories (primarily the divided, who are expressing middle-of-the-road responses on several issues and therefore do not qualify by our definitions for any ideological type).

Liberals represent a significant minority throughout the decade, in fact reaching their high point of almost 25 percent of the sample in 1980. This may seem surprising, given the apparent unpopularity of liberal policies, the collapse of many liberal presidential candidacies, and the moderation evident in the Democratic party in recent years. What appears to have happened, however, is that the ebullient fair-weather optimism of earlier years, when many citizens supported more liberal policies, has declined, leaving essentially a core of true liberals in the public. By "true liberals" we mean that the liberals we find in this decade are consistently liberal across both issue dimensions and support such major government initiatives as a guaranteed job, some form of national health insurance, and a maintenance of government services, despite adverse economic conditions.[6] To cling to such principles, given the economic

[6]As noted in the appendix, the economic questions were identical in 1972 and 1976, but two of the three questions were different in 1980. This may be a major factor in the apparent increase in the number of liberals in a year when liberals seemed to be on the defensive.

climate and the rhetoric of most political leaders in recent years, suggests that this core of liberals is an ideological group that is not easily discouraged. They are not a large enough group to establish government policy and probably not large enough to control one political party. They are committed, however, to economic intervention as well as to the advances in individual choices suggested by the liberals of the late 1960s and early 1970s. Because of this commitment, their presence in American political debates is likely to be fairly influential even though they may not be able to dominate the political system.

The 1960s trend toward populism we suggested is quite evident in this latter period. The populists are the largest category in all three years although they seem to be becoming less predominant as time passes. Again, much of the earlier support for government economic initiatives probably came as much from populists as from liberals. In other words the support for liberalism we saw in years past actually came predominantly from the populist category. The decline in levels of populism, although slight, may represent the changing nature of the U.S. population and may be quite significant for the future of American politics. At this point we note that a sizable number of Americans, the populists, have not had their particular ideological point of view expressed by political leaders in the two major political parties in recent years, although the relative success of George Wallace as an independent presidential candidate in 1968 and in the Democratic party primaries in 1972 may be attributable in large part to this group. Although many leaders like to label themselves populists because of the "common man" or "anti-bigness" connotations of the term, few leaders specifically articulate the views of this large minority. It may be, however, that many New Deal Democrats of recent years, such as the late Senator Henry M. Jackson or House Speaker Tip O'Neill, adequately represent populist views on economic issues without being perceived as excessively liberal on social issues. Even Walter F. Mondale, although clearly a liberal, seems to have appealed to voters primarily on issues of government spending and economic intervention—issues on which he could attract support from both liberals and populists.

Conservatives exist in the public at a fairly constant rate throughout the 1970s. About one-sixth of the public fits that label in all three years; the slight decline from 1976 to 1980 cannot be considered statistically significant. Nevertheless we must ask why the proportion of conservatives is not larger, given the supposed shift to the right in recent years that culminated in the election of a self-defined conservative in 1980. As with the liberals, this core group of conservatives is not large but is expressing a fairly pure statement of American conservatism: Opposition to government economic activity and opposition to the expansion of personal freedoms. For a variety of reasons conservatives are likely to be more active in politics than many of the other groups, and their views are disproportionately discussed and channeled through the political system.

The major answer to our question, though, probably lies in the evidence about libertarians. The much-noted shift to the right includes opposition both to economic activity and to changing social values. The latter trend, however, relates to the large number of populists present in the public, those people who are suspicious of changing social values or alternative lifestyles implied in guarantees of individual freedom. Opposition to economic intervention is most clearly indicated in the rising number of libertarians, the only group to show a consistent and significant increase during this period. Their level of support in 1972, just under 10 percent, is probably a reasonable estimate of true libertarian strength during the earlier decades. Our rough estimates, albeit using questions that were not quite accurate reflections of a libertarian position on personal freedoms, place them at around 10 to 15 percent in the 1950s. Our equally rough estimates for the 1960s generally place them at just under 10 percent. The rise from 1972 to 1976, however, does not reflect any methodological difficulties with the data used; the exact same six questions are used in both years. The continued increase reflected in 1980 suggests that this "simplest" of ideological views, generalized opposition to government intervention, is attracting more Americans. In *The Almanac of American Politics 1982*, Michael Barone and Grant Ujifusa make a similar estimate of the growing strength of the group that they call merely "those who are conservative on economic issues and liberal on cultural issues," estimating that group at 25 percent of the total electorate.

It is also interesting to note the relative strength of libertarians versus conservatives in our data. Conservatives outnumber libertarians by a two-to-one ratio at the beginning of the 1970s, but trail them slightly by the end of the decade. (We explore the sources of this increase in libertarian support in the next chapter.)

Finally the inattentive and divided categories suggest a few points of interest about American politics in the 1970s and 1980s. Even though our definition of an inattentive is somewhat strict (one must respond positively or negatively to four of the six issues to avoid being so classified), only 5 to 10 percent of the population now falls into that category. This probably reflects both the greater ideological nature of politics that emerged in the late 1960s and early 1970s as well as the generally increased levels of education and mass media exposure in recent decades. The divided group, which we did not deal with in the earlier analysis in this chapter, is one that is just under 20 percent in the first two surveys but barely 10 percent in 1980. Although we do not deal with this group in any significant way in this book, we should note that many of these people are probably the same as the moderate or middle-of-the-road people that political observers often suggest dominate American politics. Again we must reiterate that we do not claim that this group does not have any ideological point of view; they simply do not express opinion patterns that enable them to be categorized as liberals, conservatives, populists, or libertarians.

Having described the ideological makeup of the American public during the past few decades, and having developed detailed measures of ideologies in the 1970s period, we are in a position to look at the social and economic characteristics of the people in our four ideological categories. We can also examine the other kinds of political attitudes that these groups express. This may help us understand to what extent the public's alienation from politics in recent years reflects a continuing dilemma—that of four-way politics trying to function in a two-dimensional political system.

V. The Demographic Basis of Ideological Groups

Using our findings about the distribution of ideological types in America, we can now offer a more detailed picture of who these people are and how they behave in response to contemporary politics. In this chapter we analyze the social and demographic characteristics of our four ideological categories to gain greater insight into the composition of the groups and to offer some explanations for their ideological leanings and the changes in those tendencies in recent years. We begin by looking at generational changes and their effects on political ideologies. It is of some interest simply to know which ideological viewpoints are more accepted in different age groups. More importantly, though, we can identify groups of people who tend to share political beliefs in part because they have the shared experience of growing up in the same era and use that experience as a means to explain and interpret their political world. Next we turn to the critical variable of social class and its importance in American politics. What we propose here is that traditional social class divisions are of less importance today than previously (a point noted by many other political observers) and that the "new" class divisions we see emerging are of particular importance in the explanation of current ideological trends. The demographic descriptions of our ideological types that follow, although not as crucial for understanding the four groups, may be of interest to those who observe the shifting coalitions in American politics either for practical or theoretical purposes. We conclude this chapter with a brief recapitulation of the demographic nature of the four types and some speculation as to future trends implied by demographic changes.

The Generational Basis of American Ideology

Political beliefs do not develop at random or in a vacuum. Ideologies are partially a response to and continuation of received traditions; thus we have suggested in chapter I that our four ideological categories make sense as an evolution from the history of political thought and action. Political beliefs also form in response to perceived events, problems, and issues in the public realm. The term "political socialization" is used by political scientists to describe the process by which people learn or acquire their political attitudes, including ideological points of view. There are several major agents or sources of political socialization, including the family, the schools, peer groups, and the mass media. Research has rather consistently shown, though, that another important factor influencing an individual's political beliefs is when that person came to political maturity—a factor often called the "generational effect" (Dawson, Prewitt, and Dawson 1977; and Beck and Jennings 1979). As Karl Mannheim (1972) argued, the question to ask regarding a person's politics is not how old the person is but when the person was young. The same holds true for a generation's politics.

The major political events and conflicts and the general tenor of the political times in which a person reaches adulthood help shape his view of political issues and of the two dimensions of political belief we stress here. Put another way the generations of people who share a common set of experiences should be expected to express belief systems that reflect these experiences. This is not to argue that political beliefs once formed never change; rather landmark political events echo through generations of political belief. (The lasting effect of the Civil War on the partisan affiliations of Americans even today is probably the best example of this.) Political spokesmen often echo these experiences in their public lives. In the 1968 presidential race Hubert Humphrey's claim that government primarily should help people and Richard Nixon's rebuttal that government should make it easier for people to lift themselves up by their own efforts certainly reflected their individual reactions to the time in which they grew up. Gary Hart's 1984 primary campaign against Walter Mondale laid heavy stress on generational issues, and the response he got from baby-boom voters seemed to demonstrate that they viewed political issues very differently from older voters. Only recently has the national political leadership started to involve people born after the Depression and World War II. It is likely that as these younger people come to dominate the political debates of the future, the substance of political rhetoric also will reflect the times in which these leaders matured.

Generation and conflict between generations are often used to explain change in American politics. For example the New Left and antiwar movements of the 1960s, and the conflict these engendered, are often explained in terms of a generation gap of values and ideology between the young and old, as symbolized in the slogan, "Never trust anyone over 30." The claim that the young have become more conservative since the late 1970s has been used to explain everything from changing patterns of college enrollments to the election of Ronald Reagan. It is not surprising, then, that we find clear evidence of generational differences in the distribution of our four ideological categories. We present some evidence on this point in table 4.

Table 4 offers what is known as a cohort analysis. For each year we have divided the sample into six groups, defined by when the people in that group came to political maturity (defined as age 21 until the 1970s, thereafter as age 18). The older, pre–New Deal group, for example, includes people who were 64 or older in 1972, those 68 or older in 1976, and those age 72 and older in 1980. These of course are three different samples, not the same people being interviewed in each year, but by looking at the same cohort or generation in each year, we can estimate the extent to which generational change (the decline in size of older groups and their replacement in the population by younger generations) can explain change in the overall distribution of political attitudes.

It is not difficult to identify the landmark political events in the United States over the last half century, and we use these landmark events as the basis for our generational divisions. These divisions thus reflect the commonly accepted breaking points over the past fifty years of American politics. The oldest cohort is the generation that came to political maturity before the New Deal (over age 21 by 1930). The second cohort, the New Deal generation, turned 21 in the 1930s. The next generation is defined in terms of World War II; it is the group that reached age 21 in the 1940s. The fourth cohort is the group about which so many stereotypes have emerged, the fifties generation (who turned 21 in the 1950s). This is followed by the equally stereotyped sixties generation (who turned 21 in the 1960s). Finally the sixth and newest political generation is defined as those who turned 18 in 1972 or later, the seventies generation. Obviously the relative size of these generational groupings changes over time so that in later years the older generation constitutes a smaller proportion of the total sample and the younger categories (especially the sixties and seventies generations) contribute a larger share of the sample.

75

Table 4

GENERATIONAL SUPPORT FOR POLITICAL IDEOLOGY, BY PERCENT

Generation	Libertarian			Conservative			Populist			Liberal			Divided		
	1972	1976	1980	1972	1976	1980	1972	1976	1980	1972	1976	1980	1972	1976	1980
Pre–New Deal	4	5	12	13	18	18	41	37	34	13	6	13	14	14	14
New Deal	8	7	15	29	19	21	33	30	32	9	6	16	16	25	12
War Era	7	9	17	18	21	20	34	28	27	12	18	17	25	17	13
Fifties	13	18	20	21	22	24	22	19	26	20	14	21	20	19	7
Sixties	12	15	22	15	18	14	26	17	25	24	21	27	20	21	10
Seventies	10	21	16	18	11	11	21	17	23	30	28	35	18	19	10

NOTE: This table reads across the rows by year. For example the pre–New Deal generation in 1972 was 4 percent libertarian, 13 percent conservative, 41 percent populist, 13 percent liberal, and 14 percent divided; the remaining 15 percent were inattentive and are not presented in the table. By contrast the seventies generation in 1980 was 16 percent libertarian, 11 percent conservative, 23 percent populist, 35 percent liberal, 10 percent divided, and the remaining 5 percent not presented in the table were inattentive. All of the remaining tables in this chapter, except for table 9, also should be read this way.

Beginning with the older, pre–New Deal generation, it is evident that, despite some variations from one year to the next, populism is the largest belief system and conservatism the next largest for this group. This fact is consistent with a generational explanation of belief systems, in that those who came to political maturity before the New Deal would have had their consciousness shaped by the populist and progressive challenges to the two-party system and the preponderantly conservative viewpoint of both political parties during this era. The New Deal generation also has more populists than any other category, with a large minority of conservatives. During this period the major ideological conflicts were over economic questions; manifestations of noneconomic personal freedom issues simply were not seen as important in comparison to the fundamental question of the relationship of government to the economy. The war-era generation shows a more even distribution of ideological positions, although populism is again the plurality choice.

The fifties generation, made up of people growing up during the supposed "end of ideology," is almost evenly split among all four categories; libertarians account for 20 percent and populists for 26 percent, with conservatives and liberals each falling between those two proportions. People who came of age during the tumultuous 1960s demonstrate increased support for liberalism but only half as much support for conservatism as in the previous generational grouping. A quarter of this sixties generation is populist, and a significant 22 percent embrace libertarian ideas. By the 1970s there is a very distinct trend toward liberalism, with over one-third of this generation expressing a liberal viewpoint. Populism is slightly less important in this group than in earlier generations, although it retains the 25-percent support evident in almost every generation in every year. Finally, as with the sixties generation, libertarian views have basically supplanted conservatism for the seventies generation. The supposed trend toward conservatism among our youngest generations is more a trend toward libertarianism (support for both economic freedoms and civil liberties) than a trend toward classic conservatism.

Figure 18 presents the 1980 data from table 4 in a form that clearly demonstrates the generational basis of our current ideological distribution. In 1980, the graph makes clear, people who came to political awareness before the New Deal were still strongly supportive of economic intervention by government, but opposed to

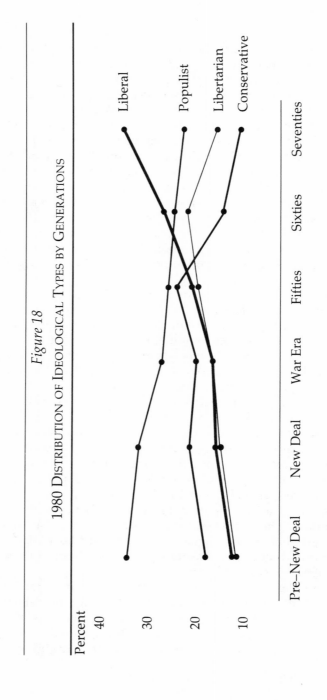

Figure 18

1980 DISTRIBUTION OF IDEOLOGICAL TYPES BY GENERATIONS

expansion of personal freedoms. The populist and progressive eras echo through the political generations. This generation also retains in 1980 its significant minority of conservatives. In moving to the turning point of 20th-century American politics, the New Deal period, we find an interesting clarification of the usual theory that the experience of the Great Depression and the New Deal laid the basis for modern American liberalism and the dominance of the Democratic party. People of the New Deal generation, like their predecessors, strongly favor government economic intervention, their "liberalism" is really better understood as populism. These older Americans retain their faith in economic intervention forty and fifty years later, but do not support the extension of individual liberties associated with contemporary liberals and Democrats. The inability of presidential candidate George McGovern to hold together the New Deal coalition in 1972 reflects this conflict, as does the fact that Walter Mondale retained the support of older voters even in the 1984 primaries that he lost to Gary Hart, who was perceived as being more socially liberal.

World War II was a time in which domestic issues were secondary concerns; only toward the end of the 1940s did conflicts over the extension of government activity again dominate political discussions. People who came of age during the war show a tendency toward more equal ideological division. Populism still dominates, but all three of the other viewpoints increase their proportion of adherents. This trend continues with the fifties generation; the end of ideology was really the fractionalization of ideology, as all four ideologies command major segments of support in the population. The 1960s, with their turbulent debates over lifestyles and generational changes as well as the unraveling of the Keynesian economic system, apparently created very few conservatives. By no means did all of the sixties generation become liberals, however, and it is not surprising that growing social liberalism and the increasing difficulties of government economic management brougth forth an unprecedented number of libertarians during that decade. Finally, coming of political age in the uncertain 1970s seems to spread out the support levels for the four groups again, although liberals are more numerous than the other types.

We can therefore speculate that much of the ideological change we see through the 1970s truly reflects changes in the composition of the population, with some clear trends for each ideological view. Liberalism rises steadily as we move across generations while conservatism seems to have peaked in the fifties generation and then declined sharply. Populism, dominant earlier in the century, demonstrates a steady if not precipitous decline. The libertarian view becomes more widespread through this generational evolution until the 1970s, when it drops again.

The key question of course is whether the younger generations will retain these ideological tendencies as they grow older. The indication from our cohort analysis here is that (within the limits of using only three surveys across eight years) the ideological leanings or earlier groups seem to have been maintained throughout the aging process. If that is the case with the younger groups, ideological distributions in the future may be quite different from what they have been. Specifically we should see a continued decline of populism and rise in the proportion of liberal and libertarian supporters. To the extent that the New Deal coalition of support for the Democratic party in fact drew from the populist category we have identified, our analysis illuminates the much-heralded "collapse" of that coalition. The populist viewpoint has declined as the New Deal cohort shrinks in size. In one sense this shrinking means that there is no longer a New Deal coalition to be reestablished. To the extent that contemporary Democrats stress liberal positions on social issues, they are at odds with their (shrinking) traditional source of support among our populist category. A retreat from liberal positions on cultural and lifestyle issues, though, would probably cause Democratic losses among younger liberals and libertarians.

Although the ideological leanings of each cohort or generation seem fairly stable throughout the 1970s, there is one exception to this pattern that can be mentioned, although the small size of each sample category prohibits making sweeping generalizations here. It is evident from the percentages in table 4 for each generation's support for each ideology that there is one consistent set of changes through the 1970s: an increase in libertarian sentiment among each of the generations except the most recent one (whose members, of course, are still very much in their formative political years). The pre–New Deal generation, for example, increases its level of libertarian support from 4 percent to 12 percent between 1972 and 1980. The sixties generation increases its level from 12 percent to 22 percent. The fifties generation goes from 13 percent to 20 percent. The New Deal and war-era generations roughly double their support of libertarian views. Thus most of the ideological change visible is that of generations moving into the electorate, but there is this evidence that some members of earlier generations are actually changing their positions toward libertarianism, a shift that perhaps signals an acceptance of the vast lifestyle changes since the 1960s and a disillusionment with government involvement in the economy.

A Changing Class Conflict

Historically the United States has not had the distinct class lines or resulting class conflict in politics of many nations. Nevertheless most analyses of political divisions in America do show some degree of class differences in support for parties and ideologies. Since the New Deal, Democrats and liberals have gathered support for their interventionist economic policies from the lower classes, while Republicans and conservatives have represented the interests of the wealthy and, to some extent, the middle classes. The class divisions between the two parties weakened in the 1940s and 1950s in a process that Sundquist calls "convergence" (1983). Explanations of more recent political trends have suggested that this traditional New Deal class division in political support may have been turned upside down, with the wealthier classes being more supportive of economic liberalism and with hostility toward such action emerging from the threatened middle class, especially the lower middle class (for example see Harris 1973; and Ladd with Hadley 1978).

With the weakness of class divisions in the United States has come disagreement among political analysts over the most appropriate ways to define and measure class or socioeconomic status. Rather than enter into this debate, we have used several indicators of class. We examine our four ideological categories using class self-identification, union membership, income, and education separately.

Using our four ideological categories, we find little evidence of class conflict in the traditional sense of rich versus poor. The old-style ideological divisions along class lines appear, if at all, only in a very muted way in our analysis. Distinctions emerge most strongly when we look at education as an indicator of class position. Table 5 presents the ideological leanings of people who define themselves as feeling closer to either the "working class" or the "middle class," a roughly equal division of the sample in all three years under study. (Almost no one in these national samples will choose the labels "upper class" or "lower class" to describe themselves.) The

Table 5

Social Class Identification of Ideological Types, by Percent

Class Label	Libertarian 1972	1976	1980	Conservative 1972	1976	1980	Populist 1972	1976	1980	Liberal 1972	1976	1980	Divided 1972	1976	1980
Working Class	6	9	12	19	17	16	38	28	32	15	15	25	16	19	10
Middle Class	13	18	23	17	20	19	21	19	20	21	18	23	24	20	12

Note: Percentages of people refusing to choose between the two class labels were 3 percent in 1972, 4 percent in 1976, and 7 percent in 1980. Inattentives omitted.

Table 6

Ideological Types by Annual Income Level, by Percent

Annual Income Levels	Divided 1972	1976	1980	Libertarian 1972	1976	1980	Conservative 1972	1976	1980	Populist 1972	1976	1980	Liberal 1972	1976	1980
0–4,999	11	12	9	3	6	5	14	9	13	44	44	42	16	10	19
5,000–9,999	17	20	12	9	9	8	21	15	18	32	29	33	16	18	25
10,000–14,999	25	21	13	13	12	14	19	21	14	25	21	28	15	18	27
15,000–19,999	26	22	11	9	17	14	20	24	21	20	15	22	23	18	28
20,000–24,999	19	26	10	14	15	20	14	25	21	16	12	24	32	18	23
25,000–34,999	43	14	9	18	30	22	7	23	20	11	9	22	21	22	26
35,000 & above	29	22	8	25	33	36	25	22	15	4	7	11	13	15	28

Note: Inattentives omitted.

most notable finding here is that the differences between the two self-defined classes are so small. By 1980 the two classes are all but indistinguishable in terms of the proportion who are either liberal or conservative by our definition; about one-fourth are liberal and about one-fifth are conservative in both the working and middle classes. Rather the differences show up most clearly in the libertarian-populist division, a distinction that would be lost in the usual liberal-conservative analysis. Populists, only one-fifth of the middle class, constitute about one-third of the working class, while libertarian views are twice as popular among the middle class as among the working class.

Union membership also is traditionally seen as an indicator of class position, with the working class more likely to be union members and the middle class less likely to be. The actual differences in terms of union support among our ideological types, however, is almost negligible. In 1980, 25 percent of the total sample are union members or have a union member in the household, but this proportion is evenly distributed across the four ideological types: 22 percent of conservatives are union members, as are 23 percent of the libertarians, 25 percent of the liberals, and 29 percent of the populists. These figures are almost identical in 1972 and 1976. This in part may reflect the decline in membership among the traditional blue-collar labor unions and the increased unionization of white-collar workers, who may consider themselves middle class despite their union membership. Thus we find relatively little to distinguish our four categories or to explain their attitudes if we either think of class as being a self-defined phenomenon or rely on union membership as an indicator of being working class.

Income level is often used as the most basic indicator of class or socioeconomic status in the United States, and there are clear income differences for populists and libertarians. Table 6 presents the distribution of ideological types according to income level. Although there are some variations across the three years of data as presented in this table, it is useful to consider figure 19, which charts the findings for 1980, as a summary of the relationship evident between income and ideology. (Note that some of the income categories at the more wealthy end of the scale are very small, especially in 1972; the smaller number of respondents in those cells means that the percentages presented there are less reliable and are likely to fluctuate more from one year to the next than would be the case for the income categories with more respondents in them.)

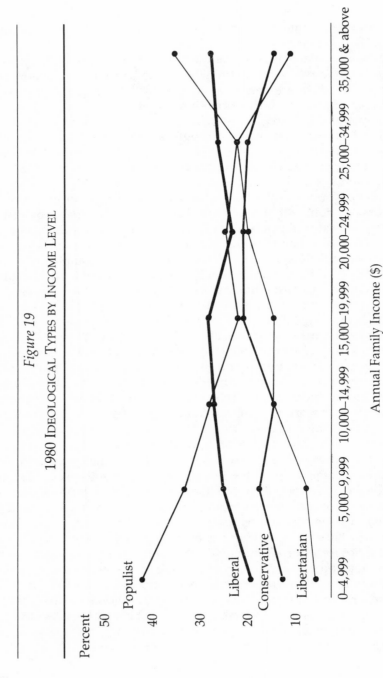

Figure 19

1980 IDEOLOGICAL TYPES BY INCOME LEVEL

84

Populism is an ideological viewpoint with definite class or at least economic connotations. Given the history of populist movements in the United States, it is not surprising to find that populism predominates among low-income groups. Populism just about preempts other ideologies in the lower-income category and is the largest in the next-to-bottom income group. For these households living on less than $10,000 per year, it is the dominant ideology, and it declines in strength regularly as one moves up the income ladder. It should be noted, however, that populism retains a strong group of adherents in the middle-income ranges: About 25 percent of those with incomes ranging from $10,000 to $25,000 per year express a populist ideology. In the highest income group, however, populism drops to an insignificant percentage.

The strength of libertarian support is the reverse: The proportion of libertarian supporters increases directly as income level increases. Almost nonexistent in the lower levels, libertarianism claims the support of significant minorities in the middle income brackets, about 20 percent of those with upper-middle incomes, and the lion's share (36 percent) of those with incomes over $35,000 per year. Conservatism, often thought to be the ideology of the wealthy, demonstrates some relationship to income but by no means the clear connection evident for libertarianism. Conservatives never rise above 21 percent or drop below 13 percent in any income segment, but their support is clearly the highest in the middle-to-upper income ranges; 20 to 21 percent of those with incomes of $15,000 to $35,000 per year are conservatives.

Liberalism is the most evenly distributed ideological category across income levels. Beyond the lowest income category, liberals claim about 25 percent of each income group; except for the very poor, differences in income levels make no difference in the proportion of liberals. The inverted class pyramid suggested earlier in this chapter is not quite an accurate depiction of support for liberalism. In the lowest income category the support for economic intervention seen in the work of earlier analyses is attributable mainly to populists who do not share the liberals' support for expanded personal liberties. The liberal point of view then has almost the same degree of support from both middle-income and upper-income citizens throughout the population.

Another way to analyze these results is to describe briefly the ideological conflict that exists within different income classes. To generalize and simplify, we can say that populism dominates the lower-income classes, with liberalism a distant second and little support for conservatism or libertarianism. In the middle-income segments of society, though, the ideological divisions are much more even. In fact, in the range of incomes from $20,000 to $35,000 per year, there is almost a four-way tie in terms of the proportion of supporters for each ideological view. In the upper-income segment of the sample, libertarians predominate, although a significant number of liberals also exist here; conservatism and populism represent the views of small minorities in this class. Thus it is libertarianism and populism that are more clearly connected with income differences, whereas liberalism and conservatism are more evenly divided across classes. Apparently, contrary to the conventional wisdom, it is not economic issues but social issues that divide most clearly along income lines, with upper-income people being more socially liberal than those with lower incomes.

Another way to look at social class differences is to examine the opinions of various educational groupings. Many observers have noted that the rise of the middle class and the expansion of affluence during the 1950s and 1960s would have minimized the importance of income as a distinguishing ideological device. Others have noted that the American public is becoming a more educated, technological, and postindustrial society, meaning that class divisions may reflect educational background more than income distinctions (for example see Bell 1973), or even that "education is the key factor in defining today's class divisions" (Ladd 1978, p. 53). Although we see some differences in ideological distribution across income levels, differences are much more apparent when we examine educational groups, as depicted for 1972 through 1980 in table 7 and summarized for 1980 in figure 20. Support for libertarian ideas is directly related to educational attainment; people with less than a high school education include almost no libertarians, but one-third of people with college degrees or beyond are libertarians. An even more extreme pattern emerges for populists, who claim half the people with grade school educations, one-third of those with high school educations, but fewer than one-tenth of those with college degrees. In terms of education, conservatism is the most evenly distributed ideology; the proportion of conservatives ranges only from 13 percent among the most educated to 18 percent among those with some college, with other education groups falling between these two figures. Liberalism is associated with education about as strongly as libertarianism, although it attracts a slightly larger minority

Table 7

EDUCATIONAL LEVEL OF IDEOLOGICAL TYPES, BY PERCENT

Educational Level	Libertarian			Conservative			Populist			Liberal			Divided		
	1972	1976	1980	1972	1976	1980	1972	1976	1980	1972	1976	1980	1972	1976	1980
Grade School	3	3	4	20	16	16	45	43	49	9	7	11	10	9	6
High School	8	11	12	20	19	16	33	27	32	14	13	22	21	21	13
Some College	17	19	26	13	19	18	19	12	15	27	23	31	22	23	8
College Degree	17	20	32	18	17	17	15	8	7	25	30	34	24	22	10
Advanced Degree	7	33	34	10	17	13	10	8	9	51	27	33	22	13	11

NOTE: The small number of respondents in the advanced degree category in 1972 (n = 41) makes the results for advanced degree people in 1972 unreliable. Inattentives omitted.

Table 8

DISTRIBUTION OF IDEOLOGICAL TYPES BY REGION, BY PERCENT

Region	Libertarian			Conservative			Populist			Liberal			Divided		
	1972	1976	1980	1972	1976	1980	1972	1976	1980	1972	1976	1980	1972	1976	1980
Northeast	9	12	17	14	14	16	34	25	26	26	21	26	15	21	13
South	8	9	16	24	17	16	34	30	31	9	12	20	17	15	11
Midwest	10	15	17	16	23	19	29	22	26	18	14	23	22	20	8
West	13	17	23	15	17	15	19	14	17	24	22	32	25	24	11

NOTE: Inattentives omitted.

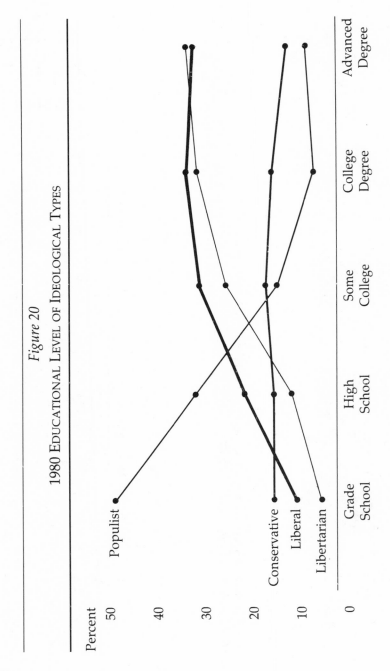

Figure 20

1980 EDUCATIONAL LEVEL OF IDEOLOGICAL TYPES

88

of people with less than a high school diploma and 22 percent of high school graduates.

To describe ideological conflicts within educational "classes" is also fairly simple; it is an exaggerated version of the differences evident within categories of income. People with less than a grade school education are predominantly populist, with a conservative minority presenting some basis conflict over economic intervention within that class. Among people who have high school diplomas (the largest category in the total sample), there is more evenly divided conflict, with populists still in the lead, but followed by liberals as a secondary group. For people who have had some college experience, liberalism is the dominant ideology, with the other three views being clustered close together in size. Among more highly educated groups the ideological division is essentially between liberals and libertarians; this professional class, people with advanced degrees, is the first in which libertarians actually have a plurality of supporters. Apparently there is strong agreement among college graduates about the importance of personal freedoms, but still much division over economic issues.

In summary social class conflict in the 1970s and 1980s is indeed quite different from the traditional class conflict based on haves versus have-nots splitting into liberal and conservative camps. The traditional measures of social class self-identification and union membership do little to distinguish between ideological types, with the one exception that libertarians are twice as likely to call themselves middle class as opposed to working class. Income differences, although still of some importance, seem less important than differences of education. Less education is associated with support for economic intervention by government and conflict over the rights of individuals; thus populists and conservatives dominate. Higher education, on the other hand, is associated with a near consensus on the desirability of extended personal freedoms but disagreement over the economic role of government, resulting in a liberal-libertarian division. It is useful to remember that the changes in overall ideological distribution (discussed in chapter IV) suggest that this may be the trend of the future. Similarly a continuing increase in the proportion of the citizenry with college and advanced degrees suggests that the liberal versus libertarian split may become the dominant one in future years, replacing what was in many ways a populist-conservative battle earlier in this century.

Additional Characteristics of Ideological Types

At this point we offer further evidence on the demographic characteristics of our four types, although this part of the analysis is aimed more at describing the groups rather than explaining their origins or patterns of increase or decline. (This section may be of more interest to the political scientist or campaign strategist than to the general reader.) Table 8 presents the distribution of ideological types in the four major regions of the United States. Patterns of regional political behavior have long been observed by historians and political scientists, especially the unique patterns of the South. Here we see that some of those regional variations can certainly be explained by our typology, although the overall pattern in Table 8 suggests a leveling of ideological regional differences during the last decade.

In 1972 the Northeast is dominated by a populist-liberal split; 60 percent of the region's citizens fall into one of the two categories, with populists slightly the more numerous. Conservatism is in a distant third place, and libertarianism is not a significant factor. By 1980, however, the populists and liberals are dead even in the Northeast, and libertarians have grown to represent 17 percent of the sample. The view that the Northeast is the stronghold of liberalism and the Democratic party makes sense in the light of these findings; economic intervention was the consensus view in the region early in the 1970s. The region is now much more evenly divided, however, and the growing number of libertarians could confuse election campaigns in this region in the future. Congressmen elected from this region usually are either liberal Democrats who unite liberal and populist voters through economic appeals or so-called maverick Republicans who could often be more accurately called libertarians.

The distinctiveness of the South is clearly portrayed in the 1972 findings. Historically populism thrived (if not succeeded) in the poor agrarian South, and it maintains its predominance through 1980; just under a third of the southerners are populists. In 1972 only conservatives constitute any notable opposition to the populists, representing what may be a leftover from the classic southern split of Bourbon conservatism versus lower-class populism that characterized southern politics for over a century. By 1980, however, there is a surprising surge of support for liberals and for libertarians, both of which claimed fewer than 10 percent of southerners eight years before, while conservatism seems to be slipping in strength. This is of course another indication of the nationalization of politics in the South, as the South more and more resembles the rest of the nation. In recent elections in the South there have usually been clashes between old-style populist candidates (Louisiana's Edwin Edwards in the 1983 gubernatorial race) and conservatives (Edwards' opponent, Republican David Treen). The occasional victory of a liberal Democrat or a more moderate Republican probably reflects the presence of small minorities of liberals and libertarians who are numerous enough in one location, such as an urban center, to elect such a "deviant" candidate. A conservative such as Jesse Helms may also be such a deviant, as his reelection campaign in 1984 may well demonstrate.

Across the decade of the 1970s the Midwest largely mirrors the national distribution of ideological types, although there is some erratic shifting in the proportion of liberals and conservatives present in this region. In 1980 the Midwest was certainly a battleground for varying ideological positions, as the variety of successful candidates for office from that region would suggest. Populists and liberals are the largest group in the region, but conservatives and libertarians are only a few percentage points behind. Unfortunately we do not have state-level surveys that could suggest some internal variations in this pattern. We can only surmise that this ideological fragmentation partly explains the wide variety of victorious candidates in this region. The Midwest has sent to Congress some of the most consistently conservative and consistently liberal senators over the years (liberals such as Birch Bayh, John Culver, and Hubert Humphrey; conservatives such as Everett Dirksen, Richard Lugar, and Robert Taft), as well as mavericks in both parties (Republicans Charles Percy and John Anderson; or Democrat John Glenn). We also see here one possible explanation for why a state such as Iowa, in a period of only a few years, could elect to the U.S. Senate liberal Dick Clark, populist Harold Hughes, and conservative Roger W. Jepsen.

Similarly the West is an ideologically fragmented region. (Most of the respondents in these national surveys who are defined as westerners in fact came from California; thus our analysis here probably is more accurate in depicting California politics than trends in the rest of the region.) At the beginning of the 1970s decade westerners are more divided than anything else, and our four ideological types are within 11 percentage points of each other. The West at this time is also the strongest region of the country for libertarians. The 1970s show a trend toward increasing liberal and libertarian support, which is slightly more pronounced in the West than that trend for the nation as a whole. Liberals are now the predominant group in the West, but libertarian supporters have moved into second position and seem to be increasing their numbers at a faster rate than liberals. The populist and conservative viewpoints have remained fairly stable in their level of support. The tumultuous politics of the state of California during this period, including the election of public officials with widely varying political philosophies and referenda results that do not fit traditional liberal-conservative interpretations, probably are a reflection of this fragmented ideological nature of the western region. Indeed this evidence from the West suggests a severe problem for political leaders that may worsen in coming years: the difficulty of building any lasting and cohesive coalition of supporters within a population that is so ideologically diverse.

An analysis of the ideological composition of racial groups shows some interesting facts about the role of blacks in American politics. As whites constitute almost 90 percent of the national sample in each year, their ideological divisions are very close to those found for the total national sample. (Hispanics, a rapidly growing but quite diverse group culturally, socially, and politically, are included in the white category.) Whites are somewhat more evenly divided, however, than the total of all groups. The 1980 distribution of whites is that 24 percent are liberal, 23 percent are populist, 20 percent are libertarian, and 18 percent are conservative. Among the remainder of the sample the distribution is very different. The 1980 distribution of nonwhites is that 47 percent are populists, 30 percent are liberal, and only 5 percent fall into each of the libertarian and conservative categories. Thus 75 percent of nonwhites (almost all blacks) agree on the need for economic intervention by government, but over 50 percent oppose expansion of personal freedoms. The suspicion often discussed in the 1960s and 1970s, that most blacks are "social conservatives" and thus unlikely to support purely liberal candidates (such as McGovern in 1972), is confirmed in these findings. Candidates who present moralistic or religious themes in their public positions (Jimmy Carter in 1976 and Jesse Jackson in 1984) provide a better representation of black views than do traditional liberals.

Table 9 presents this information on nonwhites in a slightly different form, listing the proportion of nonwhites that makes up each of the ideological categories. Presented this way the evidence serves as a reminder of the weakness of blacks in the American political system, at least as channeled through ideological debates. Only 4 percent each of libertarians and conservatives are nonwhite. Yet within the group of liberals, nonwhites constitute only 16 percent of the total group. Even among the populists, the category to which half of blacks belong, blacks contribute only about 25 percent of the group's total support in the public. Thus blacks represent a potentially significant segment in only one of the four ideological groups, populism, which historically has experienced a built-in uneasiness and difficulty in bridging racial gaps to forge an effective political coalition. This dilemma for the black populist is epitomized by the racial undercurrents of the George Wallace presidential campaigns; Jesse Jackson in 1984 was unable to attract the votes of white populists despite the similarity of his views to theirs.

Ideological differences according to gender are presented in table 10. There is no overwhelming tendency for males or females to fall into any particular ideological category, nor is any of the four types primarily a male or female group. What is evident in the 1970s is a tendency for males to be more evenly distributed across different points of view. By 1980, therefore, 24 percent of males are populists while the other three categories each claim 21 percent of males. The overall variations in support for the four categories are attributable to differences within the female half of the population. Females are slightly more likely to be liberals and populists and less likely to be conservatives or libertarians. The difficulty of building a direct ideo-

Table 9

DISTRIBUTION OF NONWHITES IN IDEOLOGICAL CATEGORY,
BY PERCENT

Ideological Category	1972	1976	1980
Libertarian	3	5	4
Conservative	6	4	4
Populist	17	19	24
Liberal	14	18	16
Divided	8	7	8
National	11	12	13

Table 10

DISTRIBUTION OF IDEOLOGICAL TYPES BY GENDER, BY PERCENT

	Libertarian			Conservative			Populist			Liberal			Divided		
	1972	1976	1980	1972	1976	1980	1972	1976	1980	1972	1976	1980	1972	1976	1980
Male	12	15	21	19	22	21	28	18	24	18	19	21	18	19	9
Female	8	12	15	18	16	13	32	27	28	17	15	27	20	19	12

NOTE: Inattentives omitted.

Table 11

DISTRIBUTION OF IDEOLOGICAL TYPES BY RELIGIOUS AFFILIATION, BY PERCENT

	Libertarian			Conservative			Populist			Liberal			Divided		
	1972	1976	1980	1972	1976	1980	1972	1976	1980	1972	1976	1980	1972	1976	1980
Protestant	10	13	18	19	19	18	31	25	27	15	14	22	19	19	10
Catholic	6	12	13	19	19	19	33	27	31	17	16	22	21	19	12
Other	7	10	17	7	13	10	23	8	9	48	39	41	16	21	19
No Religious Preference	14	21	25	6	7	8	16	9	16	39	34	37	14	20	8

NOTE: Inattentives omitted.

logical extension of a women's movement in the United States is indicated in these results. A majority of women support economic intervention, but a significant minority do not. Furthermore the two largest categories among women, populists and liberals, are opposed to each other on such personal freedoms as abortion and women's rights, precisely the types of issues around which most women's political movements have centered in recent years. It is apparent, however, that libertarian views are increasing among women (from 8 percent in 1972 to 15 percent in 1980), suggesting that in the future coalition of liberals and libertarians among women emphasizing personal freedoms could be more successful. The much-discussed "gender gap" since 1980 may rest on the dominance of economic issues as women are disproportionately affected by unemployment, deep cuts in social service programs, and the feminization of poverty. Both liberal and populist women would be expected to respond negatively to the economic conservatism of the Reagan administration. Ironically it may be the dominance of economic over social issues (abortion and ERA, for example) that allows women to agree politically in a way that differentiates them from men.

Table 11 indicates that religious differences for the most part are not translated into ideological differences in contemporary politics. Protestants make up most of the sample in each year and consequently (as was seen with whites previously) the distribution of ideology among Protestants does not differ much from the total national distribution. Catholics demonstrate a slightly greater tendency to be populists, but the differences are not very large; otherwise they distribute themselves among other ideologies about the same as do Protestants. Only for the "other" category (primarily Jewish) do we see a connection between religious affiliation and ideology; the oft-noted liberalism of American Jews is reflected in the predominance of liberals in the "other" category. The other belief systems are all underrepresented in this category, although that is only slightly true for libertarians. It may be added, however, that the group that claims no religious preference is a growing category in U.S. society. The group has doubled in size, from 5 percent in 1972 to over 10 percent in 1980, making it numerically much more important than the "other" religious preference group. Within this growing category the majority are either liberal or libertarian. Lacking even nominal religious affiliations that might generate opposition to abortion or other expanded personal freedoms, most of these people agree on supporting the expansion of personal freedoms but disagree over economic issues. Again the social categories that are growing in size contribute to the growth of liberals and libertarians as ideological groups in American politics.

Demographics and Change, 1972 to 1980

Thus far in this chapter we have presented a large amount of descriptive evidence about the four ideological types from 1972 to 1980. A brief summary is useful at this point and is presented in chart form in figure 21. Although demographic summaries such as this one, based on 1980 data only, can sometimes be misleading and form the basis of erroneous stereotypes, we can summarize our findings about the four types while being cautious not to over-simplify.

Liberals come from all income strata but in other ways they have some distinct characteristics, especially being younger and more likely than other types to have some college experience. They are

---

Figure 21

SUMMARY OF SOCIAL AND DEMOGRAPHIC TENDENCIES OF IDEOLOGICAL TYPES IN 1980

LIBERALS	LIBERTARIANS
Under age 41 (66%)	Under age 41 (55%)
Some college and college degree	Advanced and college degree
All income levels	Middle to high income
Strongest in West and Northeast	Strongest in West
84% white	Middle class
Slightly more females	96% white
More Jewish and "no religion"	More "no religion"
POPULISTS	CONSERVATIVES
New Deal generation and older	Fifties generation or older
High school diploma or less (83%)	All educational levels
Below $10,000/year income	Middle to upper income
Southern and Midwestern	Strongest in Midwest
Working class	96% white
24% nonwhite	
Slightly more females	
Slightly more Catholic	

strongest in the West and the Northeast. They are mostly white, slightly more likely to be female than male, and include a proportionately large number of Jewish or nonreligious members.

Populists, whose votes have often been misinterpreted as support for liberalism, are actually quite different from their fellow supporters of economic intervention by government. Populists come disproportionately from the pre–New Deal and New Deal generations, from lower-income and lower educational segments of the population, from those with working-class identification, and from the South and Midwest. Furthermore blacks, women, and Catholics are overrepresented among populists. In many ways this demographic portrait of populists sounds much like the standard characterization of the old Democratic party coalition. If there is a demographic opposite to the populists, it is the group that is also ideologically opposite to them, the libertarians.

Libertarians, more than any other group, look like a new type of category in American politics—a demographic category that could only have emerged in the postwar era of affluence and widespread educational attainment. In other words never before in U.S. history have there been enough people with these characteristics such that it has been possible to find one ideological viewpoint shared mainly by those in the younger age groups, raised since the 1950s, with college degrees or even higher education, with middle to high incomes, and identifying themselves with the middle class.[7] Libertarians, more than any other group, have benefited from demographic change and owe their current strength to these changes in the nature of society. They may well make up a large part of the group to which Gary Hart's 1984 campaign appealed—young urban professionals, or "yuppies."

Conservatives, on the other hand, are a category more difficult to describe as being demographically distinct. They are predominantly from the fifties generation or the older generations, have middle to upper incomes, are strongest in the Midwest, and (like the libertarians) are almost all whites. In other ways, however, they are fairly evenly distributed across various groups in the popula-

[7]This general picture is confirmed by a study (Green and Guth 1983) of active supporters of the Libertarian party. They were found to be upper-middle-income, very highly educated, frequently employed in the knowledge industries or the professions, and mostly under the age of 45—in many ways a distilled version of our more broadly defined libertarianism.

tion, especially with regard to educational level. If there is a shift from conservatism to libertarianism, as is suggested by the trends in overall support for these groups since 1972, it may be that the conservatives are what may be called a residual group. Contemporary conservatives may not be so much an identifiable class grouping but more of a collection of minorities within those social groups dominated either by populists or libertarians, both of whom share with conservatives political opinions on one of the two basic dimensions.

We have had two purposes in this analysis. The description of the characteristics of the four ideological types has allowed us to compare the types with each other and understand better the people who fit these ideological descriptions. Additionally we also have suggested that demographic change explains much of the changing distribution of ideological types from 1972 to 1980. The most critical explanatory factor is obviously age, or generational change. As we observe the changing levels of support for various groups (the decline of populists and the increased size of liberal and libertarian groups), we note a distinct connection between support for certain ideologies and the changing proportion in the population of the age, educational, and other groupings from which the ideology draws support. Populism cannot be called a dying ideology when it is still the largest of the four categories and attracts some support even in the youngest age group. However, it certainly will not be the dominant ideology of the future if its adherents come primarily from the older generations.

Other demographic changes suggest that the decline in populism reflects the changing nature of the population. Populism gathers its support primarily from the lower-income and more poorly educated elements of society. Increasing levels of education and affluence have undermined populist strength and will continue to do so in the future. Could the populist point of view become the ideological position of the large middle class that exists in the 1980s, people whose apparent affluence no longer seems as secure or as real as it once did? Our findings for 1980 suggest that this is not likely or at least is not the case now; the middle class seem more likely to move in the direction of liberalism or libertarianism, not populism.

As populism has declined as a reflection of the decaying nature of its support in various social groups, so has libertarianism prospered. The near doubling of support evident for the libertarian view in eight years (1972–80) can in large part be traced to the increasing proportion of the electorate that is from the newer political generations, is earning more income, and has high levels of education. This is not to suggest that some people have not been converted to the libertarian point of view by events of recent decades. The proportion of libertarians increased in every age group from 1972 to 1980, and the same also is true for most income brackets and most educational categories. The significant fact about libertarian growth, however, is that it is coming in exactly those demographic categories that have been growing over the past decade and are likely to continue to provide a large proportion of the electorate in future years.

The number of liberals has also increased in recent years and (although to a lesser degree than is true for libertarians) this growth comes from increases in the proportion of certain types of people in the electorate. Liberal strength is greater in the sixties and seventies generations and among those with exposure to college education. At the same time, liberalism has retained high levels of support among smaller social groups that are not growing dramatically as a proportion of the population, notably the poor, blacks, and Jews. In other words, liberalism has been able to retain both its basic level of support among small minorities of the population and at the same time is a popular ideological point of view among the population groups that are growing—the two newest political generations and the affluent, well-educated middle and upper-middle classes.

Conservatives' fortunes seem less directly connected to populational change; indeed their overall level of support in the electorate in the past decade has varied less than is the case for the other three ideological groups. On the one hand the fact that conservatism retains an appeal among many social categories (the percentage of support for conservatism varies surprisingly little across categories of income, education, or region, for example) means that the proportion of conservatives in the population is not likely to shrink drastically in the near future, just as it remained fairly constant during the 1970s. On the other hand the possibility that the slight and statistically insignificant decline in conservatives from 1976 to 1980 is a harbinger of the future is suggested by the dramatic drop in the proportion of conservatives in the political generations since the 1950s. In other words conservatives have enough supporters across many social categories and in generations recent enough (the

99

fifties generation, for example) to remain politically potent for years to come. The findings from our generational analysis, however, suggest that among the newer generations, those who will dominate the political landscape of the future, conservatism is almost completely preempted by libertarianism. Young people who oppose government activity in the economic realm usually combine that with a favorable view of personal freedoms that is not consistent with the conservative ideology.

VI. Mass Belief Systems and Political Behavior

Thus far we have described the state of American public opinion in terms of four types of mass belief systems or ideological categories. In the previous chapter we analyzed the social bases of support for those ideologies and offered some demographic explanations of the changing proportions of support for each category. This four-way analysis of American politics, however, differs from that suggested by most political observers and in some crucial ways is at odds with the way the U.S. political system is defined by political leaders in their public statements. Put more bluntly Americans live in a dichotomized political world according to conventional definitions; liberals and conservatives, Democrats and Republicans—these are the labels presented to citizens again and again by the mass media, political leaders, and political scientists. It is our aim in this chapter to describe how far mass belief systems are expressed in that dichotomous world.

What do people do when faced with the either/or choices presented to them, especially when there are two large groups, populists and libertarians, whose ideas are not even superficially addressed by most political elites? To answer this question, we first examine the crucial issue of voter turnout differences between groups and then analyze the actual voting behavior that different ideological types demonstrate in response to the choices presented them. We then look at their level of involvement in or alienation from politics in general. A diverse public, when offered simplistic and not necessarily useful choices in politics, may avoid the process, do the best they can, or develop feelings of alienation from the entire political system. It is these possibilities we explore in this chapter. Finally we present some brief evidence as to how well our four ideological labels can be used to describe the voting behavior of members of Congress. At this point we will see that populism and libertarianism do find some expression in the congressional system, although it is underrepresented as compared to the levels of public support for those views.

Ideology and Voting Behavior

It is a truism of political science that opinions must be translated into action before they can affect the American political system. The extension of this idea is that majority viewpoints may not influence government activity and that minority viewpoints may be dominant if the levels of activity vary enough between groups. Therefore we must consider our four ideological types in the same manner. How have they translated their points of view into political action through the basic mechanism of the vote? Those who vote more frequently may have more impact on the political system. Unfortunately we cannot study the voting behavior of our ideological types in every possible situation, that is in state and local elections, but we can present some interesting evidence as to how they behave in national elections.

Table 12 lists the reported voting turnout level of each of the four groups (plus the divideds and the inattentives, as they provide an interesting comparison).

Comparisons over the period from 1972 to 1980 reveal some interesting and possibly crucial trends in terms of a basic political act, that of voting in national elections. Populists vote at a slightly below average level across this time period. As populists come from those social groups that historically do not vote as often (lower educated and lower income, for example), the ideological view of populism is underrepresented in the electorate for national elections. Conversely libertarians could be expected to vote at a higher-than-average level in that they tend to be among the highly educated and more affluent types of people who do vote more often. This in fact is the case, with some variations across years. In 1980

Table 12

REPORTED VOTER TURNOUT OF IDEOLOGICAL CATEGORIES, BY
COMPARISON WITH NATIONAL AVERAGE, BY PERCENT

Ideological Category	1972	1976	1980
Libertarian	+6	+4	+10
Conservative	−1	+6	+11
Populist	−6	−5	−3
Liberal	+4	+2	−3
Divided	+8	+3	0
Inattentive	−22	−18	−34

libertarians vote at a rate 10 percent higher than that of the rest of the voting population. In the conservative and liberal categories there are interesting changes evident for the 1970s. In eight years conservatives move from slightly below to 11 percent above the national average. Liberals move in the opposite direction, shifting from an above-average to a below-average turnout level. These figures suggest that liberals are the disenchanted of the recent decade. Although they still come from social categories that are more likely to vote, their response to the changing political climate of the 1970s has been a slight withdrawal from participation. The recent success of the conservatives, especially in the 1980 presidential election, in part reflects their increasing participation, in effect filling the void left by liberal voters.

Presidential Voting, 1972 to 1980

We look now at the voting behavior of ideological types in presidential elections, presented in table 13. As a caveat to our analysis we must note that a true ideologue of course would have had some difficulty in expressing his opinions through presidential candidacies of recent years. Most political observers saw George McGovern in 1972 as presenting a fairly straightforward liberal candidacy and Ronald Reagan in 1980 as presenting the conservative opposite; otherwise, however, the ideological leanings of candidates during the 1970s have not been all that clear. Richard Nixon, Gerald Ford, John Anderson, and Jimmy Carter were often accused of being ideologically lacking, more pragmatic in their approaches to political issues. Nixon, sometimes defined as a true conservative, was at the same time a government activist, especially in regard to foreign affairs. He even instituted wage and price controls, hardly the action of a conservative. Ford, although he vetoed spending bills from the Democratic Congress, never seemed to epitomize traditional conservatism as clearly as did Reagan or Barry Goldwater. Jimmy Carter dominated presidential politics in the Democratic party through two elections and yet never attracted a definite ideological constituency; he drew from various wings of the party but never really symbolized an ideological point of view. (By our definitions Carter's moralism with regard to personal freedoms and rhetorical commitment to fiscal conservatism would label him a conservative. By his actions, however, he took few actions to limit government intervention in the economy, supported many interventionist programs, and took few initiatives to enforce his moralism, leaving his record

Table 13

VOTING BEHAVIOR OF IDEOLOGICAL TYPES IN PRESIDENTIAL ELECTIONS, BY PERCENT

Ideological Type	1972[1]		1976[2]		1980		
	Nixon	McGovern	Ford	Carter	Reagan	Carter	Anderson & Others
Libertarian	75	24	66	30	66	18	17
Conservative	84	16	65	34	78	17	5
Populist	57	42	39	61	41	57	3
Liberal	40	59	30	67	31	54	15
Divided	70	30	45	53	43	44	13

[1] 0.87 percent of sample voted for other candidates.

[2] 1.9 percent of sample voted for other candidates.

more like that of a traditional liberal, although an uncomfortable one.) John Anderson, through his independent candidacy in 1980, offered an alternative to many Americans, but the campaign itself defined his ideological views very little beyond his career-long definition as a "moderate" or liberal Republican.

How did the voters respond to these choices? In 1972 ideological choices were fairly clear for conservatives; they overwhelmingly supported Nixon over McGovern. The small proportion of libertarians that year also supported Nixon very strongly. Liberals, on the other hand, gave McGovern his highest level of support but it constituted a far-from-overwhelming endorsement; a significant number of liberals supported Nixon. It was among populists that the battle was most evenly fought; populists had to choose between two candidates who split in exactly an opposite direction from the one they would have felt comfortable with: Nixon was the social conservative populists would have liked but he attacked the economic initiatives associated with populism. McGovern was of little help to populists; his economic liberalism was less appealing when combined with lenient positions on personal freedom issues. Thus it is not surprising that populists were the most divided group in 1972.

The ideological views of presidential candidates were even less clear in 1976, as a Democrat with undefinable ideological characteristics faced a Republican whose performance in office had not excited conservative support. Each of the four ideological groups split in surprisingly similar proportions. Ford drew about 66 percent of the support of both libertarians and conservatives, apparently drawing most of his support in response to his advocacy of economic nonintervention. Carter, on the other hand, drew 67 percent support from liberals and 61 percent from populists, again apparently converting traditional Democratic arguments for economic intervention into votes. Neither candidate, however, was shut out in any ideological category; each drew at least 30 percent from each group. As we suggested in chapter II, this may be a classic case of ideological American voters looking at two unclear ideological statements from candidates and simply making the best choice they could.

The 1980 battle was more ideological in tone as Reagan clung to his articulation of conservative principles, leaving Carter defined as a liberal almost by default. Carter was not a McGovern-type liberal, however, and often sought to battle Reagan on his own ground in terms of economic minimalism. Neither stressed the expansion of personal freedoms as a goal, although Reagan did emphasize his commitment to "traditional values," often viewed as a code phrase for a less tolerant view toward personal freedom and alternative lifestyles. The situation was further confused by the presence of independent John Anderson, who offered voters an alternative to the two major party candidates without tying himself to any particular ideological point of view. The findings in table 13 indicate that Reagan did in fact cement conservatives (voting at a higher level than ever) into a voting bloc. Despite Carter's claims to conservatism, Reagan drew 78 percent of those citizens to his camp. Carter was unable to create any such ideological base. Liberals gave him barely a majority; 15 percent of them apparently protested with a vote for Anderson and 31 percent were willing to vote for a self-avowed conservative rather than stick with Carter. (The decline in turnout among liberals in 1980 is also relevant here.) Carter also slipped among the populists slightly from four years earlier. Many of this group were attracted to Reagan but few chose the Anderson alternative. Libertarians present the most intriguing voting pattern of 1980, however. In that election 66 percent of them voted for Reagan (the same percentage that had supported Ford four years earlier), apparently stressing economic issues over questions of personal liberties—as there was no candidate expressing that point of view anyway. Those who did not choose Reagan, however, split evenly between Carter and Anderson. Although a growing segment of libertarians was not yet willing to move en masse to the candidate offered by the Libertarian party, a significant number of them were willing to vote for a third alternative to the two major candidates.

This analysis of presidential voting behavior clearly indicates that ideological groups have a difficult time in American politics. Faced with alternatives that do not clearly articulate their point of view or that stress one dimension and ignore the other (usually personal freedoms), citizens with ideological viewpoints split in predictable ways, but ways that we believe express the old "lesser of two evils" adage. Only conservatives seem to have a consistent chance to be able to choose a candidate who expresses their point of view; that may very well explain their increased turnout levels. Both populists and libertarians must make do, given the choices offered to them, and, increasingly, liberals are just as disenchanted as populists with the standard-bearers of the Democratic party, supposedly their vehicle for ideological expression.

A Case Study: The Election of 1980

We believe there is a need for a more detailed description and analysis of the presidential voting behavior of ideological types in 1980. First of all we wish to reiterate the points suggested above about the relative impact of different groupings on the political process. A summary of 1980's events will highlight the importance of the varying voting behaviors we have noted. Second the 1980 election, in light of our findings presented thus far, offers an intriguing question: Given the consistently small size of the conservative category in the United States, how did a self-proclaimed conservative such as Ronald Reagan win a landslide victory in 1980? The answer is really quite simple and lies in the interplay of the factors we have just described: varying levels of turnout and levels of support for the presidential candidates.

The information in table 14 is the same as that given in tables 12 and 13 about voting turnout and presidential voting choice in 1980, but it is presented a slightly different way. The purpose of table 14 is to describe a typical or representative group of 100 American citizens in the election year of 1980. The group is apportioned among our ideological types; these 100 people are a diverse group, with populists and liberals being the two largest categories. The voting choice for these 100 citizens is actually a two-stage choice: First they decide whether or not to vote, then those who have decided to vote must choose among Reagan, Carter, and Anderson.

In many ways the most crucial event in this election year (as in most election years) was which of these citizens made that initial decision to vote. We can see that 46 of the 100 citizens did not vote and therefore are no longer relevant to our explaining what happened in the presidential election. More importantly those 46 who did not vote are not evenly distributed across ideological types. Most conservatives and libertarians decided to vote, while about half of the populists and liberals decided not to vote. Thus from the data on who actually composed the electorate, it can be seen that the differences in the proportions of the ideological groups are virtually eliminated: Libertarians and conservatives are actually about even with populists and liberals in making up the electorate.

Consider now the second stage of the decision process for the

Table 14

VOTING BEHAVIOR IN 1980 PRESIDENTIAL ELECTION

| | Ideological Types | | | | | | |
	Libertarian	Conservative	Populist	Liberal	Divided	Inattentive	Total
Electorate:							
Size of Group	18	17	26	24	10	5	100
Minus Nonvoters	-6	-6	-13	-12	-5	-4	-46
Actual Electorate	12	11	13	12	5	1	54
							Election Outcome
Presidential Choice:							
Reagan	8	9	5	3	2	1	28 (52%)*
Carter	2	2	8	8	2	0	22 (41%)*
Anderson	2	0	0	1	1	0	4 (7%)

*Figures differ slightly from the actual Reagan, Carter, and Anderson percentages because of rounding off.

remaining 54 citizens: Who did they vote for among the three candidates? Here the importance of the cohesiveness of the group is crucial; how well did they stick together to cast their votes as a bloc for their presidential favorite? It is apparent from the table that eight of the twelve libertarians and nine of the eleven conservatives voted for Ronald Reagan, giving him the bulk of his support and a basis for an easy election victory. The two groups that supported Carter, the populists and liberals, did not vote for him at such a high rate. Carter carried the populists, but not by a margin large enough to offset Reagan's advantage among conservatives and libertarians. Even the liberals, who gave Carter eight of their twelve votes, included some significant defections to Reagan (probably those who were voting on the basis of some other reason besides general ideology, such as personality differences, protest over Carter's presidency, or handling of the Iranian hostage situation, or, in the case of liberal Republicans who swallowed hard and voted for Reagan, their partisanship). The divided group made no difference in the overall outcome; they split evenly between the candidates. Finally the one of the five inattentives who voted simply added another point onto Ronald Reagan's margin. We also can note that this table summarizes the failure of the John Anderson independent candidacy: he made no headway among the core supporters for Carter and Reagan, nor was he able to translate his "independence" into inroads into the groups who would not have been clearly satisfied with the two major candidates—the libertarians, the populists, and the divided.

In short the explanation of the 1980 election results as an ideological statement rests on two simple facts: The groups that were more sympathetic to Reagan voted more heavily than those groups that could be expected to support Carter, and the Reagan-oriented groups voted more cohesively than did Carter's "natural" supporters. In other words, if populists and liberals had turned out as heavily and had stuck with Carter as strongly as conservatives and libertarians adhered to Reagan, the election would have been very close and quite possibly a Carter victory. One lesson to learn from this is that although voter turnout is still obviously crucial for liberal-oriented Democratic candidates (as the Democratic party has known for years), so is the attractiveness of the candidate. Such a candidate must be able to excite and mobilize the liberal voters (which Carter did not do), but also must be attractive enough in some way (personality, articulateness, or past record, for example) to fight inroads by the opposition into populist ranks, where such a candidate is vulnerable owing to his stands on personal freedoms.

On the other hand possibilities do exist for other types of coalitions: Consider a coalition between libertarians and liberals, perhaps in reaction to Moral Majority successes, emphasizing individual rights and a tolerant view on lifestyle issues.

The low turnout in 1980 among populists is probably a reflection of demographic tendencies in that group; populists come from the social categories that have always tended to vote less. That is not true for the liberal turnout. Liberals are generally the types of people who do vote, and their declining turnout through this period probably reflects a disenchantment with the candidates offered, the Democratic party's recent record in elections and governing, as well as a sense that they are Democrats out of touch with the supposed conservative tide sweeping the country. A candidate who could maintain the support of libertarian voters and at the same time mobilize liberals (especially the young) around issues of personal freedom would be drawing on two groups who are likely to vote and who possess the skills to participate effectively in political campaigns. Thus the future could be dominated by a liberal-libertarian conflict over economic issues or, as in the case just suggested, a liberal-libertarian alliance.

Voting for Congress, 1972 to 1980

Finally we can look at one other piece of evidence as to the voting behavior of our ideological types, although there are some limitations on how much we can conclude from this evidence. Voting for the House of Representatives can be a channel for ideological views. Unfortunately for our analysis, it can also be many other things; for example congressional voting can reflect a voter's views on the general state of the economy, a statement on the performance of the president or Congress as a whole, a vote of confidence for the local incumbent, a reflection of the incumbent's attention to local needs, or any variety of purely local issues and candidates. The data in table 15, however, suggest that even in congressional voting, our four ideological types generally split along the lines suggested by the analysis of presidential voting. Libertarians tend to vote Republican, although a large minority stay with the Democrats. Conservatives have become more and more Republican in their voting habits over the past few years, although 40 percent clung to

Table 15

Voting Behavior of Ideological Types: Votes for Democratic Congressional Candidates, by Percent

Ideological Type	1972	1976	1980
Libertarian	38	37	37
Conservative	56	45	40
Populist	56	65	64
Liberal	74	71	71
Divided	49	55	55
National	56	56	54

NOTE: Remaining percentage in each case consists almost entirely of Republican votes; the percentage of votes reported for other party candidates was only 0.6 percent in 1972, 2.7 percent in 1976, and 0.5 percent in 1980.

Democratic congressional candidates in 1980. Populists are the most split of the four groups in response to the dichotomous choices presented to them in American politics, although a majority voted Democratic (1972, 1976, and 1980). Liberals, finally, are the most cohesive of the four groups, voting over 70 percent for Democratic candidates in each year. This trend could reflect the fact that Democrats running at the congressional level often are far more liberal than the man at the top of their ticket has been in recent years. When given a clear and unequivocal liberal candidacy, liberal voters will support it.

The thrust of our argument is that in American politics, voters are facing less-than-clear choices. For libertarians and populists the choices offered by a two-party, two-ideology political system are problems rather than solutions to their need to express their political views. Choosing is easier for conservatives at the presidential level and liberals at the congressional level, although neither group has a definite and consistent political party to express their ideological views in any pure fashion.

We will now turn to more direct evidence regarding the difficult choices facing ideological types in American politics. How do these four ideological types respond to what is basically a dichotomous political world? Both ideological labels and political parties are presented to the public in either/or terms by political leaders and most of the mass media. How do liberals, conservatives, libertarians, and populists respond?

The Nature of Ideological Self-Identification and Partisanship

Politicians, journalists, commentators, and the average citizen usually discuss ideology in terms of a liberal-conservative dichotomy. This tendency has continued despite mounting evidence over the years that these labels do not explain very well what the public thinks and that there are often misunderstandings or disagreements over what the labels mean. Political scientists and professional pollsters (as discussed in chapter II) are also bound to the liberal-conservative one-dimensional approach to ideology. One manifestation of this is that in public opinion polls, pollsters and academics often ask citizens to place themselves on a liberal-conservative scale, with the options of placing themselves in the middle (thus becoming self-defined moderates or middle-of-the-roaders) or not answering the question at all. How do the four types of ideological citizens we have defined respond to such a forced choice, one that for many of them does little to describe their particular set of opinions about politics?

The figures in table 16 describe how each of the ideological groups distribute themselves across the four major possibilities in such a question in the 1972–80 period. Libertarians generally choose either the conservative or moderate label, although across time they may be moving more toward the option of not answering. Most libertarians, however, do try to make a choice, more so than does any other group. The stress on economic conditions and government activity to deal with those conditions in recent years may explain the tendency to use the liberal label less and the conservative label slightly more. Conservatives of course find the self-labeling process much easier; an increasing number of them choose the "correct" label of conservative, up to 50 percent by 1980. A significant number of them opt for either giving a moderate response or not answering the question. We suspect that such avoidance of the proper label, by either liberals or conservatives, reflects some reaction to the notion of self-labeling or else to some connotations attached to the label that the respondents wish to avoid. Only 7 percent of our conservatives "mislabel" themselves as liberals.

For populists none of the labels offered do very much to describe their opinions about politics. Half of them, possibly as a reflection of lower educational levels, decide not to respond at all. Those who do make a choice are divided among all three of the labels, although there is a slight tendency for more to call themselves conservatives.

112

Table 16

IDEOLOGICAL SELF-CLASSIFICATION BY IDEOLOGICAL TYPES, BY PERCENT

Self-Classification	Libertarian			Conservative			Populist			Liberal			Divided		
	1972	1976	1980	1972	1976	1980	1972	1976	1980	1972	1976	1980	1972	1976	1980
Liberal	23	18	15	7	7	7	10	11	11	39	43	31	15	16	15
Moderate	26	34	20	27	27	18	21	20	15	22	23	20	33	34	30
Conservative	38	37	43	35	44	50	22	22	21	16	13	16	28	29	21
No answer	14	11	22	31	22	25	46	47	53	23	21	32	24	21	34

NOTE: Reading down, this table illustrates how people in each of the ideological categories answer when asked to describe themselves as liberal, moderate, or conservative. In 1980, for instance, 15 percent of libertarians described themselves as liberals, 20 percent as moderates, and so on. Inattentives omitted.

Table 17

IDEOLOGICAL COMPOSITION OF SELF-CLASSIFIED GROUPS, BY PERCENT

Self-Classification	Libertarian			Conservative			Populist			Liberal			Divided		
	1972	1976	1980	1972	1976	1980	1972	1976	1980	1972	1976	1980	1972	1976	1980
Liberal	13	14	17	8	7	8	11	16	18	41	43	47	17	19	10
Moderate	10	17	18	20	20	15	26	19	21	16	15	27	26	26	17
Conservative	14	18	27	25	30	30	26	19	20	11	8	14	21	21	8
No answer	4	5	11	17	13	11	42	35	38	12	11	21	14	13	10

NOTE: Reading across, this table illustrates the actual ideological composition of self-classified poll respondents. For instance, of those CPS respondents who described themselves as liberal in 1980, 17 percent were actually libertarian, 8 percent were conservative, and so on. Inattentives omitted.

For them the term "conservatism" probably expresses concerns about changing social values associated with the expansion of personal freedoms. For liberals the choice of a label should be easy, but our findings indicate that it is not. A decreasing number of liberals, now less than one-third, choose the liberal label to describe themselves; we can assume that the connotations attached to the label in recent years (big spending and government deficits, with the implication of fiscal irresponsibility) inhibit their self-definition. Where do they place themselves? Although a significant 16 percent in 1980 "mislabel" themselves as conservative, most of the remainder choose not to respond, up to one-third by 1980. This finding, coupled with the lower turnout and less cohesive support for Carter in 1980, suggest that the political twists of the late 1970s have left the liberals as the most uneasy group, clinging to their opinions about the necessity for government action in the economy and expansion of personal freedoms, but not sure how to express these beliefs in a political climate generally defined as hostile to such ideas. Although increasing in size across this decade, liberals may be in a state of flux. Possibly the high proportion of young people in their ranks explains some of this apparent uncertainty. Young people may have political beliefs just like anyone else, but may not have the political experience or even sustained exposure to ideological discussions to cement their liberalism and to be able to define it precisely. (This could also explain why libertarians, also including a large number of young people, choose the simple label of "conservative," one that is more socially acceptable in current times.) Finally, although the divided category does not constitute a large segment of the public, it is interesting to observe how its members distribute themselves across a liberal-conservative continuum. An increasing number, one-third in 1980, choose not to label themselves at all, while about another third choose the basically meaningless label of "moderate." Small minorities choose either the conservative or liberal labels.

Looking at these findings in another way in table 17, we can ask how the self-defined categories gather their supporters. Who are the self-defined conservatives, for example? Conservatives, in terms of self-definition, can be almost anything: 30 percent are conservatives by our definition, 27 percent are libertarians (or as most commentators would say, are "conservative" on economic issues), 20 percent are populists (or "conservative" on issues of personal freedom), and the remainder fall into either the liberal or divided

114

categories. Self-defined liberals come predominantly from those people expressing liberal positions on both dimensions as we have defined them; about 50 percent of self-defined liberals in 1980 are liberals by definition on issue positions as well. The remainder are mostly divided into populists (18 percent) or libertarians (17 percent) by our analysis; only 8 percent of self-defined liberals actually express conservative positions on the issues. Of more interest, of course, are the other two categories. Regarding the people who either choose to be moderates or refuse to respond to the question, what are their actual opinions across the six major issues that make up the dimensions of economic and personal freedoms?

Those who call themselves moderates come from all ideological categories: the 1980 data show that 27 percent of them are liberals, 21 percent are populists, 18 percent are libertarians, 18 percent are conservatives, and 17 percent are divided. Thus if we treat moderates as a cohesive group of people whose political opinions simply lie somewhere between the liberal and conservative views, we are making a ridiculous error of analysis. The John Anderson campaign of 1980, which tried to appeal to some moderate coalition poised between Democratic liberalism and Republican conservatism, was therefore doomed to failure. The Gallup poll sometimes asks whether respondents would vote for a so-called Center Party, one that is more conservative than the Democrats but more liberal than the Republicans. It is generally found that about 25 percent of the population would support such a party. It is not clear, however, what the respondents think they would be voting for. Perhaps some of them think they would get a party that takes conservative positions on economics but avoids the social conservatism of the Republicans (what we would call a libertarian party). On the other hand some of them may envision a party that supports traditional Democratic economic activism but without McGovernite, "new politics" views on social issues. And then, of course, some may assume that the new party would manage to squeeze in between the Republicans and Democrats on each different issue. Whatever the case, it is not at all clear that there is any real basis of support for a Center Party.

Similarly those party mavericks who argue that their parties should move to the center to attract more voters can find little evidence here that such a course would benefit the party. A more moderate Democratic party, for example, would not necessarily draw many of these moderates to its camp and could lose its base of core support, the liberals, in the process. Moderates, as self-defined in public opinion surveys, do not always choose the middle position on most political issues. Their total set of opinions often places them into one of the four ideological categories, but they cannot express that in self-identification because the populist and libertarian terms are not discussed very well in American politics or because they dislike the connotations attached to one of the two standard labels. The traditional discussion of the domination of American politics by moderate voters is a mistake. The American public is not middle of the road; it is spread out all over the road, a fractionalized public facing a political system that does not translate popular opinion into public discussion very well.

Finally who are the people (about a third of the public in most of these surveys) who refuse to answer the question, because of uncertainty or ignorance of the labels, or because of an awareness that the labels simply do not make sense as descriptions of their views? The bulk of them are populists: 42 percent in 1972, 35 percent in 1976, and 38 percent in 1980. In other words we must not treat those who do not respond as political neuters or political dummies; a significant number of them believe in the two basic principles of populism, government intervention in the economy and government regulation of our personal and social behavior. Here is the clearest case of ideological views not translating into public or elite terms. Many populists exist, they have opinions on issues that fall into a reasonable ideological framework, but they are asked to call themselves liberals or conservatives. Many respond by avoiding the question. The remainder of the "no answer" group is fairly spread out across the ideological categories; 21 percent are liberals, 11 percent each are conservatives and libertarians, and 20 percent are divided—citizens for whom even the populist and libertarian labels would not permit accurate self-definition.

At this point we should make one comment on the methodology of survey research and the prospects for using that approach to understand public ideology and ideological labeling. What if a national survey organization asked a question that allowed respondents to choose among four labels (liberal, conservative, populist, and libertarian), with the option to choose none of these? We would certainly see such a question as more useful than the usual liberal-conservative dichotomy. However it would not initially generate the same kinds of proportions of supporters of each group as our analysis produced. In the first place many would still "mislabel"

116

themselves either because they have the terms confused or dislike the connotations of labeling. We see that even with liberals and conservatives; some of them choose not to label themselves in accordance with their issue positions. Second, the terms "libertarian" and "populist" are simply not part of the vocabulary of most citizens; as we have argued, politics is not presented to them in those terms by political communicators. Thus even with detailed explanations of the terms provided in the survey, it is likely that such a self-labeling question would still underrepresent both populists and libertarians. Two Opinion Research Corporation surveys in 1980 asked respondents to define themselves as liberal, conservative, libertarian, or middle-of-the-road. Only 1 percent in each survey chose libertarian, but that proportion rose to 10 percent and 12 percent after respondents were given a definition of libertarianism. Self-described libertarians came almost equally from the other three groups. Even the higher percentages, of course, are still below our estimates of those who take libertarian positions on the issues. Only after these ideological labels have existed as part of the public discourse for a few years could citizens be expected to be able to choose labels that accurately describe their belief systems.

In summary our analysis suggests that most Americans face a problem when asked to label themselves. Most attempt to choose a label that comes closest to their position on issues, on both dimensions if possible or, if that is not possible, on what is probably the more important dimension to them. Finally many of them opt for the middle category or avoid answering the question rather than choosing an erroneous label. Similarly people who hold certain mass belief views have to make another dichotomous, forced choice in American politics: partisanship.

Just as they are asked to choose between liberal and conservative labels but are left an option to choose the moderate or don't know label in response to ideology questions, survey respondents usually are asked to choose a partisan self-identification. In answer to a question that asks which party they feel closest to (not which one they vote for or are registered in), respondents can call themselves Democrats or Republicans, but are left with the option of choosing the label "independent" (which has no inherent ideological connotations and can mean whatever the citizen wants it to mean) or not answering the question at all. Table 18 shows how people in our ideological categories respond to this situation, thereby provid-

117

Table 18

PARTISAN SELF-IDENTIFICATION BY IDEOLOGICAL TYPES, BY PERCENT

Partisan Group	Libertarian			Conservative			Populist			Liberal			Divided		
	1972	1976	1980	1972	1976	1980	1972	1976	1980	1972	1976	1980	1972	1976	1980
Democrat	26	23	17	42	31	25	48	47	55	41	47	50	34	34	41
Independent	38	42	45	29	32	35	25	30	26	42	41	35	36	43	36
Republican	36	35	38	29	36	39	25	21	16	16	12	13	29	21	22
No Preference	0	0	0	1	1	1	3	2	3	1	1	2	1	1	1

ing a basis for some new explanations of partisan conflict and the public's response to the two-party system.

Partisan identification is different among ideological groups. The patterns of identification also have changed in the last decade. Libertarians, for example, demonstrate a clear pattern of partisan choice: The bulk of them classify themselves as independents, recognizing that their point of view is not adequately expressed by either major party. A large minority of libertarians identify themselves as Republicans, apparently a response to the anti–big government element of Republican party rhetoric. In fact there is an evident move away from the Democratic party over time, possibly because the party in the McGovern years of the early 1970s more clearly articulated libertarian views on one dimension, personal freedoms, than it does today. By 1980 libertarians move almost totally into the independent and Republican camps (83 percent of them). Perhaps the study of Dearborn voters by Wayman and Stockton (1980) sheds some light on partisan identification and the voting patterns of libertarians and populists. Wayman and Stockton found that while there was no correlation between views on traditional economic issues and views on "the new morality," people seemed to vote on the basis of their economic positions. Views on moral and law-and-order issues had the potential to destabilize partisanship, though they did not seem to do so in this study.

Conservatives also are moving away from the Democratic party, possibly a recognition of the stress that party has placed on economic intervention throughout this period. In 1972 more conservatives choose the Democratic label than any other, but only 25 percent of them are still with that party in 1980. They have moved to Republican affiliation (39 percent) and independent status (35 percent). Most conservatives, then, in surveying the alternatives in recent years, have concluded either that the Republican party is their proper home or that neither party is truly expressing conservative principles and they should therefore retain their independence from party labels.

Populists' and liberals' partisanship remains the most stable over time. The populists, whose ideals have usually been championed by members of the Democratic party even if they were outcasts within the party (such as George Wallace), are the most cohesive group of party adherents. About half of them in all three years (with a high of 55 percent in 1980), choose the Democratic party label, part of this of course reflecting their base in the South where Democratic affiliation is a political tradition not easily shaken by more liberal trends within the national party. Roughly 25 percent or more of the populists choose independence as a label and a declining minority choose the Republicans. Liberals, however, demonstrate the most stability through the decade, although there is a slight increase in the number who call themselves Democrats, up to 50 percent in 1980. Most of the others are independents, with only 13 percent attaching themselves to the old liberal wing of the Republican party.

These findings indicate that although attachment to the political parties has been on the decline for many years, the 1970s may have been a period of party retrenchment or clarification for many citizens. Many liberals were Democrats and many conservatives were Republicans in 1972, but over the following few years those points of view were even more clearly channeled into the political party that came closest to representing them. More conservatives moved into the Republican ranks, while slightly more liberals were choosing to call themselves Democrats, although 35 percent of each of those ideological groups remained in the independent category. The proportion of liberals and conservatives in the "wrong place" with respect to party—conservative Democrats and liberal Republicans—declined to a much less significant force during the decade (see chapter VIII). The two groups who have not found a party that even claims to express their views took two different courses of partisan action in the 1970s. Populists maintained their attachment to the Democrats, and libertarians moved away from the Democrats toward independence. If there is a group of ideological citizens who seem to be more willing and more likely to remain outside the current two-party system, it is the libertarians.

Mass Belief Systems and Political Alienation

In this chapter we have been concerned with the responses of the four ideological types to the nature of American politics as it is presented to them. We have analyzed their voting turnout, their voting for president and Congress, and their use of self-identification labels of ideology and partisanship. Much of this information, however, raises a broader question. Given the difficulty that some of our types have in matching with or expressing their views through contemporary political groups and leaders, is it likely that those groups are more alienated from the political system in a general sense?

Libertarians and populists certainly have reason to feel disenchanted or cynical about the system and politics, as the system does little to express their point of view, even in the most minimal of ways. On the other hand there is extensive evidence that Americans generally have become more alienated in recent decades as a response to such major political traumas as Vietnam, the civil rights movement, Watergate, and long-term economic discomforts. Furthermore, rather than being a product of one frustrated segment of society, such as a minority group or the poor, alienation cuts across all class, social, and political categories (for example see Schwartz 1973; Wright 1976; and Maddox 1981). If this were the case, we would expect all of our ideological categories to demonstrate equal levels of alienation. They all would have responded to the political problems and the failures of government in recent years in the same way. To answer this question concerning alienation, we must remember that alienation, or dissatisfaction with the political system, is a broad and sometimes ambiguous concept. We will observe the alienation levels of different groups, therefore, by looking at their attitudes toward political interest, feelings of control over politics, trust in government in general, and perceptions of government responsiveness.

One implication of alienation is that if one feels alienated, he ultimately loses interest in politics altogether, although interest in politics in the United States has rarely been very high, especially in the postwar era. Table 19 deals with levels of political interest. Respondents could answer that they were very interested, somewhat interested, or not very interested. The table covers only the proportion who chose the "very interested" response, one which is usually chosen on the national CPS surveys by roughly one-third

Table 19

PROPORTION OF IDEOLOGICAL TYPES WHO SAY THEY ARE VERY INTERESTED IN POLITICS, BY PERCENT

Ideological Type	1972	1976	1980
Libertarian	39	39	38
Conservative	28	39	40
Populist	25	33	24
Liberal	38	44	28
Divided	33	41	26

of the sample. Libertarians express the most consistent patterns across the 1970s, although conservatives (possibly stimulated by the presence of a more conservative candidate for president in 1980) have increased interest levels to match those of the libertarians. Populists lag behind in interest, with only about 25 percent of them expressing high levels of interest—except in 1976 when this heavily southern group's interest levels may have been inflated by the choice of a presidential candidate from the South who described himself in populist terms. Liberals demonstrate an erratic pattern over the years, being slightly above average in interest levels in 1972 (the year of a liberal presidential disaster), somewhat higher in 1976, and then undergoing a precipitous drop in 1980. This is further evidence of liberal disaffection in the latter part of the 1970s.

Political scientists have long considered one crucial component of political alienation to be the concept of political efficacy. Although the definition of the term is the object of some debate, generally it is assumed that political efficacy refers to the citizen's perceptions of how much he can influence politics through his own individual or group-channeled action. A lack of a sense of political efficacy may grow from the sense that one cannot control the political system because the system itself is not going to listen (external factors) or because the citizen himself lacks the ability (internal factors). Tables 20 and 21 offer some evidence on these points. Table 20, which gives the proportion who think that public officials do not care what most people think, describes inefficacy, or alienation, that is assumed to be the system's fault. Here we find surprisingly few distinctions among the ideological types. Libertarians demonstrate a slight increase in feelings of inefficacy, to the point

Table 20

PROPORTION OF IDEOLOGICAL TYPES WHO SAY PUBLIC OFFICIALS DON'T CARE WHAT MOST PEOPLE THINK, BY PERCENT

Ideological Type	1972	1976	1980
Libertarian	42	44	49
Conservative	51	48	51
Populist	57	61	55
Liberal	37	49	49
Divided	40	46	54

Table 21

PROPORTION OF IDEOLOGICAL TYPES WHO BELIEVE PEOPLE LIKE ME HAVE NO SAY ABOUT WHAT THE GOVERNMENT DOES, BY PERCENT

Ideological Type	1972	1976	1980
Libertarian	33	34	31
Conservative	36	36	35
Populist	49	51	45
Liberal	31	37	37
Divided	25	38	46

where about 49 percent express that feeling in 1980. The pattern for liberals is almost the same. The beliefs of conservatives (51 percent in 1980) and populists (55 percent in 1980) do not change much during the period. All four of the groups, however, are very similar by 1980; about half of each expresses doubts that public officials care what people think.

Table 20 probes the existence of internal efficacy, in this case the number of people who think that people like themselves have no say about what the government does. Here we see some distinctions among ideological types. Although liberals tend to agree with the statement slightly more in 1980, basically the findings for liberals, libertarians, and conservatives are similar; about one-third of each agrees with the statement. Populists, however, express this lack of internal efficacy at a consistently higher rate; usually about half of them do not feel that they can influence government. In other words about half of each of the ideological types believe there is some severe problem with their ability to influence government effectively, but only populists express this feeling predominantly in terms of their own inabilities. Populists are the least educated group, of course, and their perceived inadequacy probably reflects that fact. Two-thirds of liberals, libertarians, and conservatives believe that people like them (who are of course more likely to be middle-income, and well-educated) can have some influence on the system.

The data in table 22 demonstrate that levels of political trust (belief that government is run to benefit the people rather than a few) are at a fairly low level. Although there are some distinctions between ideological types, a large majority of each group believes government is run to benefit a few big interests, and all the groups except

Table 22

POLITICAL TRUST OF IDEOLOGICAL TYPES: PROPORTION WHO
SAY GOVERNMENT IS RUN TO BENEFIT A FEW BIG INTERESTS
RATHER THAN ALL THE PEOPLE, BY PERCENT

Ideological Type	1976	1980
Libertarian	62	75
Conservative	61	81
Populist	66	67
Liberal	74	63
Divided	64	73

NOTE: Data for 1972 omitted because question was asked that year of only a subset of the sample, and the subset was *not* asked all the issue questions used to define the ideological types.

the liberals express increased support for that view in 1980. Two interesting anomalies exist here. First, the phrase "run to benefit a few big interests" would seem to sum up traditional populist views of American politics, and yet agreement with that statement is less among populists than it is among libertarians and conservatives. Second, liberals, who often lament the influence of big corporations on government, agree with the statement less in 1980. This could have been a response to attacks by Reagan and conservatives on the Democratic-controlled federal government in 1980. In other words liberals were more likely to perceive "big interest influence" in 1976, when Gerald Ford was still in office, than they were after four years of a Democratic presidency. The overall point of these findings, however, is that political trust seems to have little connection to political ideology; high levels of distrust exist regardless of ideological viewpoint.

The same is true to a lesser extent of perceived government responsiveness. Table 23 lists the proportion of people who think that government simply does not pay much attention to its citizens. In 1976 there are much lower levels of agreement with that statement, but by 1980 all the types except the liberals have increased their agreement. Almost half of the libertarians and conservatives believe that government is not very responsive to citizens and slightly more populists believe it as had four years earlier. Again liberals are against the tide here: Only 32 percent of them believed government was nonresponsive in 1976 (even though a Republican

Table 23

PERCEIVED RESPONSIVENESS OF GOVERNMENT BY IDEOLOGICAL TYPE: PROPORTION WHO SAY GOVERNMENT DOES NOT PAY MUCH ATTENTION TO CITIZENS, BY PERCENT

Ideological Type	1976	1980
Libertarian	29	49
Conservative	35	48
Populist	40	44
Liberal	32	29
Divided	29	40

was in the White House) and even fewer did by 1980. In one sense this liberal belief in government responsiveness could be considered a defense of the general principle of government intervention and activity, rather than an evaluation of any particular governmental responses to citizens.

Alienation levels appear to be evenly distributed among our ideological types. Figure 22 summarizes our various measures of alienation and shows how these measures are divided among the four ideological categories in 1980. Although some differences are evident among the ideological groups, the clearest message of figure 22 is that alienation exists at about the same levels among all groups. The two groups often ignored by politicans and political groups—the populists and the libertarians—are not generally more alienated than the more "accepted" groups, the liberals and the conservatives. Alienation cuts across ideology in contemporary American politics, suggesting it is unlikely that a coalition of alienated citizens will be forged to challenge the status quo. Some may be alienated because government is doing too much, others because it is doing too little.

Even though the differences between them are not very large, we can describe some patterns across the four ideological types. In many ways libertarians and conservatives are alike in levels of alienation. Both groups exhibit about the same level of political interest (slightly higher than average) and quite a bit of agreement that the government is not responsive and is run more for a few interests rather than for the general public, but both groups also express some faith in their own ability to do something about this political situation. This latter view probably underlies the groups'

125

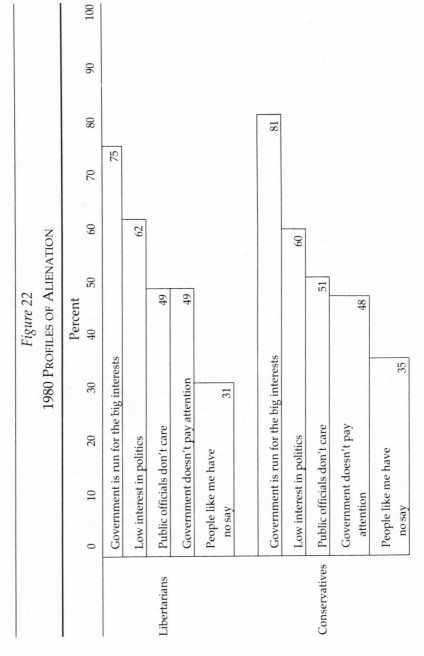

Figure 22
1980 PROFILES OF ALIENATION

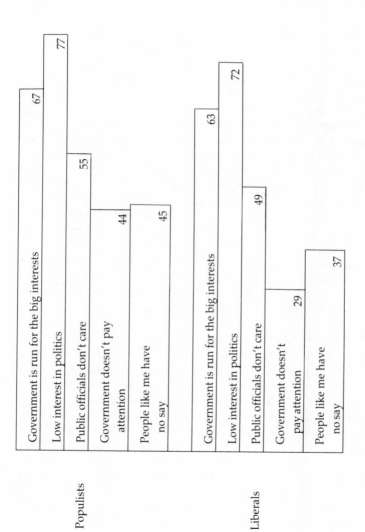

Populists

Government is run for the big interests — 67
Low interest in politics — 77
Public officials don't care — 55
Government doesn't pay attention — 44
People like me have no say — 45

Liberals

Government is run for the big interests — 63
Low interest in politics — 72
Public officials don't care — 49
Government doesn't pay attention — 29
People like me have no say — 37

higher levels of participation and their ability to affect the political system (as was evident in our analysis of the 1980 election).

Populists, however, express about the same levels of distrust of the political system and its responsiveness, but they are less interested in politics and feel that their own effectiveness is limited. Thus populists believe the same things about politics but feel less involved than other groups, and therefore they are less effective (again as demonstrated in the 1980 election).

The views of liberals are more difficult to sort out, again suggesting that liberalism is in flux in today's political system. By 1980 their interest levels had declined, quite possibly a reflection of their loss of influence in the Democratic party and the rising conservative success in national politics. Yet liberal responses to other questions indicate less of a pattern. Liberals claim that government is responsive to people's needs and that they as individuals have some degree of effectiveness in politics. At the same time, though, liberals believe—or at least a majority of them do—that government is run to benefit a few big interests. It seems that liberals are in a period of confusion, retaining their faith in government's ability to act and its general performance of those duties and obligations it has to citizens, but not being uniformly optimistic about the general thrust or success of government in recent years. Such confusion of course may simply reflect frustration. Liberals believe that government should and can do things to help the citizen, but they are frustrated by the results of government efforts to do that in recent years. One is tempted to say that liberals believe they have a good idea, but just do not understand why it will not work.

Four Ideologies in Congress

We have discussed the fact that, for American citizens, having to express their four major ideological viewpoints through a political system that defines its political parties, candidates, elections, and ideological labels only in two-dimensional form represents a major problem, one that the citizens resolve both by choosing the lesser of two evils and by retaining feelings of alienation. There is one other avenue to explore here, however: Voters may send to Congress members who express some variation of their ideological views, even though all of the members of Congress are either Democrats or Republicans and are usually labeled as either liberal or conservative. Even if voters are not always aware of the specific voting records of their congressmen, those officials may be expressing some of the more complex ideological views discussed in this book either for personal or political reasons. There may be populists or libertarians in Congress, for example, even though they do not campaign as such and are elected under other labels of ideology and partisanship.

We have some recent evidence as to the ideological makeup of Congress based on a study by *The Baron Report* (1983), which rated congressmen on separate scales of economic issues and social issues, each scale being composed of important votes in the 1982 session. Each member received a score on both economic and social issues, which represented whether he fell above or below the median rating on that scale. A member with a high score on the social issue scale, for example, voted more in support of expansion of personal freedoms on crucial votes that dealt with that dimension.[8]

By combining each congressman's rating on both scales, we can classify congressmen as liberal (voting for economic intervention and for expanded personal freedoms), conservative (voting against both), populist (supporting economic intervention but opposing expanded personal freedoms), or libertarian (supporting expanded personal freedoms but opposing economic intervention). These measures are only rough approximations of the ideological leanings of congressmen, of course, and in some cases a member may be typed a liberal, for example, when the scores are only slightly above the median on both dimensions. Nevertheless there is some expression of all four belief systems in congressional voting.

Rather than present the individual scores of all 535 members of Congress, we summarize by region the classification of both houses' members in table 24. The two most-publicized ideologies, liberalism and conservatism, do dominate both houses of Congress. In their 1982 voting records on major isssues, 72 percent of Senate members and 81 percent of House members are either liberal or conservative. Their regional background is not surprising. Liberals predominate in the East and conservatives in the South, and the two groups are fairly evenly matched in Midwest and the West. Libertarian senti-

---

[8]Some libertarians have criticized the study for having selected votes on the social issues scales, pointing out that to be defined as liberal on social issues a member of Congress had to vote not only in opposition to government restrictions on abortion, homosexuality, and press freedom but in favor of busing, gun control, and federal spending for food stamps. Thus, the critics argue, the issues chosen did not really reflect "expansion of personal freedoms" as we define it. Nevertheless the two scales still provide a useful new perspective on congressional voting analysis.

Table 24

IDEOLOGICAL CLASSIFICATION OF MEMBERS OF CONGRESS, USING 1982 ROLL CALL VOTES, BY REGION AND NUMBER OF MEMBERS

Ideological Category	Senate					Percentage of Total
	East	Midwest	West	South	Total	
Liberal	14	8	8	3	33	33
Conservative	3	10	14	12	39	39
Libertarian	6	5	3	0	14	14
Populist	1	1	1	11	14	14

	House of Representatives					Percentage of Total
	East	Midwest	West	South	Total	
Liberal	66	43	34	9	152	35
Conservative	29	55	36	80	200	46
Libertarian	2	5	0	1	8	2
Populist	17	14	4	29	64	15
Unclassified	3	4	1	2	10	2

SOURCE: *The Baron Report,* May 5, 1983.

ment is expressed by 14 of the 100 senators (a significant number) and by a handful of representatives. The Senate libertarian group comes primarily from the East, but has some representation in the West and Midwest as well. The so-called liberal wing of the Republican party could better be called a libertarian wing; Senators Packwood and Hatfield of Oregon, Percy of Illinois, Cohen of Maine, and Mathias of Maryland all can be classified by their 1982 votes more as libertarian than as liberal. In the House only eight members voted in a consistently libertarian fashion; five of them are from the Midwest and only one (Gibbons of Florida) is a Democrat. Of course the difference in the number of libertarians in the House and Senate may well be attributable to differing party cohesiveness and the votes selected for analysis rather than to widely varying beliefs.

Populists, primarily through the southern wing of the Democratic party, do have significant representation. Like the libertarians, they also have fourteen members of the Senate, including eleven of the twenty-six senators from the South. All of these populists are Democrats, a point especially important for understanding modern southern politics. In the South all Republican senators are conservatives and all but three Democrats are populists, thus reflecting both the historical trends of that region and the substance of our findings regarding public ideologies in the South presented in the previous chapter. Unlike the libertarians, the populists have about the same strength in the House as in the Senate. Fifteen percent of House members are populists, a sizable bloc of 64 members. Almost half of these are from the South, but populism in the House has a somewhat more national character than it does in the Senate. (It should be noted, though, that eight of the seventeen Eastern populists in the House are from one state, Pennsylvania.) Almost all of the populists are elected as Democrats, although five populist Republicans are from the East.

Thus liberalism and conservatism are highly overrepresented in Congress as compared to the distribution of those ideologies in the public. No doubt the nature of the ideological affiliations of the two major parties and their virtual monopoly on election to Congress explains much of this overrepresentation. In fact the small amount of representation for other points of view seems to exist primarily as a function of historical custom: the Eastern and Far Western tradition of maverick Republicans (usually called liberals or moderates, although they are libertarian in their voting) and the traditional Southern commitment to the Democratic party and therefore to some expression of populist sentiment. Given the fairly even distribution of all four ideological categories across the United States, there should be a more even spread of members of Congress to match that distribution. That there is not suggests that no major channeling of alternative points of view occurs in Congress beyond that which is supported by historical regional and partisan quirks.

Frustration and Searching in American Politics

In this chapter we have surveyed a diverse set of opinions expressed by the ideological groups that exist in the United States and have found a variety of patterns, some changing and others fairly stable. If there is one single conclusion to be drawn from these findings, it is that American ideological politics seem to be in a state of flux. Frustration extends to general government performance and responsiveness, the party system, presidential candidates, and ideological labels, and it permeates all ideological categories. This frustration is manifested in a variety of ways; some of them are more oriented toward involvement and a search of alternatives, while others, at least in the short run, are more like old-fashioned withdrawal. Libertarians seem to be remaining in the system and retaining commitment to political action or individual effectiveness while realizing that, for the time being, neither the usual ideological labels nor the party system offers them much comfort. Conservatives behave in similar ways, except that they do have a home in the Republican party, a party they are coming to dominate more and more. Populists, historically outside the mainstream of American politics despite their numbers, remain so, retaining only a commitment to the Democratic party and, somewhat weakly, to its candidates; they are as alienated as any other group, however, and do not seem very susceptible to mobilization. Liberals, finally, increasingly have moved toward the Democratic party and tend to be more optimistic in some ways about matters of responsiveness. Their behavior and attitudes as studied here, though, suggest that although they have a home in American politics, they are certainly no longer in control.

VII. Ideology and Foreign Policy

In this chapter we turn to the difficult topic of public opinion and foreign policy. Based on other studies we generally expect our ideological categories to be less directly relevant to foreign than to domestic policy questions. This cautious expectation is based on at least three problem areas in dealing with public opinion and foreign policy: (1) the marginality of foreign policy issues to most people's interest and experience, (2) the theoretical difficulties in relating positions on foreign policy to the philosophical premises of our typology in that the typology is defined primarily in domestic terms, and (3) the insufficient and incomplete survey data available. We turn first to these points.

While public opinion about foreign policy issues has received considerable attention, scholars agree that the general public has much less interest and information about foreign matters than domestic questions, except in times of international crisis. This probably is attributable in large part to the remoteness of most international questions compared to such domestic issues as unemployment or drug abuse. Outside of wartime, few citizens have direct experience with foreign governments or citizens. Foreign policy attitudes score higher than domestic policy attitudes on pollster Daniel Yankelovich's "mushiness index," meaning that people are less involved, informed, and committed to their opinions (Keene and Lockett 1981, pp. 50–51). As a result of this relatively marginal interest, public opinion on foreign policy is generally less intense and more responsive to positions expressed by policy makers, especially the president. Lacking familiarity and interest, ordinary citizens look to those they perceive as "experts" or "in charge" for interpretations of international issues and events. Consequently public opinion on foreign policy is more easily manipulated than it is on domestic issues, where citizens can compare what their government says to their everyday experiences. Perhaps the classic recent example of the manipulability of foreign policy attitudes is the shift in public assessments of mainland China. Prior to the early 1970s it was generally assumed that the United States could not recognize the People's Republic of China because the public would not tolerate relations with fanatical communists. President Nixon, however, was able not only to reverse public attitudes on this point but to make his trip to China one of the high points of his presidential popularity—and to do so while the United States was still embroiled in the Vietnam War. Thus it is often difficult to determine to what extent mass opinion on foreign policy questions grows out of ideologically based views held over time or is simply a reflection of the latest manipulation by elites.

The second problem in analysis of public opinion about foreign policy is the lack of an obvious relationship between domestic ideology and foreign affairs. While we can make some general statements about the relationship of our four ideological categories to foreign policy, the fact that our categories are primarily domestic in origin and that the context of foreign policy is so variable makes firm prediction difficult. As we will see, however, in spite of these difficulties it is possible to predict theoretically with some success a relationship between ideology and foreign policy preferences.

We cannot test our four categories in the foreign policy arena, however, as thoroughly as we would like because of the third major problem—insufficient data. While there have been several fairly detailed surveys of public opinion on foreign policy questions, these do not include sufficient numbers of questions on domestic issues to allow us to identify those people who, on these surveys, would fall into our four ideological categories. Conversely most surveys devoted to domestic issues contain few and often inadequate questions about opinions on foreign affairs. Academic and polling specialization thus present a barrier to full analysis of public opinion on foreign policy from the perspective of our ideological categories.

Some Useful Distinctions

The relative marginality of foreign policy to most citizens' lives, together with the consequent lack of intensity in public opinion about foreign affairs, has led scholars to make a number of useful distinctions concerning the relationship of ideology to opinions on foreign policy. Analysts generally distinguish between a mass public and an attentive public in regard to foreign policy questions. (This distinction is used in regard to domestic issues as well, but it is less important in that realm.) The mass public is the segment of the general population that is largely unaware of or unconcerned about all but the most important of international events or issues.

While there is disagreement about the actual size of this mass public—estimates vary from 30 to 50 percent of the population—there is general agreement that large numbers of Americans are

> minimally concerned with most foreign policy questions. . . . The general public may periodically become aroused by some crisis abroad (as clearly occurred in 1980), as a result of which a ground-swell of popular discontent may sweep the country. On the basis of experience, however, sustained public interest in foreign policy issues seldom lasts long, and the people soon become immersed once more in domestic concerns [Crabb 1983, p. 237].

The attentive public, on the other hand, is more aware of, informed about, and concerned with foreign policy questions. Again the estimated size of this group varies, but most scholars think that up to 40 percent of the population may fall into this category, with perhaps 25 percent regularly paying attention to international events. Obviously the size of these groups could be expected to change, depending upon events, and the mass and attentive publics often respond differently to events, and issues in international politics.

A second useful distinction made by scholars of public opinion is that between "valence" and "position" issues (Stokes 1966; and Schneider 1983). Position issues are those that generate conflict over alternatives—for example should we have more or less foreign aid, more or less defense spending, or greater or lesser military involvement in El Salvador. Valence issues, in their simplest sense, are those for which there is really only one side—for example peace, prosperity, security, and national strength. No one favors war, depression, insecurity, or national weakness. This does not mean that valence issues are unimportant, however; as Schneider aptly points out, "position issues are inherently divisive, in the sense that candidates and voters can take sides on them. In the case of valence issues, however, everyone is on the same side. Salience is the most important characteristic of valence issues" (1983, p. 39). Valence issues, then, become important to public opinion when the public believes, or is led to believe, that a highly valued condition (peace, prosperity, national strength) is threatened. How great the threat, how serious the problem, how deep the crisis—these are the dimensions of public perception in regard to valence issues. The relative lack of concern for or information about many specific foreign policy issues, along with the importance of valence issues in the foreign arena, help explain the fact that seemingly small changes in the wording of questions often elicit large changes in responses in public opinion polls about foreign affairs.

The Changing Context of American Foreign Policy

If public opinion, especially among the mass public and in regard to valence issues, is structured largely by the public's perception of larger international events and context, then it becomes important to consider at least the general outlines of the changing context of American foreign policy to understand the general patterns of opinion about foreign affairs in recent years.

For about twenty years following the end of World War II, cold war assumptions dominated the making of U.S. foreign policy and were generally reflected in public opinion. The valence issues seen as important during this time were national security and protection from expansionist communism. Soviet expansionism in eastern and central Europe, the establishment of a communist government in China, the Korean War, and other events led to a U.S. cold war policy of containment that saw international conflict as a consequence of communist aggression coordinated from Moscow. The United States was seen as obligated to act as a counterweight to this aggression wherever it occurred. In this context there were few positional conflicts over foreign policy questions. The mass public generally saw the valence issue of security as crucial, while the attentive public generally supported government policies. The classic study of public opinion in the 1950s found that about a third of the public held no opinion or had no familiarity with most foreign policy issues (Campbell et al. 1960, p. 173). On the other hand the attentive public, more interested in and familiar with the issues of the time, also tended to be largely supportive of governmental actions. For example John Mueller found that while initial high levels of public support for U.S. involvement in Korea clearly diminished after the Chinese entered the war, public support for U.S. involvement remained relatively high throughout the war, especially among the more educated and attentive segments of the population. The less attentive and less educated were less supportive throughout the war (Mueller 1973, pp. 44–52). Bipartisan support for presidentially initiated policies tended to blur whatever distinctions or reservations the attentive public might have held in regard to the cold war. Among the mass public, foreign policy opinions bore little relationship to opinions on domestic issues or to party identification (Campbell et al. 1960, p. 197).

During the relatively quiescent 1950s both the mass public and attentive public generally shared cold war assumptions articulated by government decision makers, supporting "toughness" in foreign policy in response to a perception of monolithic expansionism in the communist world. At the same time most Americans did not see political questions generally or foreign policy questions specifically as being particularly important or salient to their lives (Nie, Verba and Petrocik 1976, p. 104).

Vietnam of course changed this pattern. Among the many consequences of U.S. involvement in the Vietnam War was the destruction of the cold war consensus in public opinion regarding foreign policy. Divisions over Vietnam policy split the political parties, dominated congressional debate and presidential campaigns, spilled into the streets, and received extensive media attention. Given divisions among policy makers, the attentive public also divided on the issue, conflict over position issues became more intense, and the valence issues that concerned the mass public changed. International issues became more important to the large segment of society that normally is not concerned with foreign policy. If the valence issue with most salience in the 1950s had been security, it had become peace by the late 1960s. Political questions in general, including foreign policy issues, became more salient to more Americans. As conflict among decision makers was perceived and mirrored in public opinion, opinions on foreign and domestic issues showed a closer relationship to each other (support for liberal domestic positions was more associated with less hawkish views in regard to Vietnam and the cold war) (Nie, Verba and Petrocik 1976, pp. 145–73). These connections were not very strong, however, and still indicated that many people combined foreign policy opinions with domestic policy opinions in ways not definable in simple liberal-conservative terms.

The Nixon-Ford years brought policies of détente, with overtures toward China and the Soviet Union, Strategic Arms Limitation Talks, and eventual withdrawal of U.S. troops from Vietnam. Foreign policy questions, seen as important by both the mass and attentive publics during the late 1960s, faded in importance and salience for the mass public. Schneider concludes that the balance-of-power approach of Nixon and national security adviser Henry Kissinger was at least for a time "ideologically confusing" to attentive publics, in that the policies of this period stressed both détente, which appealed to liberals, and military strength, which appealed to conservatives (Schneider 1983, p. 41). By 1976 both liberal and conservative opinion was more critical of the Nixon-Kissinger policies.

Events after 1975 once again changed the context of public opinion on foreign policy. The emphasis of the Carter years on human rights, multilateral diplomacy, and arms limitation was probably less important to shifts in public opinion that were such events as the seizure of the American embassy in Iran, which seemed to symbolize lessening American power; the Soviet invasion of Afghanistan, which seemed to signal new communist expansionism; or the activities of the OPEC cartel, which seemed to dramatize the changed economic position of the United States. The valence issues of security and strength once again became salient, and the mass public responded to the Reagan emphasis on national defense. At the same time the attentive public split over such positional issues as the U.S. role in El Salvador and Nicaragua, weapons development and deployment, and defense spending. The relatively easy and successful U.S. invasion of Grenada brought the usual "rally 'round the flag" support for administration action, but the more protracted and complex involvement in Lebanon resulted in clear divisions in public opinion. Both elites and masses divided over U.S. strategy and goals in Lebanon. The lasting public reaction to the Reagan approach to foreign affairs is not yet clear.

Basic Dimensions of Foreign Policy

Despite these changes in foreign policy issues from 1945 to 1980, throughout the period analysis tended to be couched in an isolationist-internationalist terminology, implying that isolationists oppose any American involvement in world affairs and that internationalists support all or most instances of American involvement with other nations. Pure isolationism—opposition to all "entangling alliances," in Thomas Jefferson's phrase—is thought to be an enduring element of American political culture and history. A careful reading of historical debates over such questions as tariffs, trade policies, and territorial acquisition in the 18th and 19th centuries shows that the United States has never been as isolated as may have been thought. Today there is often the lingering assumption that liberals are internationalists and conservatives are isolationists. Even the most casual observer, however, soon recognizes the difficulty of such a dichotomy in the contemporary world. Certainly most conservative leaders supported increased American intervention in Vietnam, while much of the support for withdrawal from Vietnam came from liberals, but this pattern was neither unambiguous nor sustained. Recognizing this difficulty scholars have argued recently that the basic division today is not around the desirability of internationalism, but rather over the nature of internationalism.

The general argument is that the isolationist-internationalist dichotomy was a useful distinction in earlier periods, especially after World War I, but that the thrust of the United States into world affairs during and after World War II rendered the classic isolationist position largely irrelevant. Whether reluctantly or eagerly, the largest portion of the American public—most surveys would suggest somewhere between 70 and 80 percent—has come to recognize that the United States influences and is affected by events in the rest of the world. For a variety of reasons, including at least nuclear weapons and the inextricably internationalist nature of the U.S. economy, internationalism has become a consensus issue. A small portion of the American public may resist or oppose almost all U.S. world involvement, but that portion remains relatively small. For example Wittkopf and Maggiotto, using a large number of foreign policy questions and a sophisticated statistical methodology, have estimated that about 20 percent of the mass public is isolationist in that it opposes both military and cooperative international involvement for this country (1983, p. 322). On the whole, however, the largest part of the American public supports U.S involvement in the world, at least so long as the question of involvement is stated in fairly general terms or relates to areas or circumstances where U.S. involvement is already well established.

This question of whether U.S. involvement is seen as "well established" or "traditional" may well be an important one. Maggiotto and Wittkopf (1981) distinguish between what they call "hard" and "easy" foreign policy questions. "Easy" questions are those that relate to an area or issue in which U.S. involvement is of relatively long standing. "Hard" issues are those that relate to a geographic area or issue dimension seen as nontraditional. By this distinction nuclear war is "easy" while the international financial system is "hard."

In the hard areas, where U.S. involvement is seen as novel or as a radical departure from past practice, opinion is likely to be more unformed, less patterned, and perhaps more suspicious or distrust-ful. Polls that ask very specific questions about precise policy alter-natives are likely to find large percentages of "don't know" responses coupled with perhaps a larger-than-usual percentage of Americans saying that they "oppose" U.S. involvement. This pattern of responses to specific questions about precise policy alternatives in areas seen as novel is probably not comparable to 19th-century isolationism, in that it is unlikely to be a stable pattern and may well change with events, the reactions of policy makers, or simply familiarity. The by now well documented increase in public cyni-cism and distrust toward government and government officials may well be relevant here. If, as we and many others have argued, mass opinion in the area of foreign policy is particularly responsive to elite interpretation of events (especially as these relate to valence issues) and if public opinion in the United States is now less trustful of government officials, this combination may have long-term con-sequences for the patterning of public opinion in regard to foreign policy. It may in the future become more difficult for elites to convince masses that the valence issues of war, peace, or security have been changed by events. It may become more difficult for elites to bring the public to see areas of international involvement as "established" rather than "novel." If these speculations are cor-rect, the building of public consensus in support of foreign policy actions may become more and more difficult.

At present the mass public is much more divided over the ques-tion of how, not whether, the United States should be involved in the world. In what is still the post-Vietnam era, the appropriate goals and methods of foreign policy divide the public far more than does the question of whether the United States will or should be involved in or influenced by world events. (Mandelbaum and Schneider 1979 elaborate this point.)

There is general agreement among analysts that in this context of the general acceptance of internationalism, analyzing foreign policy attitudes in terms of a single dimension is misleading. While the labels vary, there is general agreement that two major issues have tended to dominate foreign policy debate in recent years. These issue dimensions are, first, the levels and kinds of military involvement that the United States should undertake and, second, the question of détente or accommodation with the Soviet Union and other non-Western nations. Barry Hughes (1978) suggests that the appropriate labels for this division are military internationalism and nonmilitary internationalism. The military internationalist sees the international arena as essentially conflictual, stresses strong military preparation, is skeptical of détente and other measures of accommodation with the Soviet Union or other communist countries, and thinks that U.S. relations with other nations should be premised primarily on concern for U.S. national security. The nonmilitary internationalist sees the possibility of international cooperation, de-emphasizes the need for extensive military expenditures, favors détente and other means of accommodation, and believes that the United States has obligations to aid other countries (especially in the Third World) for reasons going beyond the security interests of the nation. William Schneider of the American Enterprise Institute (1983) argues for a similar classification, but he uses the terms "liberal internationalism" and "conservative internationalism." Given the way we have defined the terms "liberal" and "conservative," however, it would be confusing to adopt Schneider's labels. Even the military-nonmilitary distinction is in some ways too reductionist, but at least it does not muddle the issue with the already confusing liberal and conservative labels.

The military versus nonmilitary distinction may work fairly well for describing much of the division among political leaders and spokesmen, but these categories do not cover the full range of possibilities. One characteristic of both positions is a reliance on government as the major actor in relations with other countries through alliances, military or nonmilitary aid, and military action itself. A third position, which has been articulated by libertarian spokespersons (see for example Clark 1980), is internationalist in the sense that foreign trade, cultural ties, and other forms of non-governmental international interchange are seen as positive goods, but it rejects high levels of military spending and formal alliances, whether justified in security terms or in welfare terms. These measures are seen as making war more likely at the same time that they increase the power of government at home and wreak havoc on the domestic economy. We could label this position "nongovernmental internationalism."

We must include one more major segment of the population in this categorization. Schneider labels this group "noninternationalist." This group, which is sometimes confusingly labeled "isolationist," has little or no continuing interest in international affairs or policy. It appears to retain a vague or diffuse sense of support for governmental action, especially in terms of perceived crisis, but this is not usually tied to any specific question or policy (Hughes 1978, p. 38). During "normal" or "noncrisis" periods, this group has little specific information or opinion on foreign policy questions. Noninternationalists are not pure or traditional isolationists in the sense that they automatically and specifically oppose particular international actions or in the sense that they are ideologically opposed to generalized international involvement. As Schneider says, "noninternationalists are not so much opposed as they are nonsupportive" (1983, p. 43). For this group, valence issues are primary, and noninternationalists maintain a commitment to the valence issues of peace and strength. Depending on immediate circumstance and the nature and success of elite appeals, these individuals may show short-term support for either military or nonmilitary internationalism. In the late 1960s and early 1970s, for example, this group shared the distrust of military involvement and emphasized peace along the lines of the nonmilitary internationalist position. More recently, however, the renewal of cold war tensions and the positions taken by the Reagan administration have led to some support from this group for increased military spending. Again it should be emphasized that this group is not generally interested in international issues and, given its "manipulability," is less predictable in terms of the policy direction it is most likely to support.

As a final observation we note that the varieties of internationalism may help explain survey responses that suggest a greater degree of isolationism than we contend really exists. In the 1982 Chicago Council on Foreign Relations survey, for example, only 54 percent of the public (elite support was 98 percent) agreed that it was "best to take an active part in world affairs." In the same survey, however, over 70 percent "believed the United States should play as important or a more important and powerful role as a world leader ten years from now" (Rielly 1983, p. 104). Perhaps the relatively low support for an active role stems from the ambiguity of "active role." The military internationalist may see this as a plea for more foreign aid and the nonmilitary internationalist may see it as a plea for more arms. When the question is placed in terms of continuing the present U.S. role, though, these fears or concerns are not raised as much in the public's thinking. An additional way of explaining the difference in response to this question may be that the first question may be considered a "hard" issue and the latter an "easy" issue in the sense developed by Wittkopf and Maggiotto.[9]

Foreign Policy and Ideological Types

In analysis of public opinion on foreign policy, it should be emphasized that opinion on foreign policy (more than on domestic issues) is shaped by events as interpreted by elites. Large segments of the population are usually uninterested in specific foreign issues, but they do respond when such valence issues as peace or security appear threatened. Most basically, foreign policy opinion is shaped by perceptions of world events and governmental actions, and these perceptions in turn are shaped by such demographic characteristics as education. Given this view of public opinion on foreign policy, do our four ideological categories contribute to an understanding of public opinion as it relates to foreign policy? Our analysis is a refinement of the generally accepted analysis of public opinion and foreign policy, rather than in any way a rejection of that analysis. We view ideology as adding subtle distinctions to foreign policy opinion rather than as the fundamental factor shaping that opinion. As we turn to our empirical findings, it is useful first to suggest the theoretical relationships of our four ideological categories to the four foreign policy categories outlined above.

In general liberalism has tended to extend its concern for individual development and welfare to the international sphere. Just as modern liberals argue that the state has a domestic obligation to assist individuals who do not have resources for self-development, so they also would be expected to support the idea that the U.S. government should aid people in other countries who lack economic and technical opportunities. (Thus, for example, in the early years of U.S. involvement in Vietnam, President Lyndon Johnson proposed—apparently quite seriously—a massive aid program for North Vietnam that resembled a combined TVA and War on Poverty.) The ideal of liberalism suggests that foreign policy should not

[9]Another typology that compares elite and mass attitudes has been thoroughly developed by Wittkopf and Maggiotto (1983). They use the dimensions of cooperative internationalism and militant internationalism to create four categories: accommodationists, internationalists, isolationists, and hardliners. They show the mass public to be very divided among their four categories, but show "opinion leaders" fairly evenly divided between the accommodationist and internationalist categories. The accommodationists are in some ways comparable to our "nongovernmental internationalists."

be defined narrowly in terms of national security interest, but rather should be conceived broadly to promote world well-being and peace. We would expect liberals to support nonmilitary internationalism.

We noted earlier that conservatives are less optimistic about human nature than are liberals. Early in the 20th century this distrust of human nature manifested itself in an isolationist stance intended in part to protect the United States from the decadence and corruption of the Old World and European politics. However, since the advent of the cold war this pessimism has been more focused on the evils and seductiveness of communism. To protect itself against the flaws of human nature made manifest in the world largely through communism, the United States must provide for its defense not only in the narrow sense of protecting its borders but also with the higher purpose of containing communism. This pessimism also suggests that foreign aid for economic development is suspect because it represents some of the same evils as domestic welfare programs. Thus even though conservatives have reservations about the state being too strong, they tend to support a strong military and view alliances as important and necessary for national security.

The consistency of the libertarian position makes it simpler to relate to foreign policy. Like the conservatives, libertarians tend to be skeptical of economic aid to foreign nations. The strong individualism of libertarianism, however, suggests that national boundaries should not limit the freedom of individuals to trade and interact. Basic distrust of government and the historical fear of a large military as both a threat to individual freedom and a devastating drain on the economy combine to place libertarians in the internationalist category, but with a strong emphasis on free trade and cultural exchange and opposition to worldwide military involvement and entangling alliances. Thus we would expect libertarians to be nongovernmental internationalists.

The populist category is most difficult to relate theoretically to foreign policy positions. The moralism of the populists, like that of the conservatives, has historically led to an isolationist position, but in the modern context this could be translated into support for military internationalism to contain communism. It also could manifest itself as noninternationalism. Populist attitudes toward the military are also difficult to predict. Although populists do not share libertarians' general distrust of government, they might be expected to see large military budgets as support for big corporations and the arms merchants instead of help for the working person or farmer. In other words there is no one clear and obvious extension of a populist ideology into foreign policy attitude. We suggest, therefore, that populists would respond to foreign policy events and issues in a more sporadic and "pragmatic" way; that is, only when an international event is forced upon them and is seen by them as a threat to basic values. For this reason, and because the populists are a relatively homogeneous group with lower income and education, we predict that they would generally tend to have a noninternationalist orientation.

The expected foreign policy orientations for each ideological type are summarized in figure 23.

Ideological Types and Specific Foreign Policy Issues

We turn now to an examination of our empirical findings to test our theoretical predictions. It is useful at this point to remember the limitations of the available survey data. The University of Michigan (CPS) surveys that form the basis for much of our analysis have asked relatively few foreign policy questions. Morever the several surveys that specialize in foreign policy questions unfortunately do not ask sufficient domestic questions to allow us to distinguish our ideological types in their findings. The National Opinion Research Center (NORC) surveys have asked more foreign policy questions, but these questions have not always been repeated over the years. Furthermore NORC does not ask questions about domestic policy in a sufficiently comparable way to allow us to develop our ideological types in a form exactly consistent with the Michigan studies. For relative comparisons of ideological types, however, the NORC questions seem adequate. (The NORC ques-

---

Figure 23

EXPECTED FOREIGN POLICY ORIENTATIONS OF
IDEOLOGICAL TYPES

LIBERAL	POPULIST
Nonmilitary internationalism	Noninternationalism
LIBERTARIAN	CONSERVATIVE
Nongovernmental internationalism	Military internationalism

tions used to approximate our ideological typology are presented in the appendix.) Because of these limits, however, we have only a minimal amount of data to analyze.

Fundamentally our data confirm other scholars' analyses, showing consensus in support of generalized internationalism, at least when the public is asked either broad questions about the relationship of the United States to the rest of the world or about issues or areas where U.S. involvement is longstanding. When we refine this generalized internationalism into several categories by examining nonconsensus issues, however, we find significant differences in foreign policy positions among our ideological types, in the directions we have predicted. When we examine public opinion on the most general questions of the U.S. role in the world, we find a high level of support for internationalism among all our ideological types. In both the CPS and NORC data we find support for U.S. activity in world affairs and a rejection of isolationism. Further this supportive consensus remains relatively stable over the time period we have examined.

The data in figures 24 and 25 indicate this support for internationalism. Approximately two-thirds of those interviewed rejected the view that this country would be better off if it withdrew from world affairs. This position remains remarkably constant, even during the post-Vietnam era when it was generally assumed that a new isolationism had swept over the American public. Some slight change in an isolationist direction is evident in the CPS data (figure 24), for which we have evidence only through 1976, but not in the NORC responses (figure 25), which run through 1978.[10] Nonetheless this apparent consensus may in fact be relatively superficial. Although it does give direct evidence that the post–World War I type of isolationism is largely dead, even given the Vietnam disaster, the data do not necessarily indicate that all respondents are supporting the same kind of internationalism. For example libertarians may have in mind nongovernmental internationalism whereas the conservatives are thinking of military internationalism and liberals of nonmilitary internationalism. We must look at other issues to distinguish among these different kinds of internationalism.

Figure 26 gives further evidence of the relatively high support for

[10]Initial analysis of a Gallup poll conducted for the Chicago Council on Foreign Relations in 1982 suggests that the percentage rejecting the internationalist position may now be a bit larger.

Figure 24

PROPORTION OF PEOPLE WHO DISAGREE THAT UNITED STATES
WOULD BE BETTER OFF IF WE JUST STAYED HOME AND DID
NOT CONCERN OURSELVES WITH PROBLEMS IN OTHER PARTS
OF THE WORLD

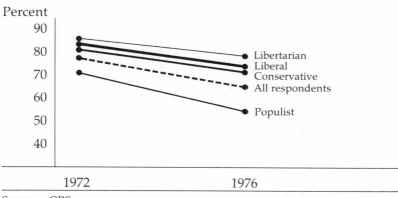

SOURCE: CPS.

Figure 25

PROPORTION OF PEOPLE WHO THINK IT WOULD BE BEST FOR
THE FUTURE OF THE UNITED STATES IF WE TAKE AN ACTIVE
PART IN WORLD AFFAIRS

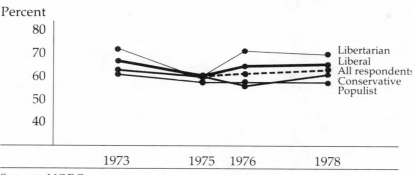

SOURCE: NORC.

internationalism, showing that about three-fourths of the population supports U.S. membership in the United Nations (despite the sharp criticism that this organization has received). Here we begin to see slight differences among our ideological types, with the greatest support for UN membership from libertarians and liberals, the least from conservatives and populists. Even among the least supportive groups, however, far more than a majority of the population favors U.S. membership in the UN.

The data in figure 27 suggest that the public has responded more to the criticism of foreign aid programs than to criticism of the United Nations, with slightly more than half of U.S. citizens being opposed to foreign aid. There is again a remarkable consistency in the post-Vietnam era for all groups except the liberals, who (perhaps because of a declining economy) show less support for foreign aid in recent years. In addition there are relatively small differences among ideological types in the direction we would predict. Populists and conservatives are the most opposed to foreign aid; liberals are the most supportive. Libertarians here seem somewhat anomalous in that nongovernmental internationalism would seem to suggest a rejection of foreign aid altogether, yet libertarians rank between liberals and conservatives in support for foreign aid.

Even though this evidence does suggest some basis for distinguishing between types of internationalism, this question, like the questions on U.S. involvement in the world, may be obscuring important differences. Even though most conservatives disapprove of foreign aid, for example, a fair percentage of conservatives say they support foreign aid. By "foreign aid," however, they may mean military aid to countries that are seen as important to a system of security alliances. The foreign aid question contains a specific condition: "Even if they don't stand for the same things we do." This phrase may suggest to conservatives a rationale for supporting repressive regimes, while liberals may interpret foreign aid to be largely for development and see the conditional clause as implying support for countries that are to the left of the United States.

Figure 28, which presents data on opposition to increased defense spending, involves a less ambiguous issue, which also relates to the different kinds of internationalism. Although again the consensus is strong, we find distinct differences among our ideological types, with liberals the most opposed and conservatives the least opposed to increased defense spending. We also see here a significant and steady decrease in opposition from 1973 to 1980, with the

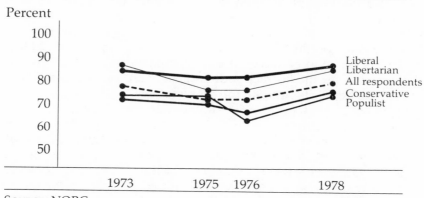

Figure 26

PROPORTION OF PEOPLE SUPPORTING UNITED STATES
MEMBERSHIP IN THE UNITED NATIONS

SOURCE: NORC.

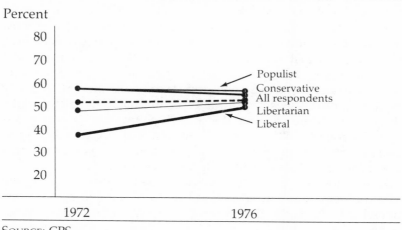

Figure 27

PROPORTION OF PEOPLE WHO DISAGREE THAT THE UNITED
STATES SHOULD GIVE HELP TO FOREIGN COUNTRIES EVEN IF
THEY DO NOT STAND FOR THE SAME THINGS WE DO

SOURCE: CPS.

149

decrease being proportionately nearly the same for all the ideological categories. As a result (except for a flip-flop between populists and libertarians from 1973 to 1975) the relative rankings of our ideological types remain the same through the decade. This suggests that although ideology does make an important difference in opinion on defense issues, people in all ideological categories tend to respond in a similar fashion to events as interpreted by elites. Once again on this question, we find that the populists and libertarians fall between the poles of support and opposition set by the conservatives and liberals, with the libertarians closer to the liberals and the populists closer to the conservatives.

Figure 29 presents data on another question, strong opposition to communism, which should distinguish between different kinds of internationalism. Here we see the same ideological ranking as on defense spending, but with even greater differences among ideological types. In 1973 more than twice as many conservatives as liberals express a strong opposition to communism, although by 1980 this ratio has lessened to three to two. Again there is evidence that all ideological types respond similarly to changing events, but that the relative rankings of the groups remain about the same over time. Populists rank just after conservatives in their opposition to communism, which can readily be explained from the general moralism and nativism of populism. The libertarian position more closely resembles the liberal position, and the explanation for this is less obvious. On the one hand the libertarian commitment to individual freedom would seem antithetical to basic communist principles as perceived in the United States. On the other hand the "live and let live" attitude of libertarians may lead to a notion that it is most important for the United States to spend its energies on its own economy and institutions. The success of these institutions will speak for itself, particularly through international trade, and therefore there is less need to directly oppose communism. The relatively high education levels of both liberals and libertarians may make them more cosmopolitan and less likely to fear countries and systems different from their own. On the kinds of foreign policy questions posed by the survey data we use, this cosmopolitanism may to some extent transcend ideological considerations.

In spite of their limitations, our data do show reasonably consistent differences among ideological types on foreign policy questions.Rather consistently liberals tend to be nonmilitary internationalists in that they are most opposed to increases in military

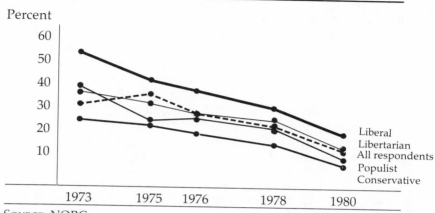

Figure 28

PROPORTION OF PEOPLE OPPOSED TO INCREASED
DEFENSE SPENDING

SOURCE: NORC.

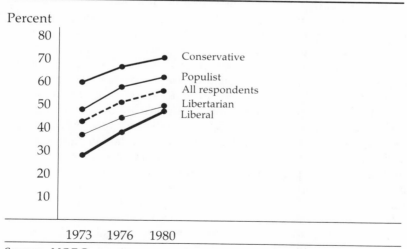

Figure 29

PROPORTION OF PEOPLE STRONGLY OPPOSED TO COMMUNISM

SOURCE: NORC.

spending, most in favor of foreign aid, least strongly opposed to communism, and most supportive of U.S. membership in the United Nations. Conservatives are consistently at the other end of the rankings, in that they are least opposed to increased defense spending, most opposed to foreign aid, most strongly opposed to communism, and least supportive of U.S. membership in the UN. As we have said, these positions are consistent with general liberal and conservative philosophy. Libertarians and populists generally fall between the liberal and conservative positions, with libertarians generally closer to the liberal position on foreign policy questions and populists closer to conservative positions, although there is occasional evidence to suggest that populists are even less internationalist than conservatives. These consistent findings give us increased confidence in our ideological categories in that they show that the categories that are defined in terms of domestic policy allow us to some extent to predict and explain differences in a nondomestic policy arena. These findings also suggest that although opinion on foreign policy is perhaps less influenced by ideology than is domestic opinion, ideology does relate to foreign policy. While elite action, world events, and other factors undoubtedly do much to structure foreign policy opinion, the people in our different ideological categories consistently respond differently to these actions and events.

Unfortunately we remain limited by our data. There are no questions that clearly tap a nongovernmental internationalist position, in that there are no questions that ask about international activity without some governmental role. Whether or not such issues would more clearly delineate libertarians remains an unanswered question. Questions about tariffs or import restrictions seem to show relatively low levels of support for a free-trade position, although support for free trade appears stronger among the demographic groups that are most heavily libertarian. We are unable to add any insight to the debate over the noninternationalist position. Among other things we would expect this group to be relatively uninformed and unconcerned about international issues. However our questions show a low percentage of "don't know" responses, and none of the questions attempt to measure degrees of concern or intensity for a given issue. The questions tend to involve major issues about which most of the public has heard opinions and has had some time in which to formulate its own opinions. Questions about strategic arms reduction, SALT talks, free trade, and the nuclear freeze question, if available, would better delineate the existence of this relatively uninvolved group. More survey work that combines questions about areas of foreign policy seen as novel or innovative (international financial questions, for example) with questions about domestic policy (so we could fully develop our ideological categories in that survey) would allow greater understanding of these points.

VIII. American Politics: A Fragmented Future?

The American public is far more ideologically divided than most political observers have recognized. Although public opinion in the United States was probably always more complex than most observers realized (or were able to demonstrate empirically), the analysis of the previous chapters describes substantial shifts that have occurred in the past two decades. Although journalists, politicians, and political scientists have persisted in discussing the public in liberal-moderate-conservative terms, very different ideological trends have been present. Populism, which probably formed the basis for Democratic party dominance in the middle of the 20th century, is on the decline, partly as a result of the changing nature of the U.S. population. Libertarianism, rarely articulated by political leaders, has nearly doubled in its number of supporters in one decade. Liberals and conservatives, rather than representing the two major ideological groupings in the public, actually have leveled off in size to include important but relatively small minorities.

What does all of this portend for the future of American politics? Many observers have noted the "coming apart" of traditional political patterns in recent years, usually citing such behaviors as the rise of split-ticket voting or the breakdown of partisanship both in the public and in Congress. These views suggest that American politics is becoming less structured, more chaotic, more unpredictable, and in general less manageable. What can our findings offer in the way of explanation, further warnings, or encouragement? In this final chapter we review our findings primarily to suggest what they mean for the future possibilities of the U.S. political system.

Many books filled with brilliant predictions of the future of American politics now gather dust in libraries; we make no claim to perfect insight or an ability to accurately read the tea leaves. We do suggest, however, that using our four-fold typology to understand the present may help us to perform better in speculating about the future.

155

The Public

The once-placid public, that mythical group of textbook citizens discussed in chapter II, has been studied more strenuously in the last thirty years than ever before. The general finding to emerge from all of this observation is that the public, to put it bluntly, has been doing some crazy things. In the past twenty-five years split-ticket voting has been on the rise, with about one-third or more of the voters casting some votes for one major party and some for the other in national elections (Maddox and Nimmo 1981, p. 403). State-level results present even stranger examples of this voter tendency; in one election the voters of a state might vote for a conservative presidential candidate, a liberal candidate for senator from the other party, and a vaguely populist governor who seems comfortable in neither party. (Perhaps the most striking such example was in 1968, when Arkansas voters gave their electoral votes to George Wallace while reelecting moderate Republican Governor Winthrop Rockefeller and liberal Democratic Senator J. William Fulbright.) Furthermore the proportion of people voting has steadily declined since 1960. Even discounting the influx of new, younger voters in the 1972 election, the decline continues, just as more citizens reach levels of education and of mass media exposure that supposedly reinforce the good citizen behavior of voter participation they learn from family and schools (Flanigan and Zingale 1983, pp. 6–11; and Abramson and Aldrich 1982).

Underlying these behaviors is a set of shifts in attitudes as reported in public opinion surveys. Citizens support the two political parties less than they used to, and those who still identify with a party are less likely to be as strong in their support. Nevertheless they have not as yet accepted any sort of challenge to that two-party system, even though independent and third-party candidacies are often presented to them, at least at the presidential level. More disturbing to observers, however, is the general alienation that provides part of the basis for disenchantment with the political parties. By almost any measure or definition, Americans of all classes, regions, and races have become more and more alienated from the political system in recent decades. Perhaps the worst is over; the civil rights struggles, Vietnam, and Watergate are now fading into history, and such turbulent events obviously create a climate conducive to alienation. What remains today, however, is a citizenry replete with people who feel unable to control the national political system,

156

question the role of the two major political parties that dominate that system, and are suspicious of politicians, bureaucrats, and even the journalists who report political activities.

What do our findings tell us about all this? The existence of an ideologically diverse public offers two ways of understanding (and perhaps accepting without worry) these trends. In the first place the basic ideological tendencies of the American public have been changing for decades. These changes reflect demographic trends (there are more of some types of people in the population and fewer of other types) as well as responses to the major events and political eras that people have experienced. When something as basic as the public's ideological views is in a state of flux, surface behavior will be a manifestation of that change. In other words, if the public were neatly divided into minorities of liberals and conservatives offset by a plurality of middle-of-the-roaders, as most observers would have us believe, we could expect the public to continue to do fairly simple and straightforward things, such as vote at the same levels, support the parties, feel trust and involvement in the system, and even vote straight-party tickets. With a changing and very diverse set of public views, however, we can reasonably expect to see various dislocations such as those that we have described and that many observers have worried about for years.

A second way of understanding recent trends in public behavior is to examine the way the public views politics as compared to the way politics is presented to the public by such political communicators as politicians, journalists, and political scientists. Here again there is a perfectly understandable situation. Only 40 percent of the public holds something like liberal or conservative viewpoints, but the political system is presented to them almost entirely in these terms. For people whose view of politics is populist or libertarian, the current political dialogue makes little sense. Furthermore, even for those who hold ideological views congruent with the way the system is usually described, there is still relatively little comfort. A so-called liberal Democratic party tries to satisfy every conceivable viewpoint and twice has nominated a presidential candidate whose ideology was murky at best. So-called conservative presidents do not behave very well either, often dismantling or downplaying some crucial elements of conservatism once in office (Goodin 1983). No wonder George Wallace's complaint of "not a dime's worth of difference" between the political parties lingers on long after his pronouncement. For a public presented with a political system and

157

political communicators who do little to take the public's definitions of politics into account, the only sane strategy is essentially to improvise in the voting booth, learning from the experience that alienation makes as much sense as anything else on the horizon.

Where does the public go from here? In the short run, of course, it continues to do what it has been doing. Alienation, distance from the parties, nonvoting, drastic shifts from one election to the other, and split-ticket voting are likely to continue, although some observers predict that Ronald Reagan's at least rhetorically more ideological presidency will sharpen political interest and bring both Reagan supporters and opponents into the polling booths in greater numbers. We do not foresee any growth in alienation or massive boycotts of elections. There is probably enough expression of liberal and conservative views through the system to prevent such trends from becoming exaggerated. Much of what happens beyond that, though, depends on the actions of political leaders. Our political system is difficult to change and its inertia must appear awesome to the typical citizen. Furthermore one of the largest categories of potential challenges to the established order is that of the populists, who make up about one-fourth of the public. As we have noted throughout this book, this group primarily includes people who traditionally have little inclination to political action. It is likely that this category of citizens will remain an alienated but unactivated buffer in politics. They will always be there to skew the overall portrait of the public (although generational change may gradually reduce their size), even if they will not provide the troops for any radical change or even a substantial challenge to politics as usual.

Much of the rest of the public, however, may behave differently. The United States is now a nation with large numbers of well-educated, fairly affluent citizens who receive a daily dosage of political awareness through the mass media. Undoubtedly many of these are waiting for a leader or a movement to channel their views, but what are the likely directions that these people might choose on their own? The first thrust will probably resemble what has occurred in the past two decades: ideological activity through the two major parties. Well-educated and involved liberals who are frustrated with the working of the system will probably channel their first efforts through the standard Democratic party apparatus, as demonstrated by the inevitable appearance every four years of "pure" liberal presidential contenders in that party. Similarly conservatives, who have had large influence in the Republican party in recent years, will more than likely continue to try to make the Republican party even more conservative; President Reagan's rightist critics within the party are often as vitriolic in their criticisms as his liberal critics outside the GOP, for example. Libertarians, however, have more of a choice. We believe that this point of view may well have a somewhat diluted impact for some time, as some try to create a strong libertarian wing in the Republican party, others commit to the new Libertarian party, and still others remain frustrated at the possibilities of either of those routes being successful. For some time to come libertarian power may be most felt at the ballot box in cases where the choice is between a Democrat and a Republican, one of whom espouses clear anti-interventionist views. The initial strength of John Anderson's independent campaign in 1980 and the surprising impact of Gary Hart's challenge to Walter Mondale in 1984, both of which showed strong appeal to under-40 voters who were often described as fiscally conservative and socially liberal, may be indications of libertarians' searching for an alternative to orthodox liberal and conservative politicians.

In general, however, we can make the following prediction about how the public will behave in the future: It will continue to refuse to play along with political leaders. In other words the United States is now a nation of citizens who are mostly well-educated and politically conscious if not astute, and who have ideological viewpoints that are of some use to them in responding to politics. The public may be attracted to a particularly persuasive leader now and then, or even to a powerfully simple idea or issue, but its intransigence and moderate level of healthy skepticism is not likely to disappear. John Naisbitt, in his popular *Megatrends*, claims that the wave of citizen action in the future will be through the referendum and initiative. As government fails to respond—or to respond quickly enough—to citizen demands, the populace will simply put issues on the ballot using the initiative process available in about half the states. An activated ideological group in one state, for example, could easily gather the usual requisite signatures to put a proposal on the ballot and then weld together a coalition of supporters to pass the measure. Indeed politically disenfranchised libertarians have already been using the initiative on a wide scale, from nuclear freeze and tax-cut proposals in a number of states, to transportation deregulation in Alaska and Colorado, to marijuana decriminalization in California. For an ideologically diverse public, this approach makes sense and probably will increase in use in future years. Most citizen political action, however, probably will still be channeled through the political parties and interest groups.

Political Parties

The political parties in the United States have always been the major mechanism for citizens to express their ideological preferences. Accordingly we have commented frequently in this book on the role of the parties and have speculated throughout as to the difficulty of expressing four ideological views through two parties that often resist ideological definition. At this point we provide another description of the ideological makeup of the current parties and suggest some alternatives.

Figure 30 presents in a different form some of the information discussed in chapter VI as the ideological makeup of the parties. Here, however, we list the ideological composition of the supporters of the two major parties (party identifiers) and of the group that labels itself "independent." Much has been written about the so-called liberal and conservative wings of the Democratic party, for example; here we see some of the problems with this conventional wisdom.

The Democratic party's reputation for economic interventionism is reflected in the views of its supporters; two-thirds of the party identifiers are either populists or liberals. In general, however, the Democrats are as divided a group as ever, with populists being the largest category (here the influence of the South in the party is maintained). The conservative wing of the party accounts for but one-tenth of the party's supporters and the libertarians are only a tiny percentage. Given the overall trends in the size of the demographic groups expressing each ideological viewpoint, it is likely that the future Democratic party will be split down the middle between populists (who are a declining group) and liberals (who are increasing in number). Thus the Democrats should be able to forge a continued consensus in support of a government active in economic affairs. Social issues and lifestyle questions still have the power to rip the party apart, as they did in the late 1960s and early 1970s.

The Republican party is a much more complicated entity than is often assumed (remember here we are referring to Republican supporters in the public, not necessarily party activists). For a party with a small number of adherents in the electorate, it is surprisingly divided, with almost equal numbers of conservative and libertarian

160

Figure 30

IDEOLOGICAL COMPOSITION OF PARTY IDENTIFIERS IN 1980

Democrats					
Liberals 30%	Populists 37%	Cons. 11%	Libt. 7%	Divided & Inattentive 15%

Republicans			
Liberals 13%	Populists 18%	Conservatives 27%	Libertarians 29%	Divided & Inattentive 13%

Independents				
Liberals 25%	Populists 20%	Cons. 17%	Libertarians 23%	Divided & Inattentive 15%

SOURCE: CPS.

161

supporters. Here the potential for future conflict is obvious. As libertarians become more aware of their strength and consider the Republican party as a possible vehicle for their views, there could be a split comparable in intensity to the old conservative-moderate split that dominated the party's presidential politics in 1952 and again in 1964. Whether or not such a split occurs depends in part on how many libertarians who presently identify with the Republican party decide to use the GOP as a vehicle. If a substantial number of them decide not to pursue active politics or move into a separate political party, the libertarian wing would be reduced to a thorn in the side of the party rather than a major threat to its current conservative leadership. The term "liberal wing" of the Republican party is clearly a misnomer. Only 13 percent of Republican identifiers are classified as liberals in issue terms. Combine this 13 percent with the 18 percent who are populists, however, and it becomes evident that even among Republican supporters, more than 30 percent of them support the notion of government intervention in the economy. Assuming this proportion does not decline dramatically, the Republican party is likely to continue to contain a moderating force as well as ideologically divisive elements.

Finally the composition of those labeled as independents indicates that any attempt to weld together a coalition of independents or to forge a new party out of that group is certainly doomed to failure. Independents are as diverse as the American public; all they share is a self-label that symbolizes disenchantment or uninvolvement with the two major parties. It makes more sense to view these independents as made up of several segments, each of which could be attracted to the two major parties or to a new party. They are not a mass that could be organized into a new party or independent movement, such as those led by Eugene McCarthy in 1976 or John Anderson in 1980. Indeed the large number of libertarian independents suggests a potential for substantial support for that new party or some other alternative political vehicle. The parties that should have attracted the liberal and conservative independents obviously have not done so, suggesting that at the least the existing parties need to do some sort of major image-building to bring these people into their fold.

The party system of the future appears to be headed for more confusion. The Democratic party will continue to be plagued by a liberal-populist division, and will be forced to downplay individual liberties issues and emphasize traditional economic policies to hold

162

itself together. The Wallace revolt of 1968 and the McGovern movement of 1972, however, suggest that both populists and liberals periodically will demand that issues other than economic ones be considered. As these noneconomic issues also tend to be highly emotional—and non-compromisable, such as abortion or women's rights—the Democratic party cannot be expected to remain at peace for very long.

The Republicans also may see an end to the relative ideological peace they have known since the ending of the Goldwater-Rockefeller battles of the early 1960s. Although the Reagan challenges of 1976 and 1980 were ideologically based and led to tough battles within the party, the differences among the supporters of various Republican candidates in those years were often only of degree of conservatism, or they were based on personality and candidate style. In the future there could be true ideological clashes again, as younger libertarians within the party attempt to move it away from social conservatism. Neither libertarians nor conservatives can dominate the party on their own; therefore any presidential candidacy would have to build an uneasy alliance with one of the small liberal or populist wings of the party. Ronald Reagan may be the last Republican leader who does not have to fight a severe ideological battle to lead his party.

In the face of such ideological diversity among party supporters, leaders in each party may well be tempted to nominate relatively unknown presidential candidates, whose issue positions are unclear and who can emphasize personal as opposed to issue appeal. However, as the Jimmy Carter experience demonstrates, this approach may help win presidential elections, but it is very difficult for such a candidate to govern once he is in office.

What of the alternatives to the two major parties? Independents, as we have seen, do not constitute a movement in and of themselves. The ideological diversity of independents means that they may be a potential source of supporters for other parties. Third parties, as they are usually called, have always faced a number of logistical and legal obstacles in the United States: The single-member, plurality election system penalizes them,[11] ballot access is often

[11]A single-member plurality system means that one member of the House of Representatives, for example, is elected from each congressional district. So if a Democrat wins 40 percent of the vote, a Republican wins 30 percent, and a Libertarian wins 30 percent, the Democrats win the seat and the other parties get nothing. A proportional system, used in some democracies outside the United States, elects members to a parliament, for example, over a larger geographic area and assigns

163

extremely difficult, and both funding and media attention are difficult to obtain. Each limitation reinforces the others. A major reason why third parties are often believed to be doomed in American politics is of course that the public will not vote for them, preferring not to "throw away a vote" on someone who will not win or is too "radical." There is still a general suspicion of third parties among the public, but this suspicion may lessen in the changed circumstances of contemporary politics. The trends in political behavior described here are changes that political observers never expected to happen. Therefore third-party possibilities should be seriously considered regardless of either their past failures or past public reactions to them. Discounting for the moment the limitations of the political and electoral system itself, what chances do third parties have in the future?

The numerically strongest source of third party support is the one least likely to emerge. Populism, that combination of economic interventionism and social moralism, has demonstrated two important characteristics in the last one hundred years. First there have been periodic populist revolts leading to a third-party movement or to the threat of one. (The People's Party of the 1880s was the first; Wallace's American Independent Party of 1968—which, contrary to the common perception, took interventionist positions on economic issues in its platform—was the latest.) We can probably expect continued outbursts of populist rhetoric and third-party attempts. The second characteristic, however, is that these populist parties have never survived as serious political parties. They either die from the inattention of their leaders, split themselves apart from racial divisions (recall that populists are mostly poor whites and poor blacks), or have their ideas confiscated by one of the major parties. History, therefore, is not on the side of a populist party succeeding, although that does not mean that it could not happen.

Three factors militate against a populist party today, however, even assuming that leaders emerged. First, populist supporters are racially divided today as much as they were in the populist parties that tried to become an alternative party in the South in the 1890s. Overt racial tensions of course are subdued today. For example,

---

seats to the party in proportion to their percentage of the vote. If the same voting results as suggested above occurred at the state level in a state with ten House members, the Democrats would win 4 seats, the Republicans 3 seats, and the Libertarians 3 seats.

former Arkansas governor Orval Faubus, who ordered the National Guard to stop school integration in Little Rock in 1957, in 1984 praised presidential candidate Jesse Jackson, citing in particular Jackson's stands on interest rates and utility rates—two classic populist issues of economic intervention. Despite such statements, it still seems unlikely that Faubus supporters and Jackson supporters could be combined into a working coalition. Like white populist candidates before, Jackson has yet to demonstrate that a black populist can create such a coalition. Second, to begin and maintain a new political party against all the odds requires a great deal of effort from a large number of people. Populist supporters come from the groups in society, the poor and uneducated, who are least likely to have the inclination or the resources to take on such a task. Finally, the populist point of view is still expressed through the Democratic party to some degree. Populist Southern whites, for example, were annoyed by the "radicalism" of their party in 1968 and voted for Wallace. More annoyed by the McGovern takeover of their party in 1972, many voted for the Republican candidate, Richard Nixon. Many of them, though, did return to the party for a Southern favorite son in 1976 and 1980. The populist Southern wing of the Democratic party, despite Carter's defeat in 1980, now finds itself more legitimized and accepted than it has been since the 1950s. So long as a Southern presidential candidacy is taken seriously and social issues are debated within the party, populists are likely to stay within the Democratic party rather than form the basis for a new movement.

There also could be ideological alternatives to the two major parties for liberals and conservatives as well. In any election year, in fact, there are a number of third parties on the ballot in at least a few states, and many claim that they should be the true home of liberals or conservatives. These parties have rarely been very effective in American politics, however, and we do not see that fact changing, for several reasons. The images and leaders these parties present are seen by both the public and political communicators as disruptive and vaguely violent in nature. The public probably will continue to reject them as much for their connotations of violence or militarism as for their extreme ideological views. Furthermore, as discussed in chapter I, the ideological points of view we find in the public all fall comfortably—at least at the present—within the basic American consensus, which is based on the assumptions of classical liberalism. Historically many third-party movements, such as the Communist party of the 1930s or the States Rights party of the 1960s, have threatened to move the political debate into another arena, offering fundamental challenges to the basic tenets of the American consensus. Beyond these general limits, the nature of third-party appeal is likely to be different for conservatives and for liberals.

In the case of conservatives, the appeal of a third party is limited by several factors. There are periodic third-party movements that are often mistakenly labeled as conservative, the Wallace movement of 1968 being the most notable example. It is apparent, though, that these are populist outbursts, not attempts to build a purely conservative alternative. In addition there are regular rumors of the formation of a major third party to promote the conservative creed, but such rumors rarely attract defections from the ranks of conservative spokesmen. The two most well known conservative spokesmen of recent decades, Barry Goldwater and Ronald Reagan, have shown little or no interest in third-party attempts. Such leaders have recognized that although the Republican party may not be entirely their own, conservatives have used it quite successfully to channel their views. So long as that is the case, there is little incentive for conservatives to support third parties outside the political mainstream, whether these be populist movements that satisfy only part of their ideological needs or any proposed new conservative party that would necessarily begin as an even smaller minority party than the Republicans are.

The communication of liberal ideology through third parties is more problematic, both historically and in the contemporary arena. Like the periodic populist third-party explosions, political parties claiming to extend liberal ideas to deal with the exigencies of particular time periods have achieved some vote-getting success in the past: the Socialist candidacies of Eugene Debs early in the century, Socialist and Communist parties in the 1930s, and Henry Wallace's Progressive Party of 1948. Two points are worth noting about these movements. First they did achieve something more akin to legitimacy and success than most radical parties have, both in terms of winning votes or electing officials, as well as ultimately having some of their programs accepted by the two major parties. Second, however, liberals seem no more likely to be attracted by such movements than are conservatives, except in fairly distressed times. When the immediate hard times have passed or the Democratic party offers watered-down versions of the third-party proposals, liberals flow back into the major party ranks. Liberals are not likely to expand the meager ranks of the various socialist or leftist parties that maintain positions on the ballot of many states.

Liberals have the Democratic party as a channel for their ideology. Their future within the party, though, is somewhat more clouded than is that of conservatives in the Republican party. Even though it is "their" party, liberals are in a minority in Democratic ranks, trailing the populists. In the last few years, there have been a variety of new approaches to liberalism, such as "neo-liberalism," the "Atari Democrats," and use of the term "progressive" to define a presidential candidate as liberal without saying he is liberal (Morris Udall insisted on using the term in 1976, for example). These are essentially modifications and semantic gestures within the basic framework of Democratic party liberalism, designed to appeal more to those outside the fold than to true supporters. Only the Citizens Party, which offered its first presidential candidate in 1980, has emerged as a recent alternative party for liberals. The combination of environmentalism as a major concern with the otherwise traditional liberal views on economic and individual liberties stressed by Citizens Party activists, hints at the entrance of a new dimension or domain of issues in American politics. Given the inability of the system to deal effectively with two issue dimensions in the past, the prognosis is not good for its chances of handling a third. It seems more likely that environmental issues will continue to be articulated through interest-group activities rather than be integrated into an ideological political party platform.

Libertarian views, as discussed in chapter I, are in many ways the easiest to define and communicate. Thus it is not surprising that these views underlie the most likely third-party success: the Libertarian party. We do not expect the Libertarian party to displace one of the major parties—nor even to achieve a third force status such as the Liberals in Britain or the Free Democrats in Germany have maintained since World War II—unless electoral laws are changed to allow third parties an equal chance to win seats in Congress. The Libertarian party, however, has several distinct advantages. First is a clear ideology that carries no offensive or foreign connotations. In some ways socialism is fairly simple, but Americans hate the word and its connotations, and see it as vaguely foreign in origin. Libertarianism is simple (government should be minimized in its involvement in our lives) and is clearly in the American classical liberal tradition. Libertarians undoubtedly have some problems explaining the full implications of their views to the public, but they begin with fewer strikes against them than most third parties.

The Libertarian party faces the challenge of convincing those who might be responsive to their views (18 percent of the public in 1980) to join their ranks, but they do not have to convert large numbers of people to become a major political force. Building on the most rapidly growing ideological viewpoint, rather than on one that is tiny or declining, is a clear advantage. As discussed in chapter V, libertarians are found most often among those groups that will constitute a larger portion of the public in the future: the sixties and seventies generations, the well-educated, and the affluent. The groups that are growing as a proportion of the electorate are the groups where the party's appeal should be strongest. Finally the Libertarian party appeals to a segment of the public that has few alternatives within the existing party system. There are few libertarians among the Democrats. They are a large minority in the Republican party, but for them to control that party would mean a series of difficult battles with an entrenched conservative leadership. Libertarian voters cannot say to the Libertarian party that their sentiments are already being expressed; the party, unlike many third-party attempts, does in fact fill an ideological void. The people we identify as having libertarian views, however, would not necessarily support the Libertarian party if they perceive the party as being too extreme or irrelevant to current political debate, or its efforts as being too futile in the present political context.

Interest-Group Politics

Many citizens and political observers today deplore the dominance of so-called interest-group politics or special-interest politics in the U.S. political system. Usually these complaints refer to the influence of interest-group activities in the legislative process (Congress is dominated by special interests), in financing elections (interest-group money and political action committees win elections), or in posing intractable demands to political candidates (one must satisfy every single-issue group on its particular issue or risk losing its support or incurring its wrath). What does our ideological analysis tell us about the future, as well as the present state, of interest-group politics?

First there are ideological interest groups that could be a channel for the communication of the four major viewpoints we have discussed. For years the Americans for Democratic Action for liberals and the Americans for Constitutional Action for conservatives have fulfilled that role, primarily through ratings of congressmen as to their ideological purity. In recent years New Right groups have become more vocal and active proponents of the conservative creed, although their newness seems to reflect mainly their intense opposition to expanded individual liberties. Populists and libertarians have not had such traditional groups to express their interests. Despite election successes claimed by the New Right, these ideological groups have not usually been very prominent on the American political scene and even the New Right seems to have peaked. Why is this?

The standard political science answer would be that this is just more evidence that Americans are not very ideological and reject such political activity; Americans are pragmatic and prefer to deal with one issue at a time or with social and economic group differences. There is some plausibility to this view, but it would be more accurate to say that Americans do not like ideological stridency. As with the leftist and rightist political parties discussed above, the public is more offended by the tactics (the New Right's shrillness and targeting of opponents generated something of a backlash, for example) of ideological groups and their tendency to rate people on a scale of purity rather than by the ideological nature of group activities. Furthermore the lack of success attributed to ideological interest groups may also rest on the peculiar nature of such groups in the U.S. system. If one wishes to act politically with regard to one specific issue, a group concern, or a set of such issues as civil liberties, one will choose interest-group activities. If one wishes to express a broader set of concerns, something approaching an ideology, then one turns to the political party as the normal instrument used in a democracy. Ideological interest groups are neither fish nor fowl, neither group nor party, and consequently they may seem to many citizens not to fit into the U.S. political system.

Beyond organized ideological groups, then, what does our typology of ideologies suggest about the future of interest-group politics? First the fragmented ideological nature of the public as we have described it provides good reason to believe that the high level of interest-group activity will continue—and perhaps increase. Coalitions are difficult to build within a diverse public. Political parties can respond but do so only very slowly, with a tremendous amount of low-level organizational activity. It makes more sense for most citizens to concentrate on one particular issue or set of grievances at a time if they are to have some immediate impact on the political system. A poll by the Advisory Commission on Intergovernmental Relations has found young people much more likely than older voters to say that "organized groups concerned with specific issues such as business, labor, environmental and civil rights groups" represent their political interests better than the political parties. Although voters over 65 prefer the parties by a ratio of three to two, those under 35 opted for interest groups by more than two to one ("Opinion Outlook" 1984). It is interesting to note that, since the 1960s, two major citizen-initiated movements have emerged: the tax revolt and the nuclear freeze campaign. Both draw in part from the two ideological groups that are increasing in size, the libertarians (who could easily support a tax revolt or a nuclear freeze) and the liberals (who predominantly support some limitation on nuclear weapons). In both cases, however, success depended on putting together a coalition with other ideological groups that could agree with them on that one particular issue. A fragmented and divided public often has no choice but to focus its immediate demands and concerns through interest groups.

Finally the single-issue group, such as an anti-abortion movement or the nuclear freeze movement, is much more likely than traditional interest groups to attract supporters now and in the future. Traditionally business, labor, and professional groups have been important in American politics. Even these, however, are too broad in their orientation to encompass ideological variations. A business group, for example, may represent some people who believe in government activity to benefit business (tax laws, tariffs, or bailouts of business, for example) and other people who believe that what is best for business is minimal government activity. Similarly a labor union or professional group may include members who cut across the ideological spectrum and who could not agree on many issues other than those very narrowly affecting their particular trade. (Members of labor unions, it is useful to recall, are as ideologically diverse as the general public.) Thus political leaders face a public that is more likely to organize along the lines of one issue at a time; the days of dealing with large-scale interest groups are probably dwindling away. The immediate implication of this is more confusion in the political system and more headaches for politicians trying to please a hodgepodge of single-issue groups. In the long run, however, one potential benefit would be that political leaders them-

170

selves may take the initiative to seek new coalitions of interests, based on taking the public's ideological orientations seriously. In other words the fragmented nature of citizen demands on politicians may force the politicians to become more ideological to survive and simplify their roles. This is not to suggest that the problems of the American political system would be solved if political leaders simply responded to public opinion. Rather it is to argue that if the alternatives framed by political leaders more adequately coincided with the varieties of beliefs that are held by the public, then public cynicism, alienation, and nonparticipation would lessen.

The Presidency

The presidency is the focal point of American politics for much of the public. Citizens pay more attention to presidential elections than any others and vote in them more regularly. They also receive a steady diet of information from the mass media that focuses on the president as the major actor in national politics, whether they get their information from an elite publication such as the *New York Times* (Gans 1980, chapter 1), from television (Graber 1978, chapter 3) or from the glossy pages of *People* magazine (Maddox and Robins 1981). The four-way ideological division we find in the public therefore should have some impact on the presidency. One way to consider this impact is to use the concept of presidential coalitions. To win a party nomination and then the general election, a presidential candidate must build a coalition of supporters, people from different groups in society with differing political views. To maintain some credibility while in office, the president must continue to satisfy a coalition of supporters in the public, one that may or may not be the same coalition that put him in office. Finally, to deal with Congress effectively, he must build or maintain some coalition of supporters in that institution. The first two types of presidential coalitions are examined here; congressional coalitions are the subject of the following section.

To speak of building coalitions to win a party nomination is a slight exaggeration. Party nominations often are won because a candidate solidifies and activates the support of one major segment of his party rather than putting together supporters from varied groups. The George McGovern candidacy of 1972, a solidification of the most liberal and anti-war segment of the party, and the Barry Goldwater conservative nomination victory in 1964, are the most obvious examples. Another tactic is to dominate one part of the

171

party, as Ronald Reagan did with conservatives in 1980, but attract just enough of the other types of supporters to demolish the chances of other contenders. We do see some attempts at cutting across ideological groups within a party to capture a nomination: Jimmy Carter in 1976 drew some support from various wings of the Democratic party (again, just enough to preempt any other candidate's claim to front-runner status), as did Richard Nixon in 1968, when neither the Rockefeller nor the Goldwater-Reagan wing of the party had enough strength to dislodge him.

Given the composition of party supporters (who, despite recent reforms, will still be the predominant element in the nomination process) in Democratic and Republican parties, what are the likely strategies that will be successful in the future? First of all the capture of a party nomination by an ideological purist who mobilizes one of the larger segments of his party is still very possible. For the Democrats this most likely means that a liberal ideologue could receive the nomination if he were able to activate that 30 percent of the party's supporters who share his ideology. Capture of the party by a populist candidate seems less likely, despite the plurality of populists among Democratic identifiers. Populists, as we have seen, often do not vote. Furthermore the uneasy alliance of blacks and whites is rare in Democratic nomination battles; Jimmy Carter in 1976 came closest to maintaining such a combination.

Similarly a Republican candidate who pleases the conservative wing and activates it during the nomination struggle can use such a strategy to achieve victory, as Reagan did in 1980. As Republicans have not internally debated issues of personal freedom in recent years, such a candidate generally can count on a combination of conservatives and libertarians who share his opposition to government economic intervention. One future possibility, which has not occurred in the past, is a libertarian candidate winning the Republican nomination. With libertarians making up 29 percent of the party's identifiers, coming primarily from the demographic groups likely to participate in politics, a presidential candidate expressing libertarian views could conceivably capture the Republican nomination. Such a candidate also would probably have to attract just enough of the tiny liberal wing by his stands on personal freedoms and some defectors from the conservative group by his classic anti-interventionist positions on the economy, but far stranger combinations have occurred in past nomination battles.

The best strategy suggested by the ideological composition of the two parties is a nonideological one. Analysts often decry the tendency of presidential candidates to try to be all things to all people, to appear to be satisfying all points of view by taking no point of view themselves. The fragmentation of ideological approaches in both parties, however, suggests that this is a sound if unfortunate strategy for winning a presidential nomination. No one ideological group can guarantee nomination in either party. Furthermore, unless one is willing to use the McGovern approach (solidify one group, ride them to the nomination, and thence to disaster in the general election), taking a clear ideological position in the future will cement support among one group but likely offend other groups. The Carter approach of de-emphasizing ideology then may be the best route to a nomination. But can it win future general elections?

Assuming that we continue the pattern of the usual two-way presidential contests between a Democrat and a Republican, how are presidential coalitions to be built with such a diverse public? Basically our portrait of the public suggests that several standard features will continue in this typical form of election. Conservatives will more or less enthusiastically support the Republican nominee; liberals will support the Democrat, although with varying degrees of intensity. Two major ideological groups, populists and libertarians, will be attracted in part to both candidates. As we saw in our analysis of the 1980 election, turnout levels are crucial. If a candidate draws heavy turnout from his natural ideological constituency, he then is less dependent on the votes of the two groups without a natural spokesman. Thus a successful strategy in future campaigns would be to solidify and activate the ideological minority that is already in the candidate's camp, just as Democratic campaigns for years concentrated on activating their majority group of supporters through turnout drives rather than trying to convert Republicans. We may see here a paradoxical situation that is somewhat the reverse of past patterns. A candidate may need to de-emphasize ideology to win the nomination, but stress it more in the general election to activate the core of supporters he must have to win.

In the hypothetical case of the takeover of one or both parties by its outsiders—populists in the Democratic party or libertarians in the Republican party—we would still expect activation of the ideological core group to be crucial. We have seen how libertarian support for Reagan and the corresponding populist disaffection from Carter in 1980 magnified the advantage Reagan held because conservatives were participatory and enthusiastic for him while

Carter's liberals were not. A populist candidate would face something more of a problem here, given the traditionally low populist involvement. A candidate who succeeded in motivating populists and could also hold enough liberals would almost certainly win. A Republican libertarian, on the other hand, could more easily try to reach out to other groups. Libertarians vote at high levels and have supported Republicans in the past (as the lesser of two evils or because they see economic issues as most important), so that a libertarian candidate could just about assume active, participating support from his natural constituency. This libertarian Republican could then attempt to mollify the fears of conservatives about his positions on personal freedoms or stress those views and try to convert some liberals to his cause. This type of strategy might appeal to a moderate Republican such as Sen. Robert Packwood of Oregon or a younger person such as Ripon Society chairman Rep. Jim Leach of Iowa. Such a candidate could attract conservative support with his advocacy of fiscal responsibility and deregulation, for instance, while reaching out to libertarians—and to liberals in the general election—with his stands on individual rights. An election strategy of this type would be risky, and it would certainly be unlike any that has occurred.

Winning the nomination and the election do not guarantee that a president can govern. He also must continue to maintain a coalition of support within the public, if not for specific policies, then at least for his general approach to governing. A high level of public support for the president, communicated through public opinion measures of his popularity, is almost essential for presenting him to the Congress, the bureaucracy, and to some parts of world opinion as an effective spokesman for what the public really wants. A diverse and divided public makes this difficult. If a president stresses economic intervention, he offends libertarians and conservatives (34 percent of the public). If he stresses support for personal freedoms and individual life style choices, he offends conservatives and populists (43 percent of the public). The list of examples could go on. What is a president to do? The prime strategy is avoidance, often by stressing foreign policy concerns, as most recent presidents have come to do by the end of their first term. As mentioned in the previous chapter, the emphasis on foreign policy moves the public-presidential interaction into a different arena, one in which ideological views are not as directly relevant to public opinion. Furthermore the public tendency to defer to the president or rally 'round him when there are perceived external threats makes the president's coalition-building much easier in the foreign arena.

In the domestic arena most recent presidents have stressed economic issues rather than personal freedoms. Immediate necessity, such as high inflation or unemployment, often dictates this approach. By dealing with one dimension at a time, and by choosing the economic (as Reagan so clearly did), the president ties himself more closely to the citizen's pocketbook and is less likely to be caught in the difficulty of being able to please no one but his own core of ideological supporters. Although this has been the pattern of recent presidents and probably will continue in the future, one factor may reduce the effectiveness of this approach. Liberals and libertarians, who agree on the need for expansion of personal freedoms, are the two groups that are growing in size, partly because of their strength in the younger age groups who constitute an increasingly larger share of the public. By 1980 these two groups accounted for 42 percent of the population. As these trends continue there may be a demand from the public that the president take a stronger stand on personal freedoms, and presidential recognition that something approaching half of the citizens want government to get out of the business of regulating lifestyles. In other words, as the number of citizens concerned with the protection of personal freedoms increases, it becomes more feasible for a president to base his coalition in part on satisfying those people.

Congress

To consider the future impact of an ideologically diverse public on Congress, we must first briefly look at the present role of ideology in Congress. A congressman's ideological orientations or those of his constituents make up only one of the influences on how a congressman behaves in his voting, committee activity, and communication with citizens back home. Generally congressmen try to cement relationships with the electorate by concentrating on constituent service, doing favors, and helping citizens in their dealings with the government. As congressmen cast votes on legislative proposals, they take into account such factors as their party leaders, the position of the president, compromises with opponents, and ties to other legislators. Historically, however, Congress has been organized by political parties and voting has generally divided along party lines, making party the major channel for expressing ideological views. The U.S. Congress has only rarely resembled the British system with its cohesive political parties composed of members who always vote together on major issues. Given the lack of party organizational discipline, loyalty to the party has always been a tentative phenomenon among members of Congress.

Furthermore, from the late 1930s until very recently, the two major congressional parties have consistently been internally divided, largely along geographic and ideological lines. Democrats from outside the South generally have voted together in a fairly liberal direction. Since the 1930s, though, southern Democrats have often voted with their conservative colleagues from the Republican party to form the so-called conservative coalition, which occasionally has dominated Congress even when the Democrats hold a nominal majority. This label is probably misleading, however. Many southern Democrats were of the old populist variety (John Sparkman of Alabama was a classic example) who often supported New Deal economic legislation and its continuation but voted against any legislation to expand personal freedoms for blacks. In the last two decades many of these populist southern Democrats have left the House and Senate, often to be replaced by conservative Republicans. In the late 1960s and early 1970s electoral trends seemed to be producing conservative Republicans and more liberal Democrats from the South (the latter largely from the growing metropolitan areas or from areas with large black populations), but by the late 1970s another pattern was becoming more evident in Congress. A number of factors combined to produce a Congress composed of 535 individuals not held together by any broader ideological grouping and incapable of being led by anyone. Voters paid less and less attention to party labels, local party organizations withered away, the mass media became more crucial electoral communications devices, campaign contributions came more from political action committees, and internal "reforms" increased the institutional leverage of individual congressmen. As a result, Congress came more and more to resemble a collection of 535 individual entrepreneurs.

Congress is supposed to be the branch of national government that most closely and, in the case of the House, most quickly mirrors shifts in public opinion. The most dramatic change in the nature of Congress would come if third parties were successful in winning congressional elections. Assuming that the Democratic party remains the major vehicle for liberals and the Republican party plays a similar role for conservatives, new parties supporting populist and

176

libertarian views would unravel the traditional organizing mechanism of Congress. But they might add a new dimension of stability and predictability in Congress. As we have said, the prospects for a populist party seem bleak. The primary source of support for such a party would be in the South, where populism still finds expression in the Democratic party. Probably the best chance for a southern-based populist party that could elect members to Congress (or convert incumbents) was lost when George Wallace let the American Independent Party apparatus of 1968 wither into fringe status. But a Libertarian party is alive and active throughout the nation. Even here, however, the party's best hope for acquiring a presence in Congress would be through conversion of current members, especially those in the Republican party, such as Ron Paul of Texas or Mark Hatfield of Oregon, who have demonstrated a libertarian voting record. Libertarians could be elected to Congress, but, like all third parties, they face the limits of the single-member-district system as well as the role of the two major parties in the internal organization of Congress. Libertarians could do well in hundreds of congressional districts across the country but not elect a single member if they did not win a plurality in any district. The 1983 election in Great Britain (which also uses the single-member-district method) is an indication of what could happen here in the United States: The fledgling Social Democratic party won 25 percent of the total popular votes, but only 3.5 percent of the seats in Parliament. Although it faces these barriers, the Libertarian party does seem to stand the best chance to emerge in Congress as a third force similar to the role of the Liberals in Great Britain.

Barring any major growth in third parties winning congressional elections, how might the public's diverse ideological leanings be expressed in Congress? One standard route for the communication of district views within the two-party Congress has been the formation of "caucuses," loose alliances of members who share some common concern that is different from that of either party. Beginning with the Democratic Study Group (made up of House liberals) in the 1950s, there are now dozens of these caucuses in Congress. Some of these organizations are clearly designed to protect a single interest (the Steel Caucus, for example), but others more nearly resemble their progenitor, the DSG, in that they attempt to define positions over a broad range of issues and provide a measure of ideological cohesion among their members for the purposes of voting, bargaining over legislative provisions, and influencing lead-

177

ership selection. These caucuses, born of the need to find some cohesion in an increasingly atomistic House and Senate, could be the seeds of future ideological organizations in Congress,

Finally the president is often described as the major legislative leader in Congress. Through his budget proposals, State of the Union address and other messages, foreign policy proposals, and constant interaction with Congress, he defines much of the legislative agenda, telling congressmen what to talk about if not what to do. Presidential strategies for building coalitions in Congress will have much to do with the extent to which ideological diversity is communicated through national politics. The president of course can use some of the same approaches in Congress that he uses to build coalitions among the public, although foreign policy presently is not as useful in manipulating Congress as it was in the pre-Vietnam era. By focusing on one issue dimension at a time, a president can create a coalition of support that may cross party lines but temporarily unite members of ideological groupings in Congress, as President Reagan did during the early months of his administration. The Reagan experience in fact may be typical of the future. Such coalitions may be created very quickly and be successful for a time, but they are inherently unstable. More than in the past, future presidents will have to rebuild their coalitions periodically, depending upon the type of issue being discussed as well as the ideological composition of Congress. As with the creation of coalitions within the public, future presidents may find it more feasible to create temporary congressional coalitions to deal with issues of personal freedom or individual liberties. Regardless of which dimension is stressed, however, the more the four ideological viewpoints are reflected in Congress, the more temporary and unstable those presidential support coalitions will become.

From Here to There

Where does all this leave us? We have described in detail the ideology, characteristics, and behavior of four major groups in the American public: the populists, liberals, libertarians, and conservatives. In this chapter we have suggested how these groups may communicate their ideas through the major institutions of politics in the United States. What in general is likely to happen in the future? What does this say about what should be happening in politics now? The answers to these questions lie in an examination

178

of the possibilities for change and in the direction or nature of that change.

As to the possibilities of change, there has been evidence in recent years of the power of citizen-initiated political movements. These will probably continue as a diverse public supports new political parties, different uses of interest groups, and ballot initiatives to allow more direct public participation in policy making. The real challenge now, however, is to those who "because of their active role in generating messages relevant to the regulation of conflict" can be labeled political communicators (Nimmo 1978, p. 12). As used here, this term refers to politicians, journalists, political practitioners and consultants, spokesmen for interest groups, and opinion leaders. The challenge is simply to begin to take the public seriously. We believe that members of the public do have ideological viewpoints and, even though they may not be able to label themselves or articulate those views as well as the political communicators do, their ideological views make sense. What is lacking is not ideas or ideologies in the public but the willingness of communicators to accept these ideas as useful ways of viewing politics. These communicators are the ones who have insisted most on discussing politics in dichotomous terms, regardless of whether that dichotomy accurately describes public opinion. They also make up a political elite that does not understand why membership in parties and groups declines, why voters are bored or alienated, and why most citizens complain when they have to consume political news or advertisements. When political communicators begin to take the mass belief systems as serious points of view and realize that new labels and terms may make communication about politics easier, we can begin to see some ideological element appear in the general discussion about politics. Sadly enough these professional "talkers" about politics probably will change their terminology and analysis only when they see that it will make their jobs easier. At least at that point, though, the process of political communication can in fact become easier and more meaningful.

Furthermore the use of ideological labels by citizens is definitely related to the use of the mass media (television, newspapers, and magazines). People who pay more attention to the mass media are more likely to choose the liberal and conservative labels for themselves rather than the "moderate" or "don't know" labels. This holds true even for those people with higher levels of education (Maddox and Wattier 1980). Thus ideological labels are in a sense legitimized by journalists' use of them. The public's ability to recognize that their own belief systems are in fact legitimate may be limited by the fact that journalists generally do not use the populist or libertarian labels. (The term "populist" is used more often in the mass media but usually to denote a campaign style rather than an ideological framework.)

As to the nature or direction of the change we may see in the future, we can conclude on a slightly optimistic note. Many political observers lament the current state of the system: Voters behave in strange ways, alienation is rampant, the solid two-party system is breaking down, institutions themselves seem to become more divided and less predictable each year. In other words they see American politics moving from simplicity and dichotomy to chaos and atomism. In response many observers suggest changes and reforms, such as a stronger party system, return of power to the professional politicians, tighter leadership in Congress or even a parliamentary system, or a new realignment of voters under the two major parties. All of these suggestions of course are for a return to the past, a return to simplicity, dichotomy, and structure.

We may have to recognize that we will never return to that simpler, more structured politics in the United States. Given the economic and demographic changes of recent years, it is unlikely that issues of personal freedom will be subordinated to economic issues as they have been often in the past. Thus politics will be more complicated as we attempt to resolve both kinds of issues at once. Furthermore the notion of a dichotomous and therefore organizable world may be a leftover 19th-century idea, one that makes little sense late in the 20th century. Finally we cannot create a mass society that includes a large number of people with high levels of education and almost complete saturation with mass media coverage of politics and then expect all these citizens to behave as mindless sheep. We have created, even fostered, diversity, and now we need a political system that can deal with it.

To say that we cannot return to a simpler structure of politics is not to say that we must remain in an atomistic state. Four ideological categories, for example, are not so easy to deal with as two, but they are easier to deal with than none at all. The public may not be as simple to describe as is often thought or assumed, but we can describe it and analyze its behavior. An institution such as Congress also may never be quite as neatly structured as it once was, but it does not have to be a collection of unconnected individuals. To accept diversity as the basic characteristic of American politics may not be as easy as accepting dichotomy, but it is realistic.

Appendix: Methodology

Sources of Survey Data

The survey data in this book were made available through the Inter-University Consortium for Political and Social Research (University of Michigan, Ann Arbor, Michigan), which gathers survey data collected by other institutions and individuals and makes that data available for use by researchers at all institutions that are consortium members. The data are not analyzed by the consortium, only transmitted in raw form. Thus the consortium is not responsible for the analyses or interpretations presented by any researcher.

Our primary analyses in this book are based on the studies known as the American National Election Studies, a series of biennial national surveys conducted by the Survey Research Center (since 1970 known as the Center for Political Studies) at the University of Michigan. All of these surveys are nationwide, multistage cross-sectional samples, designed to be representative of the voting-age citizenry of the contiguous United States, which means citizens from all regions of the country over age 21 prior to 1970 and over age 18 since 1970. Sampling is done by beginning with a sample of large geographical units (such as congressional districts), and then choosing at random smaller units, such as city blocks or segments of rural areas. Then each of those segments or blocks, a random selection of housing units is made and one person from each selected housing unit is interviewed in person, the person being chosen again in a random way. Interviews in presidential election years are done before the election; an attempt is then made to go back to as many of these people as possible for a post-election interview, which asks both some of the same questions and some new questions. Most of the questions used in our study were asked on pre-election interviews, although some (obviously reported voting behavior, for example) were included in post-election interviews.

The sample sizes for each of the CPS studies used for our analysis are as follows:

Year	Sample Size	Year	Sample Size
1952	1,899	1968	1,673
1956	1,762	1972	2,705
1960	1,181	1976	2,248
1964	1,834	1980	1,614

The National Opinion Research Center (NORC) studies, also made available through the consortium, were used as a secondary source of data, primarily to chart changes in opinion on issues (especially foreign policy) not included very often in the Center for Political Studies surveys. The NORC data used are known as the General Social Surveys, a national survey conducted every year from 1972 through 1980, except for 1979. Like the CPS surveys, each is considered a representative sample of all citizens of voting age in the contiguous United States. The selection process of people to be interviewed is similar to that of the CPS studies (although the specific sampling technique is block quota sampling through 1974 and full probability sampling since 1975) in terms of representativeness and the use of personal, rather than telephone, interviewing. The sample size for each of the NORC studies used is:

Year	Sample Size	Year	Sample Size
1972	1,613	1976	1,499
1973	1,504	1977	1,530
1974	1,484	1978	1,532
1975	1,490	1980	1,468

For those who are interested in the mechanics of survey research or the nature of secondary analysis of surveys (what we have done in this book, i.e. use survey data collected by others but analyzed for our purposes), standard reference works are Leslie Kish, *Survey Sampling* (New York: John Wiley, 1965), and Herbert H. Hyman, *Secondary Analysis of Sample Surveys* (New York: John Wiley, 1972).

Wording of Important Questions

For an exact listing of the wording of all questions used in this analysis, consult either James A. Davis, Tom W. Smith, and C. Bruce Stephenson, *General Social Survey Cumulative File, 1972–1980* (Ann Arbor, Mich.: ICPSR, 1981) for the NORC questions; or Warren E. Miller, Arthur H. Miller, and Edward J. Schneider, *American National Election Studies Data Sourcebook 1952–1978* (Cambridge, Mass.: Harvard University Press, 1980) for the CPS questions. For the convenience of the reader, however, we present below the exact wordings for those questions used to define the ideological types in each year, including those used in chapter IV to estimate the size of the types prior to 1972. The final section of this appendix describes how these questions were combined to form scales of economic intervention and personal freedoms attitudes, and how these were combined to form definitions of ideological types. Following each is a summary of how we recoded the responses into pro or con categories for each issue.

Economic Intervention Questions

1952

Government housing aid: Some people think the national government should do more in trying to deal with such problems as unemployment, education, housing, and so on. Others think that the government is already doing too much. On the whole would you say that what the government has done has been about right, too much, or not enough? Pro (about right, should do more, definitely should do more, should do more on some, don't know or the same on others). Con (should do less, definitely should do less, should do more on some, less on others, should do less on some, don't know or same on others).

1956

Government health care: The government ought to help people get doctors and hospital care at low cost. Pro (agree strongly, agree but not very strongly). Con (disagree strongly, disagree but not very strongly). Neutral (not sure, it depends).

Government job: The government in Washington ought to see to it that everybody who wants to work can find a job. Pro (agree strongly, agree but not very strongly). Con (disagree strongly, disagree but not very strongly). Neutral (not sure, it depends).

Power and housing: The government should leave things like electric power and housing for private businessmen to handle. Pro (agree strongly, agree but not very strongly). Con (disagree, disagree but not very strongly). Neutral (not sure, it depends).

1960

Government health care: same as 1956

Government job: same as 1956

Power and housing: same as 1956

1964

Government health care: Some say the government in Washington ought to help people get doctors and hospital care at low cost, others say the government should not get involved in this. Pro (should help people get doctors and hospital care at low cost). Con (stay out of this). Neutral (other, depends).

Government job: In general, some people feel that the government should see to it that every person has a job and a good standard of living. Others think the government should just let each person get ahead on his own. Pro (should see to it that every person has a job and a good standard of living). Con (should let each person get ahead on his own). Neutral (other, depends).

Power: Some people think it's all right for the government to own some power plants while others think the production of electricity should be left to private business. Pro (government own power plants). Con (leave this to private business). Neutral (other, depends).

1968

Government power: Some people are afraid the government in Washington is getting too powerful for the good of the country and the individual person. Others feel that government in Washington is not getting too strong for the good of the country. Pro (the government has not gotten too strong). Con (the government is getting too powerful). Neutral (other, depends).

Government health care: same as 1964

Government job: same as 1964

1972

Government health insurance: There is much concern today about the rapid rise in medical and hospital costs. Some feel there should be a government insurance plan which would cover all medical and hospital expenses. Others feel that medical expenses should be paid by individuals and through private insurance like Blue Cross. Where would you place yourself on this scale [respondent is presented with a seven-point scale ranging from government insurance plan (1) to private insurance plan (7)], or haven't you thought much about it? Pro (1, 2, 3). Con (5, 6, 7). Neutral (4).

Government job: Some people feel that the government in Washington should see to it that every person has a job and a good standard of living. Others think that the government should just let each person get ahead on his own. And, of course, other people have opinions somewhere in between. Suppose people

186

who believe that government should see to it that every person has a job and a good standard of living are at one end of this scale—at point number 1. And suppose that people who believe that the government should let each person get ahead on his own are at the other end—at point number 7. Where would you place yourself on this scale, or haven't you thought much about it? Pro (1, 2, 3). Con (5, 6, 7). Neutral (4).

Progressive taxation: As you know, in our tax system people who earn a lot of money already have to pay higher rates of income tax than those who earn less. Some people think that those with high incomes should pay even more of their income into taxes than they do now. Others think that the rates shouldn't be different at all—that everyone should pay the same portion of their income, no matter how much they make. Where would you place yourself on this scale [ranging from 1 (increase the tax rate for high income) to 7 (have the same tax rate for everyone)] or haven't you thought much about this? Pro (1, 2, 3). Con (5, 6, 7). Neutral (4).

1976

Government health insurance: same as 1972

Government job: same as 1972

Progressive taxation: same as 1972

1980

Government power: same as 1968

Government job: same as 1972

Government spending/services: Some people think the government should provide fewer services, even in areas such as health and education, in order to reduce spending. Other people feel it is important for the government to continue the services it now provides even if it means no reduction in spending. Where would you place yourself on this scale [respondent given a scale ranging from 1 (government should provide many fewer services; reduce spending a lot) to 7 (government should continue to provide services; no reduction in spending)], or haven't you thought much about this? Pro (5, 6, 7). Con (1, 2, 3). Neutral (4).

Personal Freedoms Questions

1952

Government aid to blacks: There is a lot of talk these days about discrimination. That is people having trouble getting jobs because of their race. Do you think the government ought to take an interest in whether Negroes have trouble in getting jobs or should it stay out of this problem? Pro (national government should pass laws and do other things too, national government should pass laws, state government should pass laws and do other things too, state government should pass laws, government should do other things only, government should take an interest, national government should stay out but state government should take action). Con (national and state government should stay out, favor restrictive legislation including clear anti-Negro statements).

1956

Desegregation: The government in Washington should stay out of the question of whether white and colored children go to the same school. Pro (disagree strongly, disagree but not very strongly). Con (agree strongly, agree but not very strongly). Neutral (not sure, it depends).

Fire Communist worker: The government ought to fire any government worker who is accused of being a Communist even though they don't prove it. Pro (disagree strongly, disagree but not very strongly). Con (agree strongly, agree but not very strongly). Neutral (not sure, it depends).

1960

Desegregation: same as 1956

1964

Desegregation: Some people say that the government in Washington should see to it that white and Negro children are allowed to go to the same schools. Others claim that this is not the government's business. Pro (see to it that whites and Negro children go to the same schools). Con (stay out of this area as it is none of its business). Neutral (other, depends).

School prayer: Some people think it is all right for the public schools to start each day with prayer. Others feel that religion does not belong in the public schools but should be taken care of by the family and the church. Pro (religion does not belong in the schools). Con (schools should be allowed to start each day with a prayer). Neutral (other, depends).

1968

Desegregation: same as 1964
School prayer: same as 1964

188

1972

Women's role: Recently there has been a lot of talk about women's rights. Some people feel that women should have an equal role with men in running business, industry, and government. Others feel that women's place is in the home. Where would you place yourself on this scale [respondent presented a seven-point scale ranging from 1 (women and men should have an equal role) to 7 (women's place is in the home)], or haven't you thought much about this? Pro (1, 2, 3). Con (5, 6, 7). Neutral (4).

Abortion: Still on the subject of women's rights, there has been some discussion about abortion during recent years. Which one of the opinions on this card best agrees with your view? Pro (abortion should be permitted if due to personal reasons the woman would have difficulty in caring for the child, abortion should never be forbidden since one should not require a woman to have a child she doesn't want). Con (abortion should never be permitted, abortion should be permitted only if the life and health of the woman is in danger).

Legalization of marijuana: Some people think that the use of marijuana should be made legal. Others think that the penalties for using marijuana should be set higher than they are now. Where would you place yourself on this scale [respondent presented a scale ranging from 1 (make use of marijuana legal) to 7 (set penalties higher than they are now)], or haven't you thought much about it? Pro (1, 2, 3). Con (5, 6, 7). Neutral (4).

1976

Women's role: same as 1972

Abortion: same as 1972

Legalization of marijuana: same as 1972

1980

School prayer: same as 1964

Women's role: same as 1972

Abortion: same as 1972

Definition of Ideological Types

The following procedure was used for defining each respondent in the CPS surveys of 1972, 1976, and 1980 as a member of one type or another. Initially any respondent who did not answer or responded "don't know" to more than two of the six issues used to measure economic and personal freedoms issues was classified as "inattentive" and was no longer included in the classification process. Furthermore anyone who chose a neutral or middle position on more than two of the six issues was defined as "divided" and excluded from further consideration. Of those who were left after excluding these two groups, a separate scale was created for their support/opposition to economic intervention (by counting the number of "con" responses on those issues), and another scale was created for their support/opposition on personal freedoms issues (by counting the number of responses supporting the expansion of personal freedoms). Those who supported two or three of the three economic interventions and two or three of the three expansions of personal freedom were classified as "liberals." Those who supported two or three of the three economic interventions but opposed two or three of the three personal freedoms issues were classified as "populists." Those who opposed two or three of the three economic interventions and supported two or three of the three personal freedoms expansions were called "libertarians." Finally those who opposed two or three of the three economic interventions and opposed two or three of the three expansions of personal freedoms were classified as "conservatives."

Thus all members of the samples were classified by use of the two scales. Those who fit our definition as liberal, conservative, libertarian, or populist were defined as such. Those who responded to fewer than four of the six questions in each year were defined as inattentive. The divided group included the remainder of the respondents, those who took neutral or middle-range positions on too many issues to fit any of the other definitions of ideological type.

NORC Data Used for Ideological Types

For purposes of analyzing foreign policy linkages with our ideological types, we used the NORC data in chapter VII only. Here we were not concerned with the distribution of types but simply with roughly estimating who could be classified as liberal, libertarian, populist, and conservative so we could observe any tendencies they demonstrate toward foreign policy issues. We used six questions, three from the economic and three from the personal freedoms areas, just as with the CPS data. We also combined the responses as described in the previous section. We consider these results as only estimates however, because of the nature of the economic issues questions used by NORC. The questions asked refer to

190

spending levels for "improving and protecting the nation's health," "solving the problems of the big cities," and "welfare." For each of these items, the respondents were asked if they thought we were spending too little, about right, or too much. They could also respond that they did not know. Beyond the ambiguity of some of these items (especially welfare), it is very possible that biases would enter into people's responses. The term welfare has negative connotations for many people, while improving the nation's health is something most would support. Thus we believe that it is quite possible that these questions do not very accurately measure someone's general support or opposition in regard to economic intervention by the government. They were the best questions available from the NORC series, however, and provided the only estimate of this dimension we could use.

The questions used to measure the personal freedoms dimension were more straightforward and, in some cases, superior to the ones we used from the CPS data for this dimension. They are listed below.

1. Do you think the use of marijuana should be made legal or not? (Should, should not, don't know.)

2. Which of these statements comes closest to your feelings about pornography laws?
   a) There should be laws against the distribution of pornography whatever the age.
   b) There should be laws against the distribution of pornography to persons under 18.
   c) There should be no laws forbidding the distribution of pornography.
   d) Don't know.

3. Please tell me whether or not you think it should be possible for a pregnant woman to obtain a legal abortion if there is a strong chance of serious defect in the baby. (Yes, no, don't know.)

The question on abortion is one of a series of questions asking under what conditions the respondent believes it should be permitted. We chose this particular one over the other possible conditions (she is married and does not want any more children, the woman's own health is seriously endangered by the pregnancy, the family has a very low income and cannot afford any more children, she became pregnant because of rape, she is not married and does not want to marry the man) simply because the responses were more evenly divided and therefore more closely resembled the responses on the CPS abortion question.

References

Abramson, Paul R. and John H. Aldrich. 1982. "The Decline of Electoral Participation in America," *American Political Science Review*, 76 (September): 502–21.

The Baron Report. 1982. (May 10).

The Baron Report. 1983. (May 5).

Barone, Michael and Grant Ujifusa. 1981. *The Almanac of American Politics 1982* (Washington, D.C.: Barone & Co.).

Beck, Paul Allen and M. Kent Jennings. 1979. "Political Periods and Political Participation," *American Political Science Review*, 73 (September): 737–50.

Bell, Daniel. 1973. *The Coming of Post-Industrial Society: A Venture in Social Forecasting* (New York: Basic Books).

Berelson, Bernard R., Paul F. Lazarsfeld, and William N. McPhee. 1954. *Voting* (Chicago: University of Chicago Press).

Bishop, George F. and Stephen E. Bennett. 1978. "The Changing Structure of Mass Belief Systems: Fact or Artifact?" *Journal of Politics*, 40 (August): 781–887.

Bramsted, E. K. and K. J. Melhuish. 1978. *Western Liberalism: A History in Documents from Locke to Croce* (New York: Longman).

Brown, Steven R. 1970. "Consistency and Persistence of Ideology: Some Experimental Results," *Public Opinion Quarterly*, 34 (Spring): 60–68.

Burnham, Walter Dean. 1970. *Critical Elections and the Mainsprings of American Politics* (New York: Norton).

Campbell, Angus, et al. 1960. *The American Voter* (New York: John Wiley and Sons).

Campbell, Angus, Gerald Gurin, and Warren Miller. 1954. *The Voter Decides* (Evanston, Illinois: Row, Peterson and Co.).

Clark, Ed. 1980. *A New Beginning* (Ottawa, Illinois: Caroline House).

Clausen, Aage. 1973. *How Congressmen Decide: A Policy Focus* (New York: St. Martin's Press).

Conover, Pamela Johnson and Stanley Feldman. 1981. "The Origins and Meaning of Liberal/Conservative Self-Identification," *American Journal of Political Science*, 25 (November): 617–45.

Converse, Philip. 1964. "The Nature of Belief Systems in Mass Politics," in David Apter, ed., *Ideology and Discontent* (New York: The Free Press of Glencoe).

Crabb, Cecil V. 1983. *American Foreign Policy in the Nuclear Age* (New York: Harper and Row).

Davis, James A. 1980. "Conservative Weather in a Liberalizing Climate: Change in Selected NORC General Social Survey Items, 1972–78," *Social Forces*, 58: 1129–56.

Dawson, Richard E., Kenneth Prewitt, and Karen S. Dawson. 1977. *Political Socialization*, 2d ed. (Boston: Little Brown and Co.).

Dolbeare, Kenneth M. and Patricia Dolbeare. 1971. *American Ideologies* (Chicago: Markham).

Field, John Osgood and Ronald E. Anderson. 1969. "Ideology in the Public's Conception of the 1964 Presidential Election," *Public Opinion Quarterly*, 33: 380–98.

193

Flanigan, William H. and Nancy H. Zingale. 1983. *Political Behavior of the American Electorate*, 5th ed. (Boston: Allyn and Bacon).

Gans, Herbert J. 1980. *Deciding What's News* (New York: Vintage).

Goodin, Robert E. 1983. "Voting Through the Looking Glass," *American Political Science Review*, 77 (June): 420–34.

Graber, Doris. 1980. *Mass Media and American Politics* (Washington, D.C.: Congressional Quarterly Press).

Green, John C. and James L. Guth. 1983. "The Socialization of a Third Party Elite: The Case of the Libertarians," paper prepared for the annual meeting of the South Carolina Political Science Association.

Green, T. H. 1964. *The Political Theory of T. H. Green*, John Rodman, ed. (New York: Appleton-Century-Crofts).

Harris, Louis. 1973. *The Anguish of Change* (New York: Norton).

Hart, David M. n.d. "The Humane Studies Review: A Research and Study Guide," Vol. 1, No. 1 (Menlo Park, California: Institute for Humane Studies).

Hartz, Louis. 1955. *The Liberal Tradition in America* (New York: Harcourt, Brace Co.).

Herzon, Frederick D. 1980. "Ideology, Constraint, and Public Opinion: The Case of Lawyers," *American Journal of Political Science*, 24 (May): 233–58.

Hess, Karl. 1975. *Dear America* (New York: William Morrow and Co.).

Hobbes, Thomas. 1968 (originally published in 1651). *Leviathan*, Michael Oakeshott, ed. (New York: Collier Books).

Holm, John D. and John P. Robinson. 1978. "Ideological Identification and the American Voter," *Public Opinion Quarterly*, 42: 235–46.

Hughes, Barry B. 1978. *The Domestic Context of American Foreign Policy* (San Francisco: W. H. Freeman).

Keene, Karlyn H. and Victoria A. Lockett. 1981. "An Editors' Report on the Yankelovich, Skelly and White 'Mushiness Index,' " *Public Opinion* (April/May): 50–51.

Key, V. O., Jr., with Milton Cummings. 1966. *The Responsible Electorate* (Cambridge, Massachusetts: Harvard University Press).

Kirkpatrick, Samuel A. and Melvin E. Jones. 1970. "Vote Direction and Issue Cleavage in 1968," *Social Science Quarterly*, 51: 689–705.

Kleppner, Paul. 1970. *The Cross of Culture* (New York: Free Press).

Kleppner, Paul. 1978. "From Ethnoreligious Conflict to 'Social Harmony': Coalitional and Party Transformations in the 1890s," in *Emerging Coalitions in American Politics*, Seymour Martin Lipset, ed. (San Francisco: Institute for Contemporary Studies).

Knoke, David. 1979. "Stratification and the Dimension of American Political Orientations," *American Journal of Political Science*, 23 (November): 772–91.

Kritzer, Herbert M. 1978. "Ideology and American Political Elites," *Public Opinion Quarterly*, 42: 484–502.

Ladd, Everett, Jr., 1978. "The New Lines are Drawn: Class and Ideology in America," *Public Opinion* (July/August): 48–53.

Ladd, Everett, Jr., 1978a. "The New Lines are Drawn: Class and Ideology Part II," *Public Opinion* (September/October).

Ladd, Everett Carll and Charles D. Hadley. 1978. *Transformations of the American Party System*, 2nd ed. (New York: Norton).

Lane, Robert E. 1962. *Political Ideology* (New York: Free Press).

Lazarsfeld, Paul, Bernard Berelson, and Hazel Gaudet. 1944. *The People's Choice* (New York: Columbia University Press).

194

LeBlanc, Hugh L. and Mary Beth Merrin. 1977. "Mass Belief Systems Revisited," *Journal of Politics*, 39 (November): 1082–87.

Levering, Ralph B. 1978. *The Public and American Foreign Policy* (New York: William Morrow).

Levitin, Teresa E. and Warren E. Miller. 1979. "Ideological Interpretations of Presidential Elections," *American Political Science Review*, 73 (September): 751–71.

Lippmann, Walter. 1965 (originally published in 1922). *Public Opinion* (New York: Free Press).

Lipset, Seymour Martin. 1959. *Political Man* (Garden City, New York: Doubleday).

Lipsitz, Lewis. 1970. "The Grievances of the Poor," in Phillip Green and Sanford Levinson, eds., *Power and Community: Dissenting Essays in Political Science* (New York: Random House).

Locke, John. 1965 (originally published in 1689). *Two Treatises of Government*, Peter Laslett, ed. (New York: Cambridge University Press).

Machan, Tibor R. 1974. *The Libertarian Alternative* (Chicago: Nelson Hall).

MacRae, Duncan, Jr. 1958. *Dimensions of Congressional Voting: A Statistical Study of the House of Representatives in the Eighty-First Congress.* (Berkeley: University of California Press).

Maddox, William S. 1981. "The Citizen's Role and Voter Turnout," *Sociological Focus*, 14 (October): 287–96.

Maddox, William S. and Dan Nimmo. 1981. "In Search of the Ticket-Splitter," *Social Science Quarterly*, 62 (September): 401–08.

Maddox, William S. and Robert Robins. 1981. "How *People* Magazine Covers Political Figures," *Journalism Quarterly*, 58 (Spring): 113–15.

Maddox, William S. and Mark Wattier. 1980. "Mass Media Use and Socialization to the Electoral Process," paper presented at the annual meeting of the Midwest Association of Public Opinion Research, Chicago. (December).

Madison, James. 1961. "Federalist Number 10," in Roy P. Fairfield, ed., *The Federalist Papers* (New York: Anchor Books).

Maggiotto, Michael A. and Eugene Wittkopf. 1981. "American Public Attitudes Toward Foreign Policy," *International Studies Quarterly*, 25: 601–31.

Mandelbaum, Michael and William Schneider. 1979. "The New Internationalisms: Public Opinion and American Foreign Policy," in Kenneth A. Oye, et al., eds., *Eagle Entangled* (New York: Longman).

Mannheim, Karl. 1972. "The Problem of Generations," in *The New Pilgrims: Youth Protest in Transition,* ed. Philip G. Altbach and Robert S. Laufer. (New York: David McKay Co.)

Marcus, George E., David Tabb, and John L. Sullivan. 1974. "The Application of Individual Differences Scaling to the Measurement of Political Ideology," *American Journal of Political Science*, 18: 405–20.

Mayhew, David R. 1966. *Party Loyalty Among Congressmen* (Cambridge, Massachusetts: Harvard University Press).

Mill, John Stuart. 1947 (originally published in 1859). *On Liberty*, Alburey Castell, ed. (Northbrook, Illinois: AHM Publishing).

Miller, Arthur H. 1978. "The Majority Party Reunited? A Comparison of the 1972 and 1976 Elections," in Jeff Fishel, ed., *Parties and Elections in an Anti-Party Age* (Bloomington, Indiana: Indiana University Press).

Miller, Arthur H. and Warren E. Miller. 1975. "Issues, Candidates, and Partisan

Division in the 1972 American Presidential Election," *British Journal of Political Science*, 5: 393–434.

Miller, Warren E. and Teresa E. Levitin. 1976. *Leadership and Change* (Englewood Cliffs, New Jersey: Winthrop).

Miller, Warren E., Arthur H. Miller and Edward J. Schneider. 1980. *American National Election Studies Data Sourcebook 1952–1978* (Cambridge, Massachusetts: Harvard University Press).

Minar, David M. 1964. *Ideas and Politics: The American Experience* (Homewood, Illinois: Dorsey).

Mueller, John. 1973. *War, Presidents and Public Opinion* (New York: Wiley).

Naisbitt, John. 1982. *Megatrends: Ten New Directions Transforming Our Lives* (New York: Warner Books).

Natchez, Peter B. and Irvin C. Bupp. 1968. "Candidates, Issues, and Voters," *Public Policy*, 17 (Summer): 409–37.

Nathan, James A. and James K. Oliver. 1983. *Foreign Policy Making and the American Political System* (Boston: Little Brown).

Nelson, Brian R. 1982. *Western Political Thought: From Socrates to the Age of Ideology* (Englewood Cliffs, Jew Jersey: Prentice-Hall).

Nie, Norman H. and Kristi Anderson. 1974. "Mass Belief Systems Revisited: Political Change and Attitude Structure," *Journal of Politics*, 36: 540–87.

Nie, Norman H., Sidney Verba, and John R. Petrocik. 1976. *The Changing American Voter* (Cambridge, Massachusetts: Harvard University Press).

Nimmo, Dan. 1978. *Political Communication and Public Opinion in America* (Santa Monica, California: Goodyear Publishing).

Nimmo, Dan and James E. Combs. 1980. *Subliminal Politics: Myths and Mythmakers in America* (Englewood Cliffs, New Jersey: Prentice-Hall).

Nozick, Robert. 1974. *Anarchy, State, and Utopia* (New York: Basic Books).

"Opinion Outlook." 1984. *National Journal* (March 17).

Page, Benjamin I. 1978. *Choices and Echoes in Presidential Elections: Rational Man and Electoral Democracy* (Chicago: University of Chicago Press).

Palmer, Bruce. 1980. *Man Over Money: The Southern Populist Critique of American Capitalism* (Chapel Hill: University of North Carolina Press).

Phillips, Kevin P. 1982. *Post-Conservative America: People, Politics, and Ideology in a Time of Crisis* (New York: Random House).

Pierce, John C. 1970. "Party Identification and the Changing Role of Ideology in American Politics," *Midwest Journal of Political Science*, 14: 25–42.

Pomper, Gerald M. 1972. "From Confusion to Clarity: Issues and American Voters, 1956–1968," *American Political Science Review*, 66 (June): 415–28.

Pomper, Gerald M. 1975. *Voters' Choice* (New York: Dodd, Mead & Co.).

Repass, David E. 1971. "Issue Salience and Party Choice," *American Political Science Review*, 65 (June): 386–400.

Rielly, John E. 1983. "American Opinion: Continuity, not Reaganism," *Foreign Policy*, 50: 86–104.

Robinson, John and John Holm. 1980. "Ideological Voting is Alive and Well," *Public Opinion* (April/May): 52–58.

Schneider, William. 1983. "Conservatism, Not Interventionism: Trends in Foreign Policy Opinion, 1974–1983," in Kenneth A. Oye, et al., eds., *Eagle Defiant* (Boston: Little Brown).

Schubert, Glendon. 1965. *The Judicial Mind: The Attitudes and Ideologies of Supreme Court Justices, 1946–1963* (Evanston, Illinois: Northwestern University Press).

Schwartz, David C. 1973. *Political Alienation and Political Behavior* (Chicago: Aldine Publishing).

Sennett, Richard and Jonathan Cobb. 1972. *The Hidden Injuries of Class* (New York: Vintage Books).

Stack, John. 1983. *Critical Issues in American Foreign Policy* (Guilford, Connecticut: Dushkin).

Stimson, James A. 1975. "Belief Systems: Constraint, Complexity, and the 1972 Election," *American Journal of Political Science*, 19: 393–417.

Stokes, Donald E. 1966. "Spatial Models of Party Competition," in Angus Campbell, et al., *Elections and the Political Order* (New York: Wiley).

Stouffer, Samuel. 1955. *Communism, Conformity and Civil Liberties* (Garden City, New York: Doubleday).

Sullivan, John L., James E. Piereson, and George E. Marcus. 1978. "Ideological Constraints in the Mass Public: A Methodological Critique and Some New Findings," *American Journal of Political Science*, 22 (May): 234–49.

Sundquist, James L. 1983. *Dynamics of the Party System*, Revised ed. (Washington, D.C.: Brookings Institution).

Truman, David S. 1959. *The Congressional Party: A Case Study* (New York: Wiley).

Turner, Julius. 1951. *Party and Constituency* (Baltimore: Johns Hopkins University Press).

Wayman, Frank Whelon and Ronald R. Stockton. 1980. "The Structure and Stability of Political Attitudes: Findings from the 1974–76 Dearborn Panel Study," paper prepared for the annual meeting of the American Political Science Association.

Wittkopf, Eugene and Michael A. Maggiotto. 1983. "Elites and Masses: A Comparative Analysis of Attitudes Toward America's World Role," *Journal of Politics*, 45 (May): 303–34.

Wright, James D. 1976. *The Dissent of the Governed*. (New York: Academic Press).

Wyckoff, Mikel L. 1979. "Alternative Approaches to the Study of Political Belief Systems: A Defense of the Traditional Paradigm," paper presented at the annual meeting of the 1979 Midwest Political Science Association, Chicago. (April.)

Index

Afghanistan, 138
Americans for Democratic Action, viii
Anderson, John, viii, xiii, xiv, 16, 91, 103, 105, 106, 107, 109, 159, 162

Baron, Alan, viii, xi
Barone, Michael, xi, xiv, 70
Bayh, Birch, 91
Behavioral movement, 23
Bisnow, Mark, viii
Brown, Jerry, xiv, 16
Burnham, Walter Dean, 24
Bush, George, xii

Caddell, Pat, xiii–xiv
Carter, Jimmy, xii, 92, 103, 105, 106, 107, 109, 114, 138, 163, 165, 172, 173, 174
Center for Political Studies (CPS), 35, 183
China, People's Republic of, 134, 137
Citizens party, 2, 167
Clark, Dick, 91
Clark, Ed, xiii, xiv, 141
Classical liberalism, 7–12, 14
Cohen, William, 130
Combs, James, 23, 24, 29
Commoner, Barry, 19, 20
Communist party, 166
Conable, Barber, 16
Congress, U.S.:
  caucuses, 177–78
  party cohesiveness, 175–76
  third party potential, 176–77
  voting for, 110, 111 tbl
  voting patterns, 32–33, 128–29, 130 tbl, 131
Conservatism (see also Conservatives; Liberal-conservative continuum):
  communism, opposition to, 150, 151 fig
  congressional voting reflecting, 129–31
  defense spending, 148, 150, 151 fig
  definition of, 4, 5 fig, 16–18
  foreign aid, 148, 149 fig
  foreign policy orientation, 144, 145 fig
  government responsiveness, perception of, 124, 125 tbl
  internationalism, 146, 147 fig
  1960's, 65, 66 tbl, 67
  1970's, 68 fig, 69–70
  Republican party as channel for, 158–59
  third party, possible creation of, 166
  United Nations, involvement in, 148, 149 fig
Conservatives (see also Conservatism):
  alienation, levels, 125, 126 fig, 127 fig
  Congress, voting for, 110, 111 tbl
  demographics of, 97–98, 99–100
  educational levels, 86 tbl, 88 fig, 89
  gender differences, 93, 94 tbl, 95
  generational differences, 75, 76 tbl, 77, 78 fig, 79–80
  income levels 85–86
  party identification, 118 tbl, 119–120
  political efficacy, 122 tbl, 123
  political interest, 121 tbl, 122
  political trust, 123, 124 tbl
  presidential voting, 105–7, 108 tbl
  racial differences, 92, 93 tbl
  regional differences, 87 tbl, 90–2
  religious differences, 94 tbl, 95
  self-identification, 112, 113 tbls, 114–17
  voter turnout, 102 tbl, 103
Converse, Philip, 25–26
CPS. See Center for Political Studies
Culver, John, 91

Daley, Richard, vii
Davis, James A., 43

199

Long, Huey, 20
Lugar, Richard, 91
Luther, Martin, 8

McCarthy, Eugene, xiv, 162
McGovern, George, 14, 79, 92, 103, 105, 119, 163, 165, 171, 173
Madison, James, 11
Mannheim, Karl, xv, 74
Mass belief systems:
  characteristics of, 5–7
  issue voter, 26–28
  liberal-conservative continuum used to evaluate, 28–30
  multidimensional aspects, 4, 30–34
  nonideological citizen, 25–6, 27, 28
  party realignments, 25
  textbook citizen, 23–25
Mass media, 179–80
Mathias, Charles McC., 130
Medieval consensus, 8
Mercantilism, 10
Mill, John Stuart, 11, 13
Modern liberalism. *See* Liberalism
Mondale, Walter F., xiv, 69, 74, 79, 159
Moral Majority, 54, 110
Mueller, John, 136

Naisbitt, John, 159
National Conservative Political Action Committee, 54
National Opinion Research Center (NORC), 36, 184
New Right, xii, 3, 54
Nicaragua, 138
Nimmo, Dan, 23, 24, 29
Nixon, Richard, 74, 103, 105, 134, 137, 138, 165, 172
NORC. *See* National Opinion Research Center

O'Neill, Tip, 69
Orwell, George, vii

Packwood, Robert, xii, 130, 174
Paul, Ron, 177
Percy, Charles, 91, 130
Personal freedoms:
  abortion, 50, 51 fig
  civil rights, 46 fig, 47 fig, 48 fig, 62

defendants' rights, 50 fig
freedom of speech, 54, 55 fig
ideological positions, 4, 5 fig
liberal-conservative continuum evaluation of, 33–34
marijuana legalization, 52, 53 fig, 54
prayer in schools, 49 fig
presidential stances on, 175
public opinion regarding, 45–54, 55 fig
survey questions, 187–89
women's rights, 51, 52 fig
Phillips, Kevin, 17
Political behavior:
  alienation levels, 125–28
  cohesiveness of ideological groups, 109–10
  Congress, voting for, 110, 111 tbl
  Congressional voting patterns, 32–33, 128–29, 130 tbl, 131
  government responsiveness, perception of, 124, 125 tbl
  party identification, 117, 118 tbl, 119–20
  political efficacy, 122 tbl, 123
  political interest, 121 tbl, 122
  political trust, 123, 124 tbl
  presidential voting, 103, 104 tbl, 105–7, 108 tbl, 109–10
  self-identification, 112, 113 tbls, 114–17
  voter turnout, 102 tbl, 103
Political communicators, 179
Political socialization, 74
Populism (*see also* Populists):
  communism, opposition to, 150, 151 fig
  congressional voting reflecting, 129–31
  defense spending, 148, 150, 151 fig
  definition of, 4, 5 fig, 18–20
  foreign aid, 148, 149 fig
  foreign policy orientation, 144, 145 fig
  government responsiveness, perception of, 124, 125 tbl
  internationalism, 146, 147 figs
  1950's, 62, 63 tbl
  1960's, 65–67
  1970's, 68 fig, 69
  third party, possible creation of, 164–65
  United Nations, involvement in, 148, 149 fig
Populists (*see also* Populism):
  alienation levels, 125–28
  Congress, voting for, 110, 111 tbl
  Democratic party, involvement in, 65, 67, 165
  demographics of, 97
  educational levels, 86–89

202

About the Authors

William S. Maddox is associate professor of political science at the University of Central Florida.

Stuart A. Lilie is associate professor and chairman of the department of political science at the University of Central Florida.

Cato Institute

Founded in 1977, the Cato Institute is a public policy research foundation dedicated to broadening the parameters of policy debate to allow consideration of more options that are consistent with the traditional American principles of limited government, individual liberty, and peace. Toward that goal, the Institute strives to achieve a greater involvement of the intelligent, concerned lay public in questions of policy and the proper role of government.

The Institute is named for *Cato's Letters*, pamphlets that were widely read in the American Colonies in the early eighteenth century and played a major role in laying the philosophical foundation for the revolution that followed. Since that revolution, civil and economic liberties have been eroded as the number and complexity of social problems have grown. Today virtually no aspect of human life is free from the domination of a governing class of politico-economic interests. A pervasive intolerance for individual rights is shown by government's arbitrary intrusions into private economic transactions and its disregard for civil liberties.

To counter this trend the Cato Institute undertakes an extensive publications program dealing with the complete spectrum of policy issues. Books, monographs, and shorter studies are commissioned to examine the federal budget, social security, regulation, NATO, international trade, and a myriad of other issues. Major policy conferences are held throughout the year from which papers are published thrice yearly in the *Cato Journal*. The Institute maintains an informal joint publishing arrangement with the Johns Hopkins University Press.

In order to maintain an independent posture, the Cato Institute accepts no government funding. Contributions are received from foundations, corporations, and individuals, and other revenue is generated from the sale of publications. The Institute is a non-profit, tax-exempt, educational foundation under Section 501(c)3 of the Internal Revenue Code.

CATO INSTITUTE
224 Second St., S.E.
Washington, D.C. 20003

1 & 2 PETER

A SELF-STUDY GUIDE

Irving L. Jensen

MOODY PRESS

CHICAGO

Contents

Introduction

Down through the ages Christians have been in need of inspiration, exhortation, and warning to strengthen their souls and to guard them against perils from without and perils from within. Shortly before Peter denied his Master, Christ told him, "Simon, Simon, behold, Satan hath desired to have you, that he may sift you as wheat: but I have prayed for thee, that thy faith fail not: and when thou art converted, *strengthen thy brethren*" (Luke 22:31-32, emphasis added). Little did Peter know at that time how he would eventually be used of God to strengthen, through these two inspired epistles, not only believers of his own generation but believers of all generations to come.

As you study the epistles of Peter, make it your high aim to learn that which will help you to grow in grace and in the knowledge of Christ (2 Peter 3:18). This is your strongest fortification against every peril and device of Satan.

Some Suggestions for Study

1. *Paragraph-by-paragraph study.* This procedure of study is consistently fostered in these self-study books. Studying by paragraphs should always precede verse-by-verse study, so that you will not lose your bearing in details of the Bible text.

2. *Word study.* The epistles of Peter use an unusually large amount of strong key words, worthy of much individual attention. Suggestions will be given for such word studies. Meditate on implied as well as explicit meanings of important words of the Bible text.

3. *Jotting things down.* Someone has said that the pencil is one of the best eyes. Throughout the manual you are urged to record your observations. The analytical chart, suggested in some lessons, can be a productive work sheet for organizing one's study

of a chapter of the Bible. The analytical chart method is described in detail in my book *Independent Bible Study.*

4. *Independent study.* The emphasis here is always: first see for yourself what the Bible text says; then go to commentaries for help. Most of the directions of this manual are geared to encourage original, firsthand study.

5. *The Bible, your textbook.* Whatever *version* of the Bible you use, choose an *edition* with large print and wide margins. Also, make many notations on the pages of your Bible as you study —underlining, cross references, notes, etc.

6. *Attitude of dependency.* Depend on the Holy Spirit to throw light on the Scriptures that He inspired. Meditate on words and phrases that He calls to your attention in the course of your study. Continually ask the question, What can I learn from this? And always have an eager attitude to obey God's Word to you.

Lesson 1
The Man Peter

The recommended order of study of any book of the Bible is background, survey, and analysis. Background and survey are of an introductory nature. Analysis, which is a careful scrutiny of every part of a particular Bible book, takes up most of one's study of the Bible text.

This lesson is devoted to one phase of the general background of Peter's epistles—that of Peter's biography. Further background and survey of 1 Peter is the subject of Lesson 2. Analysis of the Bible text of 1 Peter follows, beginning with Lesson 3. The same order is followed in the latter half of this manual.

* * *

Peter wrote only two New Testament books. It is interesting to observe that of the notable "triumvirate" of New Testament writers—Paul, apostle of faith; John, apostle of love; and Peter, apostle of hope—the man who does not appear in the gospels (Paul) wrote most of the New Testament books, and the man who is most prominent in the gospels (Peter) wrote the least number of New Testament books.[1]

For some Bible books, we cannot be sure of the identity of authorship (e.g., Hebrews). For some books whose authorship is known, we have sparse biographical information concerning the author (e.g., Jude). However, in the case of 1 and 2 Peter, the gospels and Acts furnish much information concerning the life and character of those epistles' author.

Peter is one of the most interesting characters of the New Testament. More personal information is given by the New Testa-

1. Paul wrote thirteen epistles (fourteen, if he wrote Hebrews); Peter, two; John, five books (the gospel, three epistles, Revelation).

ment concerning Peter than concerning any of the other apostles. Spend much time in this part of the lesson, reading all Bible verses cited, so that you can become intimately acquainted with the man who was inspired to write such marvelous books for God's people.

I. NAME

Originally Peter's name was Simon (a common Greek name), the Hebrew equivalent being Symeon (Acts 15:14). Jesus gave Simon a new name, prophetically pointing to his future status and position among the Christian circle. That new name was Cephas (Aramaic), or Peter (Greek; John 1:42; consult an exhaustive concordance to observe how frequently the name *Peter* appears in the New Testament, as over against only six references to the Aramaic name Cephas. It may be noted here that there is no other Peter in the New Testament.)

II. BIRTH

We do not know the date of Peter's birth. His father was a Jew named John or Jonas (also Jona). (Read John 1:42; 21:15-17; Matt. 16:17.) Peter had at least one brother, whose name was Andrew. The family's hometown was Bethsaida of Galilee (John 1:44), located near the north shore of the Sea of Tiberias (Galilee). (See map, p. 94.)

III. FOUR PERIODS OF LIFE

The biography of Peter can be divided into four parts: (1) pre-gospel period, (2) gospel period, (3) early church period, (4) later life period. The highlights of each of these are shown below.

A. Pre-gospel Period

1. *Education*. Peter probably had the normal elementary education of a Jewish boy in a small town. The description "unlearned and ignorant" of Acts 4:13 is better translated "without schooling or skill" (Berkeley) and refers to the fact that Peter did not have rabbinical training. What amazed the rulers and people was the fact that unschooled laymen such as Peter and John preached and performed with such mighty power.

2. *Occupation*. Many boys raised in the environs of the Sea of Galilee eventually entered the fishing trade. Peter and his brother, Andrew, were among these. When Jesus first met them, they were

busy about their trade (Matt. 4:18). James and John were partners with Peter and Andrew (Luke 5:10), who were living at this time in the coastal town of Capernaum (cf. Mark 1:29).

3. *Marital status.* From Mark 1:30 and 1 Corinthians 9:5 we learn that Peter was a married man during the period of the gospels. We do not know if he had children. (The gospels and Acts provide comparatively little information concerning the families of the disciples and apostles.)

B. Gospel Period

The highlights of Peter's life during Jesus' public ministry are listed below. Be sure to read all the Bible passages cited.

1. *Connection with John the Baptist.* Peter likely attended the preaching services of John the Baptist, as did Andrew (cf. John 1:35-37, 41-42).

2. *There were three calls by Jesus to Peter.*
   (a) The new-name call: "Thou shalt be called" (John 1:42)
   (b) The new-vocation call: "Thou shalt catch men" (Luke 5:1-11)
   (c) The new-association call: "He ordained twelve" (Matt. 3:13-19)

   What three aspects of this ordination are mentioned in Mark 3:14-15? It is interesting to observe that in the four passages where the names of the twelve apostles are listed, Peter's name heads each list (Matt. 10:2-4; Mark 3:16-19; Luke 6:14-16; Acts 1:13-14). At least two reasons may be given for this priority: (1) Peter was among the first disciples called by Jesus for the evangelistic ministry, and (2) Peter's natural aggressiveness made him the spokesman and leader of the group, at least in an unofficial way. Two examples of Peter acting as spokesman are given in John 6:66-69 and Matthew 16:16-20.

3. *Peter was one of Jesus' "inner circle."* It was natural for Jesus to have in His company from time to time a small segment of the twelve disciples. Peter, James, and John composed this inner circle. The gospels record three occasions when these three were the only apostles accompanying Him. Read the passages and determine the reasons for the limited company:
   (a) At the house of Jairus—Mark 5:37 (Luke 8:51)
   (b) Mount of Transfiguration—Matthew 17:1 (Mark 9:2; Luke 9:28)
   (c) Garden of Gethsemane—Matthew 26:37 (Mark 14:33)

4. *Peter was a prominent character during Jesus' passion week.* Read carefully each of the following passages, and record below

8

(a) an identification of the occasion and (b) what is revealed about Peter's character.

Passage	Occasion	Peter's Character
Mark 11:21		
Mark 13:3		
Luke 22:8		
John 13:1-11		
Matthew 26:33-46		
John 18:10-11		
Matthew 26:58, 69-75		
Luke 22:61-62		

5. *Key role among apostles.* Peter also played a key role among the apostles during the forty days between Jesus' resurrection and ascension. Before Peter could begin to minister as a "rock" in the gospel's witness, he needed to be restored to fellowship with Christ, which had been broken during the week of Jesus' trial. Read the following passages, and note what is said about Peter in each case:

John 20:1-10 (Luke 24:12; Mark 16:7):

_____

1 Corinthians 15:5:

_____

John 21:1-23:

_____

In your own words describe the "new " Peter as of the end of the gospel account.

_____

_____

C. Early Church Period

The most active and eventful period of Peter's life was during the years of the first twelve chapters of Acts, or A.D. 30 to A.D. 47. Chart

9

A shows the major events and movements of those chapters, and also indicates that Peter was *the* main character in chapters 1-7 and that in chapters 8-12 he shared the spotlight with such men as Philip, Barnabas, and Paul.[2]

ACTIVE PERIOD OF PETER'S LIFE   **Chart A**
Acts 1—12

1	3	8:1b	9:32	12
Church Is Born	Church Grows Through Testing	Church Is Scattered	Church Embraces Gentiles	
Jerusalem		Judea and Samaria		
Peter		Philip—Barnabas—Peter—Paul		

The following passages of Acts reveal the place of leadership and responsibility that Peter filled in the small group of twelve chosen apostles and in the larger group of the local congregation of believers in Jerusalem.[3]

1. *Leader of the twelve apostles* (1:15-26).
2. *Powerful preacher* (2:14-40; 5:42; 8:25; 10:34-43).
3. *Miracle-worker* (3:1–4:22; 5:12-16; 9:32-43).
4. *Other experiences* (identify them).
5:1-11

_____

5:17-41

_____

8:14-24

_____

12:1-19 (Except for the reappearance of Peter in chapter 15 in connection with the Jerusalem Council, we might say that Peter fades

2. For a survey chart of the rulers (emperors, procurators, and high priests) during the years of the Acts, see Irving L. Jensen, *Acts: An Inductive Study* (Chicago: Moody, 1968), p. 247.
3. The original group of twelve was reduced to eleven with the alienation and death of Judas (Acts 1:16-20) but was restored to twelve when Matthias was selected to replace Judas (Acts 1:23-26).

out of the action of Acts at 12:17: "And he [Peter] departed and went to another place.")

5. *Apostle to the Gentiles* (10:1–11:18).

6. *Speaker at the Jerusalem Council* (15:6-11; cf. vv. 12-29). This is the last reference to Peter in Acts. What he was doing while Paul was engaged in missionary journeys and other experiences of Acts 13-28 is the subject of the next era of his life, which we shall call the Later-Life Period.

D. Later-Life Period

From a few New Testament references to Peter after the Jerusalem Council, the following reconstruction of his latter life may be made:

1. *Evangelistic ministry to Jews* (Gal. 2:7-9).

2. *A visit to the church at Antioch (in Syria).* Here Paul rebuked Peter for his inconsistency in the manner of fellowshiping with Gentiles and with Jews.[4] Read Galatians 2:11-21. What harm was Peter doing?

_____

_____

_____

3. *Evangelistic tour of northern Asia Minor.* There is a strong possibility that the northern provinces of Asia Minor not evangelized by Paul were the areas where Peter ministered the gospel as an itinerant evangelist after the Jerusalem Council. This would partly explain Peter's references to believers living in Pontus, Galatia, Cappadocia, Asia, and Bithynia in 1 Pet. 1:1.[5] Peter probably ministered to both Jews and Gentiles at this time.

4. *Arrival at Rome.* It is generally believed that Peter came to Rome shortly after Paul's release from his first imprisonment.

5. *Writing of the epistles.* The two epistles of Peter were written at this time, with perhaps only a short interval between them. At the time of his second letter, Peter knew his death was imminent (2 Pet. 1:14).

---

4. Peter's behavior on this occasion has been identified in various versions as "insincerity" (*Revised Standard*), "deception" (Phillips), and "playing false" (*New English Bible*).

5. Of Peter's relationship to the churches in these areas, Tenney writes, "While there is no statement on record that Peter founded or even visited these churches, there is nothing to preclude his doing so" (Merrill C. Tenney, *New Testament Survey*, rev. ed. [Grand Rapids: Eerdmans, 1961], p. 345).

IV. DEATH

According to tradition, Peter was martyred by Nero in A.D. 67, about the same time his "beloved brother Paul" (2 Pet. 3:15) also was martyred. Origen says that Peter's death was by crucifixion and that the apostle requested that he be crucified head downward, because he felt unworthy to die as Christ had died.

V. THE CHARACTER AND PERSONALITY OF PETER

The character and personality of Peter have been scrutinized perhaps more than those of any other man or woman of the Bible. It is a happy circumstance that the New Testament reveals so much about this interesting man.

A man's character may change radically in his lifetime, such as happens in the conversion of his soul. His basic temperament, however, is part of his permanent image.[6] For example, Peter was always an aggressive man, full of energy. In his early days as a disciple of Jesus, this brought on unfortunate consequences, such as Peter's rash act of cutting off the ear of the high priest's servant Malchus (John 18:10-11). After Pentecost, Peter was still the man of action, but that basic temperament had undergone some radical experiences, including the Holy Spirit's baptism (Acts 2). This gave birth to a new passion and a mature vision, so that now the aggressive Peter was the powerful preacher and courageous leader of the earliest New Testament church community. Peter in Acts is a different *character* from the Peter found in the gospels, but his basic temperament is essentially the same.

Four passages of Scripture should be studied in connection with Peter's character-biography. These are shown on Chart B. Read them carefully, and try to reconstruct the things that were probably going through Peter's mind at these times.

With the above exercise as a background, study the following list of various traits that have been attributed to Peter at some time in his life. Identify each one as either pre-Pentecost, post-Pentecost, or both, from what you know of Peter.

unstable _____   hasty _____

daring _____   strong in faith _____

weak _____   stable _____

humble _____   impulsive _____

6. For an interesting and practical discussion of varieties of temperament, see O. Hallesby, *Temperament and the Christian Faith* (Minneapolis: Augsburg, n.d.).

PETER in the GOSPELS	Calling of the Twelve	John 1:41-42 (cf. Matt. 16:13-20)	PROGNOSTICATION	"Thou shalt be called Cephas"
	Calvary	Matthew 6:69-75	DEFECTION	"But he denied"
	Resurrection	John 21:15-19	RESTORATION	"Feed my sheep"
PETER in ACTS	Ascension and Pentecost	Acts 2:1-41 (cf. 1:6-8)	DEMONSTRATION	"Filled with the Holy Ghost"

energetic _____   strong in leadership (Gal. 2:9) _____

courageous _____   self-confident _____

devoted as a servant _____

The question may be asked, What kind of a man was Peter in the last decade or so of his life, after he moved out of the story of Acts in chapter 15? The gospels and Acts, of course, supply no information on this. Our sole source is the inspired writing of Peter himself during these years—the two epistles that bear his name (1 and 2 Peter). As we analyze the various chapters of these epistles (beginning in Lesson 2), we will get to know Peter more intimately, and then it is that we will have at least a partial answer to the question raised above.

* * *

SOME REVIEW QUESTIONS

1. What is significant about Peter's name?

_____

_____

_____

13

2. What were the four periods of Peter's life? Recall some of the highlights of each period.

_____

_____

_____

_____

_____

_____

3. What were Peter's three calls by Jesus? What was the significance of each call?

_____

_____

_____

4. What role does Peter play in the book of Acts?

_____

5. Reconstruct a probable biography of Peter after the Jerusalem Council of Acts 15.

_____

_____

6. What experiences of Peter are suggested by the words *prognostication*, *defection*, *restoration*, and *demonstration*?

_____

_____

_____

7. Describe in your words the character of Peter as of the time of the writing of his epistles.

_____

_____

Lesson 2
Background and Survey of 1 Peter

Focus now on the setting of the background of 1 Peter and the epistle's general contents.

I. BACKGROUND

A. Authorship

First Peter is one of those Bible books whose authorship is identified by name. "Peter, an apostle of Jesus Christ, to . . ." (1:1). As to authorship, the epistle is one of the best-attested books of the New Testament. When Peter wrote this letter he was an elderly man, as seen from 5:1: "I . . . who am also an elder" (cf. 5:5, "younger"). How else did Peter identify himself in 5:1?

B. Destination

The natural, literal meaning of 1:1 is that this epistle was sent to people who were living in various Roman provinces of northern Asia Minor, namely, Pontus, Galatia, Cappodocia, Asia, and Bithynia (see map on p. 98). They were believers (5:2) and apparently had moved to those regions because of persecution ("strangers scattered," 1:1). Peter's interest in these areas may have originated in evangelistic work to which he had devoted himself for some time between the Jerusalem council (Acts 15; A.D. 49) and the Neronian persecutions at Rome (A.D. 64). From the Acts account we learn that Paul did not evangelize northern Asia Minor on his missionary tours—in fact, on the one occasion when he began to move northward into this vicinity, he was forbidden by the Holy Spirit, who directed him to Troas and thence to Macedonia (Acts 16:6-12).

It is difficult to determine the exact background of the exiles to whom Peter wrote his epistles. Many if not most of them were Jewish believers, persecuted by dispersion (suggested by the phrase "strangers scattered," 1:1) for their Christian faith. However, there were probably Gentiles represented in the group as well, suggested by such verses as 2:10 and 4:3-4 (read these).

C. Date and Place Written

First Peter was written probably around the time of the outbreak of the Neronian persecution, or A.D. 64.

From 5:13 we may conclude that Peter wrote this epistle from Babylon. If the reference was a literal one,[1] there are two possible places of writing: (1) Babylon on the Euphrates (Mesopotamia), where it is known a colony of Jewish Christians lived as early as A.D. 36, or (2) Babylon on the Nile (a city of Egypt now know as Old Cairo).[2]

Many Bible scholars favor a symbolic interpretation of the name *Babylon*. Merrill Tenney sees Babylon here as "a mystic name for Rome, by which Christians applied to it all the evil connotations that had been historically associated with the Babylon on the Euphrates, and by which they could vent their feelings without being detected."[3] If the purpose of using "Babylon" was to disguise the actual origin, we can understand why the name as Peter used it doesn't have the *appearance* of mysterious symbolism in the context of the verse.

D. Immediate Setting

The Christians addressed by Peter in this epistle were experiencing fiery trials because of their faith (1:6-7). Slander by fellow citizens was one of those trials (2:12). Darker still were the shadows of persecution by the state that Christians throughout the Roman Empire feared. Everyone knew about those martyred by Nero in Rome. Would the fires spread to the Christians in northern Asia Minor? Peter wrote this letter not to assure the Christians that persecution would not come but to encourage them to stand true and endure

---

1. The main argument for a literal interpretation is that the whole verse (5:13) is a simple matter-of-fact salutation.
2. See G.T. Manley, ed., *The New Bible Handbook* (Chicago: Intervarsity, 1950), p. 399.
3. Merrill C. Tenney, *New Testament Survey*, p. 348.

suffering for Christ's sake and with His strength, even as the persecution grew more intense.[4]

E. Theme

The theme of 1 Peter is that of hope in the midst of severe trial. Such hope comes from a firm faith in the "God of all grace" (5:10). More reference will be made to this in the Survey section below.

II. SURVEY

Now that we have become acquainted with the various backgrounds of 1 Peter, we are ready to study the *text* of the epistle itself. Beginning with the next lesson, we will analyze the text in minute detail. Our present task of survey is to get a *general view* of the epistle as a whole.

There are three main stages of survey study: (1) making the initial acquaintance; (2) scanning the prominent individual items; and (3) searching for the integrating relationships. Don't get bogged down in any particular details in survey study. Study of details comes later, in analysis. In survey, the purpose is to see the larger things, such as general movements, turning points, and highlights.

A. Stage One: Making Initial Acquaintance

Scan 1 Peter in one sitting. You may want to do this in a modern version. The purpose of this initial quick reading is to get the feel and atmosphere of the book and catch its major purposes. Write down your first impressions of 1 Peter and any key words and phrases that stand out as of this reading. (If the key words and phrases are of a modern version, underline their equivalents in the study version that you will be using later on.)

---

4. To what extent the persecutions at Rome extended to the other lands at this time is not exactly known, but "Roman provincial governors tended to reflect the Emperor's will, and especially in any place where powerful elements were ill-disposed to Christianity there might well be a severe outbreak" (Alan M. Stibbs, *The First Epistle of Peter* [Grand Rapids: Eerdmans, 1959], p. 54). At least by the end of the century, in the time when John wrote Revelation, the churches of Asia Minor were undergoing severe persecution.

B. Stage Two: Scanning Individual Items

First mark in your study Bible any paragraph divisions shown on Chart C that do not appear in your Bible. Then read 1 Peter paragraph by paragraph, assigning a title to each paragraph and recording it on Chart C. (A paragraph title is a strong word or short phrase, preferably taken from the text itself, which serves as a clue to at least one main truth of that paragraph. See Chart C for two examples of paragraph titles.) Note: Each oblique space on Chart C represents a whole paragraph. For example, the second space represents verses 3-9 of chapter 1.

PARAGRAPH TITLES Chart C

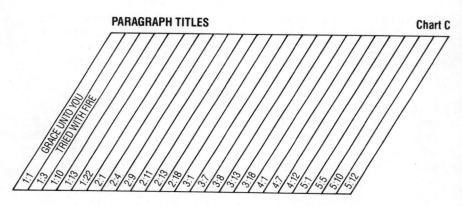

What have you observed so far about these subjects:

1. The amount of doctrine (teaching, such as 1:18-19), as compared with the amount of practical injunctions (such as the command of 2:2).

2. A comparison of the opening paragraph (1:1-2) and closing paragraph (5:12-14).

3. The opening word or phrase of each paragraph.

4. Key words and phrases. One of Peter's favorite words was *precious*. How would such a word come out of the crucible of suffering? Read the following verses where the word appears in the two epistles:

    1:7—trial of faith
    1:19—blood
    2:4—living stone
    2:6—chief cornerstone
    2:7—he (Christ)
    2 Peter 1:1—faith
    1:4—promises

C. Stage Three: Seeking Integrating Relationships

The Epistles are not unorganized ramblings of men written hastily at a camel caravan stop. The writers, in unique Spirit-inspired experiences, reflected much over what they wanted to communicate to their readers and then wrote the messages in their individual styles and vocabulary.

The organization of a book of the Bible is not always clearly discerned. This is so for 1 Peter. Whatever outline is arrived at for a Bible book, the student should not force any artificial structure upon any part of the book, just for the sake of a homogeneous or symmetrical outline. The suggestions for survey study given below have this counsel in mind.

1. Read your paragraph titles, and try to recall the general movement of 1 Peter.

2. The opening and closing paragraphs are typical salutations found in epistles. Set off these paragraphs from the others on your survey Chart C.

3. In constructing an outline, we should always look for *groups* of paragraphs of similar content. One group shows up clearly in 1 Peter—paragraphs involving servants, wives, husbands, and so forth. Locate these paragraphs in the epistle. Chart D shows this group beginning at 2:11 and ending at 3:12. Observe that the opening and closing paragraphs are directed to believers in general. The other paragraphs are addressed to more specific groups. List these:

2:11-12 _____

2:13-17 _____

3:1-6 _____

3:7 _____

3:8-12 _____

In this connection also note the appeal of subjection, or submission, directed to each group (e.g., 2:13; 2:18; 3:1; 3:7).

4. You no doubt have already observed that the subject of trial and suffering appears often in 1 Peter. Read each verse listed below, and record what is said about suffering in each case. (The first group gives the appearances of the word *suffering* in its various forms as related to Christ; the second group, as related to believers. The last group shows references to the subject of suffering.)

Group 1: Christ's suffering

1:11 _____

2:21 _____

2:23 _____

3:18 _____

4:1 _____

4:13 _____

5:1 _____

Group 2: Believer's suffering

2:19 _____

2:20 _____

3:14 _____

3:17 _____

4:1 _____

4:13 _____

4:15 _____

4:16 _____

4:19 _____

5:9 _____

5:10 _____

Group 3: Other references

1:6 _____

1:7 _____

2:12 _____

3:13 _____

3:16 _____

4:4 _____

4:12 _____

4:14 _____

In order to see where there is a concentration (if any) of references to suffering in 1 Peter, mark a small *x* on Chart C at each paragraph where each of the above references appear. It will be seen that that heaviest concentration is in the group from 3:13 to 5:11. We should keep this in mind when we make an outline for 1 Peter.

Note how early in the epistle there is reference to suffering and trial. The purpose of Peter in mentioning this in the opening paragraphs is to introduce it as one of the main subjects of the epistle. How is trial related to salvation in 1:5-9? We will be using this relationship as part of an outline in the survey Chart D.

5. There are important references to Christ's second coming in this epistle. Record each teaching below. (Other references *imply* this second coming.)

1:8 _____

1:13 _____

2:12 _____

4:7 _____

4:13 _____

5:4 _____

6. When the total structural organization of a Bible book is not clear, it is sometimes helpful to choose any one section of the book and, using it as a starting point, relate the other sections of the book to this base. The result will be an outline of one prominent theme of the book and will not necessarily represent a standard outline of content.[5] Let us apply this approach to 1 Peter. Keep referring to Chart D as you read the following:

(a) *A base section*. Let us choose 2:1-10 as our base section. In these three paragraphs are some wonderful truths basic to Christian living, namely, truths about who Christ is and about what our position is in Christ. (Read the passage.) Let us identify the section by the phrase *unique position*. Note where this appears on survey Chart D. Try to think of other representative phrases.

(b) *Related sections*

2:11-3:12. We have already scanned this section, observing that it is about specific Christian groups, appealing especially to a life of submission. Let us call this section "Life of Submission."

---

5. I consulted seven authors to compare their outlines of 1 Peter and found no two outlines alike, even as to chapter-verse dividing points. Of the seven outlines, three centered on the subject of suffering, one on salvation, two on Christian living, and one on a variety of questions.

1 PETER TRIALS, HOLY LIVING, and THE LORD'S COMING

Top section labels (with verse references):

- GRACE UNTO YOU — 1:3
- TRIED WITH FIRE — 1:10
- PROPHETS — 1:13
- HOLY — 1:22
- WORD OF GOD — 2:1
- MILK — 2:4
- LIVING STONE — 2:9
- CHOSEN GENERATION — 2:11
- PILGRIMS — 2:13
- KING — 2:18
- SERVANTS — 3:1
- WIVES — 3:7
- HUSBANDS — 3:8
- ALL — 3:13
- SUFFER FOR WELL-DOING — 3:18
- BAPTISM — 4:1
- WILL OF GOD — 4:7
- END OF ALL THINGS — 4:12
- FIERY TRIAL — 5:1 — AMEN
- ELDERS — 5:5
- YOUNGER — 5:10
- GOD OF ALL GRACE — 5:12
- GREET ONE ANOTHER — AMEN
- AMEN

1:1 — INTRODUCTION

SUFFERING AND SALVATION / THEIR OUTLOOK ON TRIALS
1:8 revelation / appearing
1:13

LIFE OF HOLINESS / HOW THEY SHOULD LIVE

UNIQUE POSITION / GOD'S CHOSEN PEOPLE
2:12 visitation

LIFE OF SUBMISSION / HOW THEY SHOULD LIVE

SUFFERING AND GLORY / THEIR OUTLOOK ON TRIALS
4:7 end
4:13 5:4 revelation

SECOND COMING

CONCLUSION

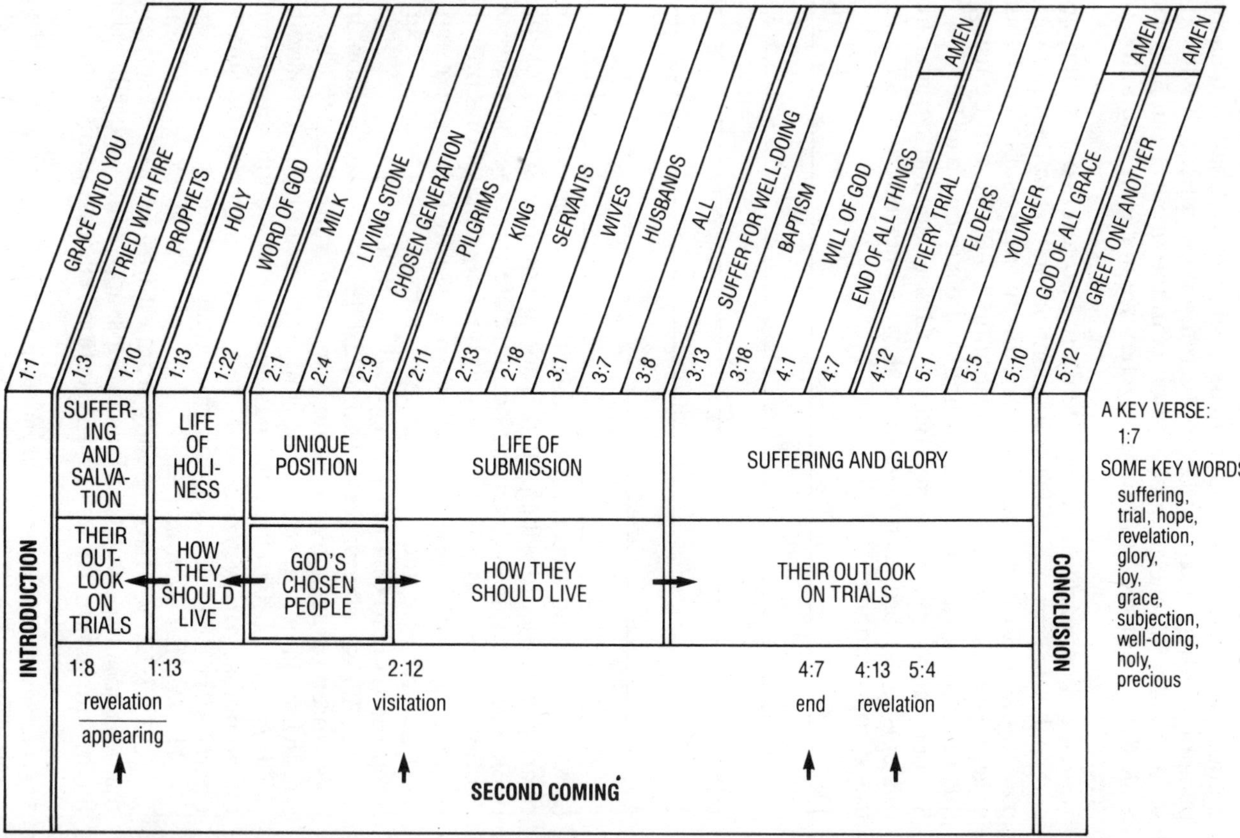

A KEY VERSE:
1:7

SOME KEY WORDS:
suffering,
trial, hope,
revelation,
glory,
joy,
grace,
subjection,
well-doing,
holy,
precious

1:13-25. A key command here is "Be ye holy" (1:15). Although other attributes appear in this section as well (e.g., "fear," v. 17; "love," v. 22), we will call this section "Life of Holiness."

3:13–5:11. Earlier in the study we observed the concentration of references to suffering in this section. Read the passage again to discover what truths are associated with that of suffering. One such truth is "glory." Underline in your Bible each reference to glory. We will call this section "Suffering and Glory."

Observe the word "Amen" at the end of 4:11. Some see here a climactic point in the passage 3:13–4:11. Compare 3:13–4:11 and 4:12–5:11, observing differences and likenesses.

1:3-12. Two subjects seem to be prominent in this section: suffering and salvation. Read the section, and observe how Peter relates the two subjects. We will call this section "Suffering and Salvation."

7. Let us now bring together on a survey chart (Chart D) the basic outline that we have arrived at in our overview of 1 Peter. Note the wording of the outline centered on "God's Chosen People," which is another way of wording the outline arrived at above. Also included on the chart is a title (reflecting three main subjects of the epistle); a key verse (look for other key verses); and key words (add to the list others that you may have observed).

As we move from lesson to lesson in our analytical study of 1 Peter, we will want to keep in mind this survey chart of the whole epistle. In doing so we will be respecting the surrounding context, which is an important principle of Bible hermeneutics (interpretation).

SOME REVIEW QUESTIONS

1. Describe the people to whom Peter wrote this epistle.

_____

_____

Where were they living?

_____

What was their relationship to Peter?

_____

What were their particular spiritual needs at this time?

_____

_____

_____

2. What is the theme of 1 Peter?

_____

_____

3. What are some important subjects reiterated in the epistle?

_____

_____

4. Reconstruct the survey chart of 1 Peter, exclusive of paragraph titles.

5. How many key words can you recall?

_____

_____

6. Write down the key verse from memory.

_____

_____

Lesson 3

Suffering and Salvation

Peter was a happy Christian when he wrote this epistle, and he wanted to share this joy. He shared it with his readers early in the manuscript. What made Peter rejoice was the wonderful realization that *salvation* was his and for eternity. Suffering and trial were only for the present; glory was forever.

As you study the opening paragraphs of the epistle, be thorough in all three areas of study, which are:

Observation—What does the text say?

Interpretation—What do the words and phrases mean?

Application—How does this meaning apply to me?

In connection with the last area, *Application*, it will help you in your study throughout Peter's epistles to think of these people:

1. Peter, the writer
2. the original readers
3. you as a Christian
4. other Christians with whom you might share this message

I. PREPARATION FOR STUDY

Bible study that is effective demands a good measure of methodicalness and organization. Each Bible student should develop his own particular methods and routines. This section of each lesson, Preparation for Study, is given to help you organize the "materials" (the Bible text itself) to be analyzed and to make related studies in other parts of the Bible as an introduction to your analysis of this particular passage.

1. Acquaint yourself with the literary device of *salutations* in New Testament epistles by reading the opening verses of various epistles (e.g., 1 Corinthians, Ephesians, 1 Timothy).

2. If you have not already done so, study the geography of Asia Minor, observing the locations of the areas mentioned in 1:1.

25

3. Read 1:1-12 in a free rendering of the New Testament such as *The Living Bible* or Phillips's version. This reading will help remind you at the beginning of your study of the text that Peter's letter was a personal message sent to Christian friends in need.

II. ANALYSIS

Segment to be analyzed: 1:1-12
Paragraph divisions: at verses 1, 3, 6, 10

A. The Opening Salutation (1:1-2)

1. Read carefully this warm greeting. About whom is more description given in these verses: Peter, or the exiles? Compare this ratio with that of Paul's salutation in his letter to Titus.
2. What are the functions of a salutation?

Does it intend to identify the main theme of the letter itself?

---

3. The first words of the salutation identify Peter as an apostle. The Greek word is *apostolos*, derived from *apo*, "from," and *stello*, "send," the combination of which means literally "one sent forth." Peter was *Christ's* apostle. What specifically was the relationship between an apostle and Christ?

---

4. The readers addressed are "strangers scattered." What is implied as to the reason for this status, in view of the context of the entire epistle, which we have already surveyed?

On the basis of this, what specifically was the relationship between such a "stranger" and Christ?

---

5. The readers are further identified as "elect" (v. 2). The word translates the Greek *eklektos*, which literally signifies "picked out," "chosen" (*ek*, "from," plus *lego*, "to gather"). What is the specific relationship of one of God's elect to Christ?

Observe from verse 2 that election is "according to the foreknowledge of God the Father." What does this suggest to you?

How would this truth of election comfort and encourage the scattered exiles of Asia Minor?

6. Record the references made in verse 2 to each Person of the Trinity.
Father:

Spirit:

Son (Jesus Christ):

This is an example of what is referred to as *economic Trinity*, having to do with the distinctive functions of each of the three Persons. What is meant by the particular work attributed to each Person of the Trinity in this verse?

Concerning the word "sanctification," two possible connotations are: *imparted holiness*, and *separation to service*. (Cf. also 2 Thess. 2:13.) The phrase "of the Spirit" may be read "by the Spirit." On the phrase "sprinkling of the blood of Jesus Christ," compare Hebrews 9:19; 10:22; 12:24.
7. The words of benediction at the end of verse 2 sound commonplace to us because of our familiarity with them from church worship services. Try to catch the import of the words as they came to the exiles in need of grace and peace, and you will have a greater appreciation of the function of such a benediction for even the twentieth century reader, *which you are!*

B. Salvation and Suffering (1:3-12)

1. Note that we are treating verses 3-12 as a group of three paragraphs, with paragraph divisions at verses 3, 6, and 10. If your study Bible does not already show divisions at these verses, mark your Bible accordingly.
2. Read the three paragraphs in your study Bible, marking with pencil or pen on the pages as you observe such things as strong words and phrases. After the reading, record your answers to these questions:

27

What is the *main* point of each paragraph?

_____

_____

What key words stand out?

_____

What is the atmosphere, or tone, of the first and second paragraphs?

_____

The last paragraph does not have as strong a tonal quality as the two preceding, but there is still a tone here. What is it?

_____

3. Observe how long the sentences are in verses 3-12 of the King James Version. What does this suggest about the content of the verses?

_____

_____

4. Who are the main characters of the first paragraph?

_____

Of the second paragraph?

_____

Of the third paragraph?

_____

5. Make a list of all the verbs (not including "is") appearing in the first two paragraphs. Record these in the space below. Note how diversified the list is. What does this tell you about the message that Peter wants to share with his readers?

_____

_____

_____

6. What Persons of the Trinity are referred to in 1:3-12? What is taught about each Person in each reference?

_____

_____

_____

7. Read the verses again, and observe which ones speak about the blessed fruits of salvation and which ones speak about the sufferings and trials of the saved person. Mark your observations in your Bible.

RELATION OF VERSES **Chart E**

```
3.          Blessed be
            the God and Father
            of our Lord Jesus Christ

                    who ("which," KJV) according to his abundant mercy
                    hath begotten us again
                    unto a lively hope
                    by the resurrection of Jesus Christ from the dead,

4.          to an inheritance
            incorruptible,
            and undefiled,
            and that fadeth not away,
            reserved in heaven
            for you,

5.                  who are kept
                    by the power of God
                    through faith
                    unto salvation ready to be revealed in the last time.

6.          Wherein ye greatly rejoice,
            though now for a season, if need be,
            ye are in heaviness through manifold testings ("temptations," KJV)

7.                  that the proving ("trial," KJV) of your faith,
                    being much more precious than of gold that perisheth,
                    thought it be proved ("tried," KJV) with fire,
                    might be found unto praise and honor and glory
                    at the appearing of Jesus Christ:

8.          whom having not seen, ye love;
            in whom, though now ye see him not,
            yet believing, ye rejoice with joy unspeakable
            and full of glory:

9.          Receiving the end of your faith,
            even the salvation of your souls.
```

8. Now concentrate your study on verses 3-9. Observe how each verse is closely connected to the verse just preceding it, even grammatically. Chart E shows the text of the King James Version. The lines connect the related words and phrases.

Here are some things to look for in these verses (whenever possible mark these in the printed text of Chart E):
   (a) all references to the benefits of salvation (e.g., hope)
   (b) references to events of last times
   (c) references to praise
   (d) references to trial
9. Chart F is an analytical chart that shows how one topical study may be derived from this segment. Use the chart as a place to record some of your own observations and as a suggester of other studies.
10. Verse-by-Verse Analysis. Keep in mind the various interrelationships of verses as you analyze each verse individually.
Verse 3. The key word is "hope." What does mercy have to do with this?

_____

How is Jesus' resurrection related to it?

_____

What if Jesus had died but had not been resurrected?

_____

Who raised Him?

_____

Verse 4. What truth does each of the four descriptions give concerning the Christian's inheritance?

_____

_____

Verse 5. The word "kept" appears as "guarded" or "protected" in some versions. From what is the Christian protected?

_____

What does faith have to do with this protection?

_____

   Observe that salvation is spoken of here with reference to the last times, when it will be unveiled for each believer. This does not take away from one's assurance of salvation now. The grand truth of salvation is large, all-inclusive, and relates to time and eternity. Three aspects of salvation are these:
   (a) *Regeneration.* Spiritual new birth takes place the moment a sinner believes. Other works of God also take place at this moment, such as justification and adoption.

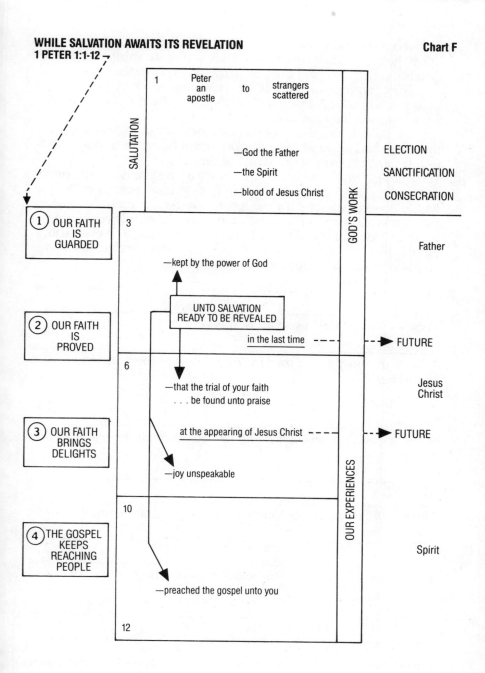

SALUTATION

1 Peter an apostle to strangers scattered

—God the Father
—the Spirit
—blood of Jesus Christ

GOD'S WORK

ELECTION

SANCTIFICATION

CONSECRATION

① OUR FAITH IS GUARDED

3

Father

—kept by the power of God

UNTO SALVATION
READY TO BE REVEALED

② OUR FAITH IS PROVED

in the last time ---- ----► FUTURE

6

Jesus Christ

—that the trial of your faith
. . . be found unto praise

③ OUR FAITH BRINGS DELIGHTS

at the appearing of Jesus Christ ---- ----► FUTURE

—joy unspeakable

OUR EXPERIENCES

10

④ THE GOSPEL KEEPS REACHING PEOPLE

Spirit

—preached the gospel unto you

12

(b) *Sanctification*. This is the continuing work of the Holy Spirit, helping the Christian to grow and mature spiritually. Someone has called this "the Christianizing of the Christian."

(c) *Glorification*. This is the crowning work of God for the believer, when he is given a new body and when his spirit is conformed to the likeness of Christ.

In view of the above descriptions of salvation, it is apparent that Peter had in mind *glorification*, when he wrote about a salvation ready to be revealed in the last time.

Verse 6. The word "wherein" may refer to the phrase of the previous verse, "in the last time,"[1] or it may have reference to the whole concept of hope for the future. (Berkeley reads, "Be cheerful on this account.") The word "temptations" of this verse can refer to any kind of testing—trials, such as suffering, and even solicitations to sin. How does Peter in this verse intend to relate "rejoice" with "heaviness"?

_____

_____

Verse 7. What is the key word of this verse?

_____

What is the purpose of *trial by fire* in view of the illustration used in this verse?

_____

_____

What do *proving* and *approving* have to do with the truths of this verse?

_____

_____

Verse 8. What two conditions for rejoicing are cited here?

_____

_____

What does the phrase "unspeakable and full of glory" mean to you?

_____

_____

1. Kenneth S. Wuest, *First Peter in the Greek New Testament* (Grand Rapids: Eerdmans, 1942), p. 24.

Verse 9. The word "end" primarily refers to the fruit, or result, of faith, whether of the present or of the future. (Cf. "result of your faith," Phillips; "harvest of your faith," *New English Bible.*) Compare this verse with the opening verse of the paragraph, verse 3.
Verses 10-12. What is said in these verses about
the prophets:

_____

angels:

_____

the Christians addressed by Peter:

_____

Why would verses 10-12 be of special encouragement to the exiles reading Peter's letter?

_____

_____

III. NOTES

1. The word "sanctification" of verse 2 is "consecrated" in the Berkeley Version. The entire verse reads, "Chosen in agreement with the foreknowledge of God the Father, and consecrated by the Spirit to be obedient to Jesus Christ, and to be sprinkled with His blood: Grace to you and peace in increasing measure."
2. *"Begotten us again"* (v. 3). This is a reference to the new birth. Compare the verse in a modern version.
3. *"Kept"* (v. 5). As a present participle, the word connotes continuous action. As Christians we are constantly being protected by the power of God.
4. *"Of which salvation the prophets have enquired and searched diligently"* (v. 10). Of this *The Wycliffe Bible Commentary* writes, "God has sometimes chosen to reveal through the sacred Scriptures mysteries beyond the comprehension of the writers (cf. Dan. 12:8, 9)."[2]

IV. FURTHER ADVANCED STUDY

1. Investigate the extent of persecution of Christians in the Roman Empire during the last half of the first century.

2. Charles F. Pfeiffer and Everett F. Harrison, eds., *The Wycliffe Bible Commentary* (Chicago: Moody, 1962), p. 1445.

2. Make word studies of the following words of the text: temptations (v. 6), trial (v. 7), love (v. 8), glory (vv. 7-8, 11) Outside sources on word studies include Bible dictionaries, encyclopedias, concordances, and specialized works such as W. E. Vine's *An Expository Dictionary of New Testament Words*; R. C. Trench, *Synonyms of the New Testament*; and R. B. Girdlestone, *Synonyms of the Old Testament*. Such works treat both the literal meaning of a word and the usage of that word in Bible times.

3. Make doctrinal studies of the following: election (v. 2), sanctification (v. 2), regeneration (v. 3), salvation (vv. 5, 9-10). Help for such studies may be found in books on doctrine, Bible encyclopedias, and commentaries.

V. APPLICATION

1. Peter loses no time in reminding his readers of the *greatness of salvation* that was theirs. How is a Christian's appreciation of and gratitude for salvation an incentive for *living* the Christian life?

_____

_____

_____

2. How are these twelve verses of chapter 1 a help to Christians undergoing persecution for their faith in Jesus Christ?

_____

_____

VI. WORDS TO PONDER

An inheritance . . . reserved in heaven for you (1:4).

Lesson 4

The Christian Pilgrimage

Peter was aware that a persecuted Christian, when overwhelmed by oppression, often crawls into a shell. Then he may hibernate as far as full Christian living is concerned. So now the apostle's burden in his letter was to stir up his readers mentally and spiritually by challenging them to *active consecrated Christian living.* There is something noble and courageous about a store owner who doesn't give up when his store and stock have been decimated by fire or storm but works with what he has, behind the sign "BUSINESS AS USUAL."

So this passage is about how Christians should live the Christian life. Peter presents basic guidelines now; later in the epistle (2:11–3:12) he treats specific rules of behavior (e.g., of servants, husbands, wives). Of the many basic commands that Peter might have chosen to write about at this point, it is interesting to observe which ones the Holy Spirit inspired him to select.

I. PREPARATION FOR STUDY

1. Peter's opening phrase, "wherefore gird up the loins," was an Oriental expression referring to a man's gathering up his long, loose robe around his waist. Of this, one writer says, "The loins were girded by gathering the long folds of the wide undergarment in a girdle in order to supply the body with a firm stay and to remove all hindrances, when the object was to work, to set out on a journey, to run, to carry a burden, to wrestle, or to go to war."[1] Read Exodus 12:11-13 to see how the Israelites were instructed to be ready to move on a moment's notice, in connection

---

1. John Peter Lange, *Commentary on the Holy Scriptures: Peter* (Grand Rapids: Zondervan, n.d.), p. 21.

with the Passover and Exodus. What do you think Peter was referring to when he said, "Gird up the loins of your mind"?
2. Peter quotes from his Bible (the Old Testament constituted the entire Scriptures in Peter's day) in verses 16, and 24. Read those Old Testament passages, noting particularly the contexts. Record your notes.
Leviticus 11:44-45

_____

19:2

_____

20:7

_____

Isaiah 40:6-8

_____

II. ANALYSIS

Segment to be analyzed: 1:13-25
Paragraph divisions: at verses 13, 17, 22 (mark these divisions in your Bible)

1. With pen or pencil in hand, read this passage, observing and underlining in your Bible all the strong words, such as *hope* and *obedient*. It may surprise you how many such words Peter is able to compact into a short space. This is typical of his writing style.
2. The list shown below includes many of the strong words of the passage. Add to the list other words that you have observed. See how many of these you can identify as to their *function* in the context.

gird	judgeth	raised
sober	fear	glory
hope	redeemed	faith
grace	precious	truth
revelation	blood	Spirit
obedient	lamb	love
lusts	foreordained	withereth
holy	manifest	word
Father	believe	gospel

3. Reread each paragraph and determine a theme or main point of each. Then work from the three paragraph themes to arrive at a theme for the whole segment.

THREE MUSTS OF THE CHRISTIAN PILGRIMAGE
1 PETER 1:13-25

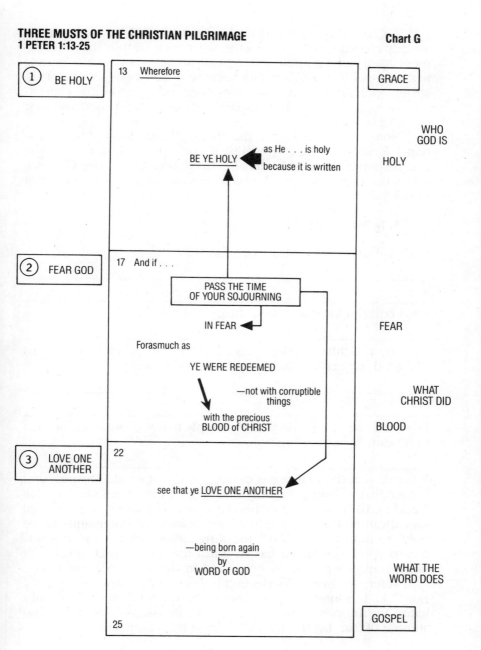

(1) BE HOLY	

13 Wherefore

GRACE

WHO
GOD IS

BE YE HOLY ← as He . . . is holy
because it is written

HOLY

(2) FEAR GOD	

17 And if . . .

PASS THE TIME
OF YOUR SOJOURNING

IN FEAR ←

FEAR

Forasmuch as

YE WERE REDEEMED

—not with corruptible
things

WHAT
CHRIST DID

with the precious
BLOOD of CHRIST

BLOOD

(3) LOVE ONE ANOTHER	

22

see that ye LOVE ONE ANOTHER

—being born again
by
WORD of GOD

WHAT THE
WORD DOES

25

GOSPEL

4. Chart G is an analytical chart of 1:13-25, with a few studies already recorded. Observe on the chart, for example, that this segment opens with a reference to grace and closes with a reference to the *gospel*. This is significant because in between (see chart) are strong command words such as *be holy* and *fear*. Use the chart as a work sheet to record other kinds of observations that you may make in your study.

Note the master title of the chart, "Three Musts of the Christian Pilgrimage." Three prominent commands chosen from the text (one per paragraph) are: Be Holy; Fear God; Love One Another. Let us pursue the subjects further, looking closely at the text in our Bibles.

A. Be Holy (1:15-16)

What are the bases for this command?

_____

_____

What contrast to holy living is made in verse 14?

_____

What do you think of when you consider God as being *holy*? (This is a good subject for discussion in group study.)

_____

_____

Does the command "Be ye holy" imply that it is possible for man to be exactly like God in holiness?

_____

It is true that the believer is clothed in Christ's righteousness and is therefore a "saint" or holy one (e.g., 1 Cor. 1:2; Eph. 1:1; Col. 1:2; Heb. 10:10; Judg. 1:3). This is positional holiness, or positional sanctification. But observe that Peter relates the command "Be ye holy" to our conduct (1:15; the King James word "conversation" means conduct). So he has in mind the experiential *process* of sanctification, growing in grace and in the knowledge of Christ. Paul refers to this as "perfecting holiness in the fear of God" (2 Cor. 7:1). It is interesting to observe the reference to fear in Paul's letter, for the next command in Peter's epistle involves this same attitude of fear. Let us now move on to this command.

38

B. Fear God (1:17)

This command is attached grammatically to two truths involving (1) a relationship to the Father (1:17) and (2) redemption by the blood of Christ (1:18-19).

1. *Relationship to the Father* (1:17)

The first two words of verse 17 may be translated "And since." Observe that God is identified in this verse as both Father and Judge. How does this combination help explain what is meant by the command "Pass the time of your sojourning here in fear"?

_____

_____

2. *Redemption by the blood of Christ* (1:18-19)

The first two words of verse 18 relate these verses about Christ's blood to the command to fear God. Study verses 18 and 19 carefully. Why should the Christian's knowledge concerning his redemption, as stated in these verses, spur him to walk in the fear of God?

_____

_____

C. Love One Another (1:22)

The command "love one another" depends on the clause preceding it, which reads (broken down into three parts):

"*seeing ye have* purified your souls"

"in obeying the truth through the Spirit"

"unto unfeigned love of the brethren"

In connection with this verse we may well ask the question, Why did Peter exhort his readers to love one another (i.e., their Christian brethren), when they were already loving the brethren? For your answer, consider these two things:

1. The two references to love are described in two different ways. What are they?

_____

_____

2. Actually, the word "love" used in both references in the King James Version appears as two different words in the original Greek text. The first reference ("unfeigned love") uses the word *phile*, defined by Kenneth Wuest as "an affection or fondness, a

purely human attachment for another, and perfectly legitimate."[2] The second reference ("love one another") uses the word *agape*, a word used of God's love (e.g., John 3:16; 1 Cor. 13; 1 John 4:8) which is an unselfish, sacrificial love by one who wants to serve the object of love without expecting something in return for it.

Read verse 22 again and determine how each phrase describes or qualifies Christians' love for each other. Record your conclusions in the spaces provided.

"purified your souls"; "pure heart":

___

"obeying the truth through the Spirit":

___

"unfeigned":

___

"fervently":

___

D. Other Truths

In the exercises above we have focused our study on three main commands of the passage 1:13-25. Let us now go through the segment and observe other truths taught in the text.

1. *Paragraph 1:13-16*
(a) What is the function of the word "wherefore" in verse 13?

___

___

(b) The words "gird up the loins of your mind, be sober" may be translated "having girded up the loins of your mind, be sober"[3] Explain this latter grammatical construction in view of the Oriental expression about girding up the loins, discussed earlier in this lesson.

___

___

___

2. Kenneth S. Wuest, *First Peter in the Greek New Testament*, p. 46.
3. Cf. Wuest, p. 35.

40

(c) What does verse 13 teach about grace and its relation to "the end"?

_____

_____

Compare this verse with 1:7 and 1:9.

_____

_____

(d) Christians are identified as "children" in verse 14. Compare verse 17. In what other ways are Christians identified by Peter in verses 1-13?

_____

_____

2. *Paragraph 1:17-21*
(a) Read the word "redeemed" (v. 18) as "set free." From what had Peter's readers been set free (v. 18*b*)?

_____

Keep in mind that the King James word "conversation" means "manner of life," or "conduct."
(b) What is taught by verse 20 about God's plan of salvation?

_____

What is the difference between a plan and the execution of that plan?

_____

What is the intent of Revelation 13:8 concerning Christ's death?

_____

_____

(c) Verse 21 tells us that it is *God* who transfers from the realm of death to the realm of glory. How does the verse relate *faith* to this truth?

_____

_____

3. *Paragraph 1:22-25*
(a) According to verse 22, how can a Christian daily cleanse his soul?

_____

_____

(b) Verse 23 brings in the subject of regeneration ("born again"), which Peter had introduced in verse 3 ("begotten us again"). According to verse 3, who is the one performing the regeneration?

_____

Through what means?

_____

Verse 23 says the new birth is "by the word of God." This could be a reference to the written word (Scripture), the incarnate Word (Christ), or both. What do you think? (Consider 1:25*b* and 2:2-3; also John 1:1; 20:31; Rom. 10:17.)

Keep in mind in your study of the phrase "word of God" that the word is likened to seed that is planted. The fruit of that seed is the new birth, and, according to the intent of verse 24 (quoting Isa. 40:6-8), both the seed and the fruit abide forever.

III. NOTES

1. *"Holy"* (1:15). W. E. Vine says that this adjective "fundamentally signifies separated (among the Greeks, dedicated to the gods), and hence, in Scripture in its moral and spiritual significance, separated from sin and therefore consecrated to God, sacred."[4]

2. *"Redeemed"* (1:18). Redemption is God's work of delivering the sinner from the bondage of sin by paying a ransom price. Here is an excellent translation of verses 18 and 19:

> For you know what was paid to set you free from the worthless manner of life you received from your ancestors. It was not something that loses its value, such as silver or gold; you were set free by the costly sacrifice of Christ, who was like a lamb without defect or spot." *(Today's English Version)*

IV. FURTHER ADVANCED STUDY

1. The lamb as a type and picture of Christ appears from time to time throughout the Bible. Chart H shows some of the key references to Christ as a lamb. Read the context of each passage cited, and make comparative studies similar to the ones shown.

2. Make a study of the subject of "fear" as it appears in the Bible. Include in your study that attitude that a Christian should have

4. W. E. Vine, *An Expository Dictionary of New Testament Words* (Westwood, N.J.: Revell, 1940), p. 226.

(e.g., 1 Pet. 1:17) and the fear he need not have (e.g., "Perfect love casteth out fear," 1 John 4:18).

THE LAMB IN SCRIPTURE   Chart H

PASSAGE	MAIN TEACHING	SETTING
1. Genesis 4:4-8 (Abel)	necessity of the lamb	for the offerer
2. Genesis 22:7-8 (Abraham and Isaac)	provision of the lamb	for another individual
3. Exodus 12:12-14 (Passover)	slaying and eating of the lamb	a family
4. Leviticus 1:10	character of the lamb	a nation
5. Isaiah 53	the lamb is a person	all elect
6. John 1:29-36	the lamb is **that** person	world
7. Acts 8:32-35	that person is **promised**	whosoever
8. 1 Peter 1:18-21	resurrection of the lamb	all time
9. Revelation 5:12-13	enthronement of the lamb	all the universe
10. Revelation 21-22	glory of the lamb	all eternity

V. APPLICATION

1. How would you describe a holy Christian life? Do you aspire to such living each day?

2. Does it make a difference *how* you live as a Christian? What attitude should undergird your behavior concerning God as Judge of every man's work?

3. What are some genuine evidences of pure, fervent love among Christians?

VI. WORDS TO PONDER

Obey God because you are His children; don't slip back into your old ways (1:14, *The Living Bible*).

43

Lesson 5

God's Chosen People

God does not command His children concerning Christian conduct without giving incentive, direction, and power. In the passage of this lesson the atmosphere is one of inspiration and encouragement, as you the reader are exhorted to

THINK ABOUT CHRIST ⟶ how precious He is

and to

THINK ABOUT WHAT GOD
MADE YOU ⟶ one of His chosen people

In the survey study of Lesson 2, we chose the passage 2:1-10 as the central, key passage of the epistle. Chart I is an excerpt from the survey Chart D, showing this key passage. This is the text of our present lesson.

GOD'S CHOSEN PEOPLE   **Chart I**

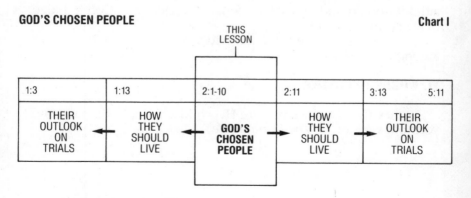

1:3	1:13	2:1-10	2:11	3:13	5:11
THEIR OUTLOOK ON TRIALS	HOW THEY SHOULD LIVE	GOD'S CHOSEN PEOPLE	HOW THEY SHOULD LIVE	THEIR OUTLOOK ON TRIALS	

I. PREPARATION FOR STUDY

1. In 1:13-25 Peter has just finished recording some strict commands of God involving holiness, fear, and love. Now he

44

moves into the bright and happy sphere of preciousness, to put God's commands in a true perspective. As you study the passage 2:1-10, keep in mind this preceding section of divine orders.

2. Peter quotes some Old Testament verses in this passage. Compare his sources, his quotes, and other New Testament verses referring to the same subjects.[1] Record your study on Chart J. For the last column (other NT verses), place these verses in the appropriate boxes: Matthew 21:42; Acts 4:11; Romans 9:32-33; 10:11; 1 Corinthians 3:11; Ephesians 2:20.

QUOTATIONS   **Chart J**

O. T. SOURCES	PETER'S QUOTES	OTHER N. T. VERSES
Isaiah 28:16	1:6	
Psalm 118:22	1:7	
Isaiah 8:14	1:8a	

II. ANALYSIS

Segment to be analyzed: 2:1-10
Paragraph divisions: at verses 1, 4, 9

1. You will observe that Peter's quotes are not exactly as they appear in your Old Testament. This can be explained partly by the fact that Peter is making a free rendering of the Old Testament passages.

Following procedures shown in earlier lessons, read the segment paragraph by paragraph, identifying a theme for each paragraph. How is the third paragraph (2:9-10) different from the second (2:4-8)?

Now read the passage verse by verse, underlining key words and phrases in your Bible. These are the "materials" for your analysis.

Paragraph 2:1-3
This is a transition paragraph, connecting what goes before (1:13-25) with what follows (2:4-10). Note the opening word "wherefore," which relates to the previous section. What is the command of this paragraph?

How is it related to the previous section of commands (1:13-25)?

Note: The phrase "of the word" (v. 2) should read as one word, "spiritual." "Milk" still refers to the Word of God, even though explicit mention of "word" is not made. Can the spiritual growth mentioned here come without *desire*?

How is verse 3 an introduction to the paragraph that follows?

Paragraph 2:4-8
This paragraph is mainly about Christ. He was introduced in verse 3 as "gracious." Now some further descriptions are given of Him. List these, and tell what each means. (Your earlier study of the Old Testament quotes should be referred to here.)
Verse 4:

Verses 6-8

_____

_____

How do you account for the fact that God's creatures (men) repudiate God's beloved Son? See verse 8 for help in answering this question.

_____

How are Christians described in verse 5?

_____

_____

As applied to Christians, how are "stones" related to "house," and how is "priesthood" related to "sacrifices" (v. 5)?

_____

_____

Paragraph 2:9-10
1. Listed in verse 9 are four pairs of significant descriptions of God's people, that is, Christians. Examine each pair and draw out of each as much of the intended meaning as you can.
(a) Chosen Generation. Who is the one who chooses? Compare verse 4.

_____

(b) Royal Priesthood. Here is the combination of king and priest. How does Jesus serve in the office of king and priest?

_____

In what sense are Christians royal priests?

_____

(c) Holy Nation. One of God's purposes in raising up the nation of Israel was that they should be an example to other nations of a true theocracy, with God on the throne. From Old Testament history we learn that Israel failed in this purpose. How can the church today, composed of all true followers of Christ, function as a *holy nation* in this world?

(d) Peculiar People. The Greek phrase translated "peculiar people" in the King James Version does not mean strange or odd people, but "people for a possession," that is, *God's own possession*. The same word for "peculiar" is used in the Greek translation of Isaiah 43:21, translated in our English versions as "This people have I formed for myself." See more on this word in the Notes section.

In what sense is the church truly God's own possession?

What are the implications and the responsibilities of this relationship?

---

2. What is the relation between these phrases:

BUT YE ARE — THAT YE SHOULD SHOW (v. 9)

Compare the use of "ye . . . are" in verse 5, studied earlier. What is taught here about accountability?

---

3. Verses 9 and 10 give three sets of before-and-after descriptions of the Christian. List these:

BEFORE	AFTER
called out of _____	into _____
were not _____	are not _____
had not _____	now _____

In writing these descriptions, Peter was no doubt thinking of the Old Testament book of Hosea. Read Hosea 1:6-9; 2:23. The names mentioned in 1:6 and 1:9 are significant:

Lo-ruhamah—"She hath not obtained mercy"

Lo-ammi—"Not my people"

Observe that Hosea 2:23 prophetically speaks of a transformation: those who had not obtained mercy becoming the objects of mercy; and those who were alienated from God becoming His people. How is such a description true today of Jews before and after their conversion to Christ?

_____

_____

How is it true of all members of the Body of Christ?

_____

In view of the transformation wrought by God in the heart and life of a person when he is saved, what should such a transformed sinner be doing to show his gratitude? (v. 9). What are some ways that you as a Christian can do this, in everyday life?

_____

_____

For a concluding study in your analysis of this segment, 2:1-10, compare the two words that appear at the beginning and end of the segment, "malice" (2:1) and "mercy" (2:10). For example, where does each one originate? Record your thoughts below.

MALICE (2:1)	MERCY (2:10)

III. NOTES

1. *"Sincere milk"* (2:2). As indicated earlier in the lesson, the phrase "of the word," which follows "sincere milk," should be translated "spiritual." The same Greek word (*logikon*) is translated "reasonable" or "spiritual" in Romans 12:1. The word "milk" is still a reference to the Word of God—spiritual food for the spirit of a man. In using the word "milk," Peter did not have in mind a comparison that the writer of Hebrews had when comparing milk and solid food. (cf. Heb. 5:11-14). Peter's sole purpose was to instill in his readers a strong thirst or desire for the Word of God, just as a newborn babe craves for milk.

Peter calls this spiritual milk (the Word) "sincere" milk, that is, without guile, or unadulterated. God's Word is not tainted with impurities. It is not weighed down with superfluous ingredients. It is God's pure, wholesome food for the Christian who wants to grow spiritually. *The Living Bible* paraphrases verses 2 and 3 thus: "If you have tasted the Lord's goodness and kindness, cry for more, as a baby cries for milk. Eat God's Word—read it, think about it—and grow strong in the Lord."

2. *"Lively stones"* (2:5). The same Greek word translates "lively" (referring to Christians) and "living" (referring to Christ). This is because of the believer's intimate identity with Christ.

3. *"Elect"* (2:6). The words "elect" (v. 6) and "chosen" (v. 4) translate the same Greek word *eklektos*, meaning "chosen out." Observe that the description "precious" (meaning "dear," cf. Luke 7:2) follows the word *eklektos* in both verses.

4. *"Confounded"* (2:6). The *American Standard Version* translates the original word as "put to shame." Another possible translation is "disappointed" (*Today's English Version*), based on a flavor of the word that has the "sense of being defeated or deceived in some hope."[2]

5. *"Peculiar"* (2:9). The *New English Bible* reads thus for this word: "a people claimed by God for his own." Wuest says that the original word speaks of a "unique, private, personal ownership of the saints by God. Each saint is God's unique possession just as if that saint were the only human being in existence."[3]

IV. FURTHER ADVANCED STUDY

1. Paul also refers to Christ as the chief cornerstone, in his epistle to the Ephesians. Compare Ephesians 2:19-22 with Peter's similar description. Among other things, note Paul's reference to "strangers and foreigners"—words that remind one of Peter's letter.

2. The subject of the mercy of God is an important subject in the Bible. With the help of a concordance and other aids (e.g., word studies), study various verses in the New Testament that refer to God's mercy. Among the verses that you will want to consider are: Ephesians 2:4; Titus 3:5; Luke 1:50, 72; Romans 12:1; 15:9; Hebrews 4:16; Galatians 6:16; 1 Timothy 1:2; 2 Timothy 1:16; Jude 21; 2 Corinthians 1:3.

V. APPLICATIONS

1. What kinds of "spiritual sacrifices" (2:5) can Christians offer to God? As a starter for answering this question, read Romans 12:1-3.

---

2. Kenneth S. Wuest, *First Peter in the Greek New Testament*, p. 55.
3. Ibid., p. 57.

2. Christian living involves the negative (e.g., separation from) and the positive (e.g., separation unto). In 2:1-2, the negative command is "laying aside"; the positive command is "desire." Can you say that one of these is basic to the other? How are the two related in practical living?

_____

_____

_____

3. Observe that desire for the Word of God (v. 2) comes from having tasted that the Lord is gracious (v. 3). Has this been your experience?
4. What are some of the *tender* words of 2:1-10? What do these words reveal about what the Christian life should be?

_____

_____

_____

VI. WORDS TO PONDER

See, I am sending Christ to be the carefully chosen, precious Cornerstone of My church, AND I WILL NEVER DISAPPOINT THOSE WHO TRUST IN HIM (2:6, *The Living Bible*).

Lesson 6

Life of Subjection

U p to this point Peter has been writing, as it were, a sermon addressed to a congregation. Now Peter moves to the counseling
room and speaks with particular groups (e.g., wives, servants)
about Christian living in their particular setting. This is the subject
of our present lesson. Chart K is an excerpt from the survey Chart
D, shown here to remind us of the location of this passage in the
entire epistle.

EXCERPT FROM CHART D **Chart K**

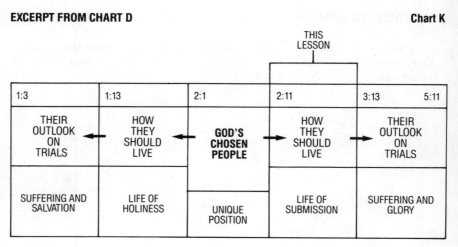

It is true that the Bible speaks to the everyday living of all people
of all time. Some parts of the Bible speak only to believers; other
parts only to unbelievers; still other portions to both believers and
unbelievers. All of Peter's epistle is directed to believers, and the

passage of this lesson is no exception.[1] For example, the servants of 2:18 are Christian slaves; the wives of 3:1 are Christian wives; and the husbands of 3:7 are Christian husbands. They were among Peter's "dearly beloved" (2:11). As you study this passage of the epistle, apply the many practical truths to twentieth-century Christians and, specifically, to yourself whenever you are involved.

I. PREPARATION FOR STUDY

1. Observe from Chart K that this passage, like 1:13-25, is about how God's chosen people should live. The earlier passage stressed holiness. The present segment stresses submission. Review 1:13-25 and keep this passage in mind as you proceed in your study of 2:11–3:12.

2. Refer to a Bible encyclopedia for a description of the profession of household servant, which was common in the first century. This type of servant is what is referred to in 2:18.

II. ANALYSIS

Segment to be analyzed: 2:11–3:12
Paragraph divisions: at verses 2:11, 13, 18; 3:1, 7, 8

Peter has just reminded his readers of their enlightened, responsible position as a chosen generation, royal priesthood, holy nation, and people of God's own possession (2:9). They were objects of God's mercy (2:10) and had received all the blessings that attend those who are the "mercied ones." Now Peter is ready to identify the demands incumbent upon God's children.

First, make paragraph divisions in your Bible according to the ones shown above. Then read 2:11–3:12 with these paragraphs in mind. Keep pencil or pen in hand and mark words and phrases in the text that strike you as being important, for whatever reason. These are the words that you will want to analyze in detail when you go through the text later on, verse by verse.

1. Acquaint yourself with the analytical Chart L, partially completed, which can be used as a work sheet to record observations and outlines.

2. Identify in each paragraph of the Bible text a particular *group* of people. Record these in the column titled "Groups." Ob-

1. This does not mean that the truths of a book addressed to Christians have no message for an unbeliever. For example, an unbeliever can learn the gospel of salvation from 1 Peter 2:24. Likewise, such a command as "Honour the king" (2:17) reflects a standard that all societies should follow in their community living.

		GROUPS	END or GOAL
(1) **TO PERSECUTORS** —good works	2:11	Pilgrims	glorify God
(2) **TO CIVIL GOVERNMENT** —obedience	13 SUBMIT		___
(3) **TO**	18 BE SUBJECT 25		___
(4) **TO**	3:1 BE IN SUBJECTION		___
(5) **TO**	7 GIVING		___
(6) **TO**	8 12	all	___

serve that the first and last paragraphs do not speak of a particular group, as do the other paragraphs. In this sense it is accurate to set off the first and last paragraphs from the other four.

3. Observe the repetition of the idea of *subjection* at the beginning of each of the central four paragraphs. The phrases appear on Chart L. Underline them in your Bible. Do you see any suggestion of subjection or submission in the first and last paragraphs? If so, record these.

On the basis of this prominent command of subjection, the master title shown on Chart L is "Life of Subjection." Keep this theme in mind as you continue your study of the paragraphs.

4. Subjection involves (1) those in subjection and (2) those over the subjects. On the basis of your study of who the subjects are (above), determine in each paragraph who they are to whom subjection is due. Complete the study already begun in the left-hand margin, as a series of paragraph points related to the master title "Life of Subjection."

5. Go through the segment once again, this time observing the attitude or relationship expected of the subjects concerning those to whom they are to be in subjection. Record your findings ("good works" and "obedience" are given as examples).

6. Here is another paragraph-to-paragraph study. Read the entire segment again, and note the references to purposes (that is, ends or goals) that justify the relationships of subjection referred to in each paragraph. This kind of reference is often introduced by the word "that" (or "in order that"). Record your observations in the far-right margin (example "glorify God" is already given).

* * *

Now we will approach the text in more detail, moving verse by verse within each paragraph. The outline followed below relates to the title "Life of Subjection."

A. Relation to Persecutors (2:11-12)

1. The word "Gentiles" has reference to the heathen pagan world, that is, to unbelievers. Whoever they are specifically, Peter says that persecution comes from them in what form? (2:12)

_____

_____

2. What relation to their persecutors did Peter urge the Christian exiles to have?

3. The opening words of verse 11 are "dearly beloved." Most versions translate the one original word in a similar manner (e.g., "dear friends," Berkeley). There is the possibility of a reference here to the exiles as beloved of God. If Peter had this in mind, how was it an echo of the previous verse, 2:10?

Also, how does it compare with the concluding words of the paragraph, referring to God (2:12)?

4. In verse 11 the exiles are called "strangers and pilgrims." Read the *Notes* of this lesson on these two designations. On the basis of the literal meanings of the word, how relevant and significant are these references?:

"abstain from fleshly lusts" (2:11)
"conversation [conduct] honest among the Gentiles" (2:12)
"your good works, which they shall behold" (2:12)

5. The phrase "day of visitation" has been variously interpreted, as seen by the following translations in different modern versions:

"When Christ returns" (*The Living Bible*)
"On the Day of his coming" (*Today's English Version*)
"On the Day of Judgment" (Goodspeed)
"In the day of inspection" (*Amplified*)
"When the Spirit influences them" (Berkeley, footnote)

What interpretation do you think best fits the context of the whole verse?

Will those who glorify God in the day of visitation be believers or unbelievers?

B. Subjection to Civil Government (2:13-17)

1. Observe the references to the highest type of earthly authority

(king) and to authorities under the highest throne. What is the reason given for obedience to civil laws?

_____

_____

2. What is one of the fruits of a law-abiding Christian, according to verse 15?

_____

What do you think Peter is referring to when he says, "The ignorance of foolish men" (v. 15)?

_____

3. "As free" (2:16). In what sense were Peter's readers a free people?

_____

According to verse 16, of what must people who are enjoying their liberty beware?

_____

_____

Compare the phrases:
As free:

_____

As servants of God:

_____

4. What do you learn from the references to God in this paragraph?

_____

_____

5. What does verse 17 teach about honor, love, and fear?

_____

_____

_____

Apply this to the contemporary scene in the world today.

C. Subjection to Masters (2:18-25)

In this paragraph Peter masterfully moves from a *problem* of the Christian servant's profession to a grand *consolation* for his soul.[2]

2. As noted earlier, the servants mentioned here were household servants.

57

Before we analyze the *context* of what Peter writes, let us observe the *form* of the writing. This will help answer some questions that will arise in our later analysis.

Read the paragraph carefully, observing how Peter moves from one subject to another. List these subjects below:

v. 18*a*: _____

v. 18*b*: _____

vv. 19-20: _____

vv. 21-23: _____

v. 24: _____

v. 25: _____

Note that the paragraph begins by referring to servants (Christian servants, that is) and concludes with a reference to their souls ("your souls"). Who is the main character in between these verses?

Jesus Christ is revealed in various ministries in the passage. Note these:

    vv. 21-23–Our Example

    v. 24–Our Atoning Sacrifice

    v. 25–Our Shepherd and Guardian[3]

That Jesus as the believer's atoning sacrifice has something to do with a Christian servant's attitude toward his master is one of Peter's main points in the paragraph. The progression of Peter's reasoning is shown in the diagram of Chart M.

So Peter's appeal to servants to maintain a good Christian testimony even in the difficult situation of a harsh master is bolstered by the warmhearted reminder to them that they became sheep of Christ's fold through an infinitely greater sacrifice than they could ever make.

Now let us study the paragraph in smaller units, verse by verse.

1. Read 2:18. Recall the phrase "servants of God" appearing in 2:16. What kind of servants are the ones of 2:18?

_____

Read the verse in some modern versions, to see other renderings of the words translated "fear" and "froward." List these.

_____

---

3. The word translated "Bishop" in the King James Version is translated by various versions as "Keeper," "Overseer," "Guardian."

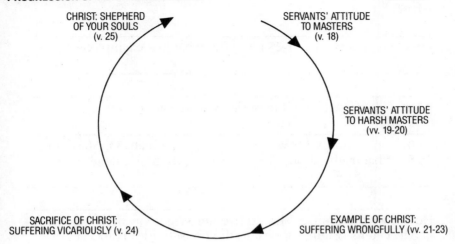

CHRIST: SHEPHERD
OF YOUR SOULS
(v. 25)

SERVANTS' ATTITUDE
TO MASTERS
(v. 18)

SERVANTS' ATTITUDE
TO HARSH MASTERS
(vv. 19-20)

SACRIFICE OF CHRIST:
SUFFERING VICARIOUSLY (v. 24)

EXAMPLE OF CHRIST:
SUFFERING WRONGFULLY (vv. 21-23)

2. Read 2:18-19. (Cf. Matt. 5:46-48; Luke 6:27-35.) What Christian virtue is needed in suffering wrongfully?

_____

What does Peter have in mind by the words "for conscience toward God"?

_____

_____

The phrases "this is thankworthy" (v. 19) and "this is acceptable" (v. 20) both translate the original text that would read literally "this is grace" (v. 19, Berkeley). What do you see of *grace* in the attitude for which Peter appeals in these verses?

_____

3. What is taught about discipleship in verse 21?

_____

_____

Compare the phrases "were ye called" and "follow his steps." What were Peter's memories of Jesus calling him to follow Him? (cf. Matt. 4:18-20).

_____

_____

4. Verse 21 says that Jesus left us an example to follow. Example of what?

How much of verses 21-25 identifies what that example is?

What does verse 24 say Christ did that we cannot do?

5. In connection with verses 22-24, read Isaiah 53; Mark 14:61; 15:5.) What truths about Christ's atoning death are taught here?

How does the phrase "should live unto righteousness" (v. 24) relate to Peter's original appeal to the household servants (v. 18)?

What does Peter mean by the phrase "being dead to sins" (v. 24)?

6. What different ministries of Christ are suggested by the titles *Shepherd* and *Bishop* (*Guardian*, Berkeley)? On *Shepherd*, read Psalm 23; John 10:11; Isaiah 40:11.

D. Subjection to Husbands (3:1-6)

Peter has two groups of Christian wives in mind as he writes this paragraph. Verses 3:1b-2 refer to wives whose husbands are unbelievers. The remaining verses are addressed to *all* Christian wives.
1. *Christian wives of unbelieving husbands* (3:1b-2). The opening words of verse 1 introduce the theme of the paragraph: "Likewise, ye wives, be in subjection to your own husbands." Then follows the reference to unbelieving husbands. For these verses, read the first appearances of "the word" as "the Word," (i.e., the Scriptures) and the second appearance of "the word" as "a word" (i.e., the wife's speech).[4] Also, read the two appearances of "conversation"

---

4. This second occurrence of "word" in the original text does not have the definite article.

60

as "conduct," or "behavior." In view of this, what is the most effective witness of a Christian woman to her husband?

_____

_____

Does this mean that the gospel should not be spoken by word at all to such a husband?

_____

2. *All Christian wives* (3:1*a*, 3-6). List all the desirable qualities of a wife whose relationship to her husband is well pleasing to God. What is the teaching underlying the instructions of verse 3 about adorning?

_____

_____

Determine the universal, timeless principle involved, and apply it to the present day in our own land.

E. Subjection to Wives (3:7)

This is a short but important paragraph about the husband's relation to his wife. What is due the wife from the husband?

_____

_____

On the phrase "dwell with them according to knowledge," compare a modern version reading.

Analyze the three reasons given for honoring the wife:
"As unto the weaker vessel":

_____

"as being heirs together of the grace of life":

_____

"that your prayers be not hindered":

_____

F. Relation to One Another (3:8-12)

With the words "Finally, be ye all" Peter comes to a concluding point in his exhortations to specific groups among the Christian exiles. What is the main exhortation here?

_____

Read 1 Corinthians 13 in connection with this passage. Why is love so important a trait in the fellowship of Christians?

What is taught in 3:9-12 about the spiritual law of returns?

III. NOTES

1. *"Strangers and pilgrims"* (2:11). The Greek word translated "strangers" has the idea of "having one's home alongside of." The word translated "pilgrims" means literally "those who settle down alongside of pagans." So Peter's command "abstain from fleshly lusts" was relevant—the Christian exiles were not to take part in the worldly engagements of their neighbors among whom they had taken up residence.

2. *"Froward"* (2:18). Some Christian servants worked in households where the masters were unfair and adverse ("froward"). An example of their harsh treatment was the buffeting (2:20) that the masters inflicted on their servants. The same kind of buffeting, or striking with fists, was inflicted on Jesus (Mark 14:65).

3. *"Hair . . . gold . . . apparel"* (3:3). Peter was here referring to extravagance for the sake of show. "Apparel" was the outer clothing of women. Secular literature of the early centuries reveals how artificial and immodest were the adornments of women in those days.

IV. FURTHER ADVANCED STUDY

Make a study of the Christian's relation to governmental authority in the first century. The book of Acts furnishes much information of this subject. Study also what Jesus said about this.

V. APPLICATIONS

On the basis of your study of this passage, write your own list of desirable traits of everyday living in today's world by each of these:

CITIZENS—relation to civil law

WORKERS—relation to foreman and employer

WIVES—relation to husbands

HUSBANDS—relation to wives

CHRISTIANS IN A LOCAL CHURCH—relation to each other

IV. WORDS TO PONDER

Christ also suffered for us, leaving us an example (2:21).

Tertullian (A.D. 122-50), Christian author of North Africa, reflected thus about Christ's example of suffering:

He Who is God,
    stooped to be born in the womb of His mother,
    and waited patiently, and grew up;
    and when grown up, was not impatient to be recognized as God.
He was baptized by His servant,
    and repelled the tempter only by words.
When He became a Teacher, He did not strive nor cry,
    nor did anyone hear His voice in the streets. . . .
He scorned no man's company; He shunned no man's table.
He conversed with publicans and sinners.
He poured out water and washed His disciples' feet.
He would not injure the Samaritan village which did not receive Him,
    when His disciples called fire from heaven to consume it.
He cured the unthankful;
He withdrew from those who plotted against Him.
He had the traitor constantly in His company and did not expose
    him.
And when He is betrayed and is brought to execution,
He is like a sheep which before his shearers is dumb,
    and a lamb that doth not open its mouth,
He who, Lord of angelic Legions,
    did not approve the sword of Peter drawn in His defense,
    . . . is spit upon, scourged, mocked, crucified. . . .
Such longsuffering . . . is found in God alone.

Lesson 7

A Christian's Attitudes in Suffering

As Peter comes to the last main division of his epistle (3:13–5:11), he returns to the theme of suffering. This is the theme with which he opened the epistle (1:3-12). Chart N shows this:

SUFFERING   **Chart N**

1:3	1:13	2:1	2:11	3:13 5:11
THEIR OUTLOOK ON TRIALS ←	HOW THEY SHOULD LIVE ←	GOD'S CHOSEN PEOPLE	→ HOW THEY SHOULD LIVE	→ THEIR OUTLOOK ON TRIALS
SUFFERING AND SALVATION	LIFE OF HOLINESS	UNIQUE POSITION	LIFE OF SUBMISSION	SUFFERING AND GLORY

Observe from the chart that in the opening section (1:3-12) suffering is related especially to the *believer's salvation*. In the closing section (3:13–5:11) suffering is related especially to *God's glory*. Read these references to glory: 4:11, 13, 14, 16; 5:1, 4, 10, 11. All but the first of these references appear in the passage of the next lesson, where the subject of glory is prominent. The passage of this lesson (3:13–4:11), with its emphasis on the Christian's *attitudes* in suffering, may be considered as introductory to the subject of glory. This function of introduction is not negated by the climax of 4:11, where a doxology with an "Amen" appears. More is said about this in the next lesson.

I. PREPARATION FOR STUDY

1. Read Genesis 6:1–7:1 (the story of Noah and the Flood) and look for indications of the long-suffering of God (e.g., Gen. 6:3) to which Peter refers in 1 Peter 3:20.

2. Read 3:15*a* thus in your Bible: "But revere Christ in your hearts as Lord" (Berkeley). This reading is based on the best Greek manuscripts, which have "Christ" rather than "God."

Also, change "conversation" to "conduct" in 3:16. By now you are aware how often this word appears in Peter's epistle.

3. Before studying the passage of this lesson, think of your own experience and situation as a Christian. Are you having to suffer for righteousness' sake? If so, in what ways?

II. ANALYSIS

Segment to be analyzed: 3:13–4:11
Paragraph divisions: at verses 3:13, 18; 4:1, 7

1. First read the four paragraphs to get a general idea of their content. Read them a second time, underlining in your Bible every reference to suffering, if you have not already done this in the survey stage of study. Note that suffering is not mentioned in the last paragraph. But how does 4:7 indirectly relate to this subject?

---

2. Try to identify a main theme for each paragraph. This may be difficult to do for some of the paragraphs, because a single theme is not always clear or prominent. Chart O is a partially completed analytical chart, showing some identifications of main paragraph content. Study these after you have made your own identifications of paragraph themes. Use the chart as a work sheet to record observations as you proceed with your analysis of the segment.

3. Record what each of the following references teaches about *suffering*:
3:13

3:14

65

A CHRISTIAN'S ATTITUDES IN SUFFERING

3:13—4:11

(1) ATTITUDE OF GOODNESS IN ACTION	3:13 —followers of good —righteousness —SANCTIFY CHRIST AS LORD IN YOUR HEARTS —good conscience —good conversation —well doing	LORDSHIP of CHRIST	Conduct **IN CHRIST**
(2) ATTITUDE OF NEWNESS OF LIFE	18 —bring us to God —quickened by the Spirit —resurection of Jesus Christ	CHRIST'S SUFFERING	
(3) ATTITUDE OF SEPARATION IN LIVING	4:1 ARM YOURSELF LIKEWISE WITH THE SAME MIND no longer to lusts of men but to the will of God	OUR SUFFERING	
(4) ATTITUDE OF SERVICE IN SUFFERING	7 —charity —hospitality —minister one to another 11	GLORY of GOD	God glorified **THROUGH CHRIST**

3:16

_____

3:17

_____

3:18

_____

4:1*a*

_____

4:1*b*

_____

4:4

_____

4:7

_____

4. What is taught about Christ in each paragraph?

_____

_____

_____

Compare "conduct in Christ" (3:16) with "God ... glorified through Jesus Christ" (4:11).

_____

5. Note the main topical study on Chart O, "A Christian's Attitudes in Suffering." What Bible text(s) in each paragraph is the basis for each of the four paragraph points recorded in the left-hand margin? What is meant by each attitude so cited?

_____

Now let us examine each paragraph individually, spending more time on particular words and phrases.

Paragraph 3:13-17
1. Note all the references to *good* in this paragraph. Why is well doing such a powerful reply to persecutors?

_____

2. Read verse 15. What kind of person might ask a believer to explain the hope he has?

_____

_____

In what spirit should such an explanation be given?

_____

_____

What is meant by "with meekness and fear"? (Cf. a modern version here; also cf. Mark 13:11; Acts 6:10; 24:25; 26:24-28.)

_____

_____

3. In verse 17 what does the phrase "if the will of God be so" refer to?

_____

_____

Paragraph 3:18-22
The middle verses of this paragraph have posed problems to Bible expositors. Before looking at the problems, let us discover the *primary* teachings of the paragraph. This is best done by observing the structure of the paragraph, which is diagrammed on Chart P.

ACTIVITY OF CHRIST   **Chart P**
3:18-22

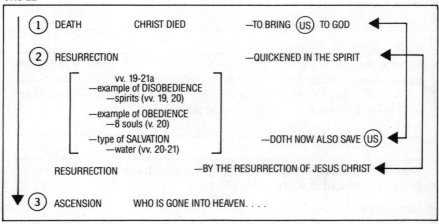

1. Whereas the first paragraph (3:13-17) is mainly about *Our Life*, this paragraph (3:18-22) is mainly about *Our Christ*. Note that the

68

main point of the paragraph is *Christ's work* in death, resurrection, and ascension. (See chart.) Observe in the text where and how these truths are presented.

2. Observe how the reader is brought into the story by the references to "us" (vv. 18, 21). Read the text and note how this is recorded on the chart.

3. Note how the middle verses (19-21*a*) serve in a parenthetical way, leading out from a reference to resurrection (quickened by the Spirit), and returning to that same subject.[1] What are the three subjects of this parenthesis, recorded on the chart? (See Notes concerning the "problem" passages.)

4. What do you think are the *main* truths of this paragraph?

_____

_____

_____

_____

_____

Paragraph 4:1-6

1. The core of this paragraph is the command of verse 1. For the meaning of the last part of this verse, compare modern versions, and study Romans 7:1-6.

2. Study the paragraph with the following outline in mind:

A. Command to the Readers
   Death to sin (4:1, 2)
   Their sinful past, as unbelievers (4:3)

B. The Readers' Unbelieving Neighbors
   Unbelievers' reactions to believers' lives (4:4)
   Unbelievers' accountability to God as Judge (4:5)

C. The Experience of Believing Martyrs[2]
   They suffered at the hands of men (4:6*a*)
   They live with God (4:6*b*)

3. How would these verses of the epistle be an encouragement and inspiration to the Christian exiles of Peter's day?

_____

_____

_____

1. The preferred reading of most versions is "spirit," not "Spirit." (The original autographs did not distinguish between small *s* and capital *S*.)
2. The thought of 4:6*a* may be this: "For, for this cause was the gospel preached also to them that are now dead." (See footnote of Berkeley Version.)

Paragraph 4:7-11

The emphasis of these verses is on what believers can give to others. List all such references. Apply these to your own life. Why is the mention of the glory of God so relevant to the discussion of Christian service?

III. NOTES

1. *"Preached unto the spirits in prison"* (3:19). Various interpretations have been offered concerning this phrase, including:

(a) Between the cross and the resurrection, Christ went to Sheol and preached the gospel of salvation to unbelievers of Noah's day, now dead.[3]

(b) Christ preached (proclaimed) judgment to these at this time.[4]

(c) The preincarnate Christ preached *through Noah* to unbelievers. When Peter was writing, these unbelievers were spiritual prisoners. (See footnote of Berkeley Version.)

(d) The preincarnate Christ preached to fallen angels.[5] A similar reference is seen in 2 Peter 2:4-5. It is interesting to observe that Peter refers again to Noah in the verses of the second epistle.

2. *"The like figure, whereunto ... baptism doth also now save us"* (3:21). The "figure," or counterpart, is "water" (last word of v. 20). Peter uses two illustrations involving water (ark, baptism) to teach that salvation depends on a heart relationship to God, not on water itself. Noah was saved in the Flood catastrophe because he walked with God (Gen. 6:9). In Peter's day a believer being baptized in water was saved because he believed in the risen Christ, Son of God. Water baptism was visible *testimony* to that faith.

Throughout the Bible, salvation is by God's grace, through man's faith. This was true even for an Israelite in Old Testament times offering an animal sacrifice. Of this, Wuest comments:

> The Old Testament Jew was saved before he brought the offering. That offering was only his outward testimony that he was placing his faith in the Lamb of God of whom these sacri-

---

3. If this were true, why did not Christ preach to *all* unbelieving dead, of all time? Or, if He did, why does Peter just cite those of Noah's day?
4. This interpretation is based on a difference between the word *kerusso*, "proclaim," and *euaggelizo*, "preach good tidings."
5. See Kenneth S. Wuest, *First Peter in the Greek New Testament*, pp. 97ff.

70

fices were a type. The moment he conceived in his heart that he would bring his offering to the Tabernacle, his faith leaped the centuries to the time when God would offer the Sacrifice that would pay for his sin.[6]

3. *"The gospel preached also to them that are dead"* (4:6). The total teaching of the Bible does not suggest a second chance to hear the gospel after death. This verse must be interpreted in light of the total teaching. The simplest paraphrase would be "the gospel preached also to them that now are dead." One writer paraphrases the entire verse something like this:

> With this end in view (i.e., the final judgment just mentioned) was the gospel preached also to those (martyrs) now dead, that they might be (as they were) judged in the flesh (and condemned to martyrdom) after the fashion of men, but might live in the Spirit according to God.[7]

IV. FURTHER ADVANCED STUDY

With the help of books on doctrine, study what the Bible teaches about the intermediate state of unbelievers. This is the period of time between death and the final judgment of Revelation 20:11-15.

V. APPLICATIONS

Enumerate some of the fruits of Christian living that will come forth for each of these attitudes:

1. being eager to do good:

_____

2. being conscious of God's presence:

_____

3. loathing wickedness:

_____

4. wanting to serve others:

_____

5. wanting to glorify God:

_____

6. Ibid., p. 108.
7. John Owen, quoted in *The Wycliffe Bible Commentary*, p. 1450.

VI. WORDS TO PONDER

If anybody asks why you believe as you do, be ready to tell him and do it in a gentle and respectful way (3:15*b*, *The Living Bible*).

Lesson 8

Suffering and Glory

Peter the apostle, as he wrote this epistle, was a healthy combination of realist and optimist. As a realist, he was conscious that
living the Christian life entailed suffering and hardship. As an optimist, he was confident that such suffering could reflect the glory
of God and that his Lord would be an ever present help and inspiration in every trial. The passage of the present lesson reveals this
mature and beautiful blend of character that was Peter's. The
twenty-two verses are a triumphant conclusion to an epistle addressed to oppressed and discouraged exiles.

I. PREPARATION FOR STUDY

Because the subject of *glory* is prominent in this segment, it
would help you to think about what the glory of God is, before
you read the passage. For example, recall the Christmas song of
angels.

> Glory to God in the highest,
> And on earth peace,
> Among men of His favor! (Luke 2:14, Berkeley)

How do you think God's glory is related to man?

_____

_____

II. ANALYSIS

Segment to be analyzed: 4:12–5:14
Paragraph divisions: at verses 4:12; 5:1, 5, 12

73

Mark the paragraph divisions in your Bible before reading the segment. In what sense does the last paragraph stand by itself? Observe the "Amen" at the end of verses 11 and 14.

Follow the study procedures of earlier lessons as you read the segment paragraph by paragraph. You may want to record observations on an analytical chart for the segment 4:12–5:11 (which is exclusive of the final paragraph of personal notes).

Make topical studies, paragraph by paragraph, of the following subjects: trials, glory, the help of God.

A. Various Trials

Concerning trials, C. H. Spurgeon once said, "You begin to reign the moment you begin to suffer well." Another has put it this way: "The richest chords require some black keys."

Learn all you can from these verses about the subject of trial. The outlines of Chart Q will assist you in looking for truths related to this subject.

TRIALS OF 4:12–5:11   **Chart Q**

4:12	5:1	5:5	5:11
Trials of Judgment —judged by the world (falsely) —judged by God (rightly)	Trials of Service —the load of responsibility —the demand of integrity	Trials of Submission —subjection (to one another) (to God) —but resistance (vs. Satan)	

B. Glory

Observe what is said in each paragraph about the glory of God. Record this below.

4:13

_____

4:14

_____

4:16

_____

5:4

_____

5:10

_____

5:11

_____

How is the believer brought into the stream of God's glory?

_____

What effect should this have on him?

_____

_____

C. The Help of God

Observe that each paragraph closes with a reference to the God-head. What kind of divine help is suggested by each of these phrases:
"faithful Creator" (4:19):

_____

"chief Shepherd" (5:4):

_____

"God of all grace" (5:10):

_____

Be sure to study the context of the phrases. (We will return to these phrases later in the lesson.)

* * *

Let us move now from the topical studies suggested above, to paragraph and verse studies.

Paragraph 4:12-19
1. The phrase "fiery trial" repeats a truth given earlier in the epis-tle. Where was that reference made?

_____

The Greek word (*purousei*) translated "fiery" appears in the Greek Old Testament as "furnace" in Proverbs 27:21 and "smelt-

75

ed" in Psalm 66:10. Read these verses for a picture of the purpose of God in giving His children such intense trial.

2. To what was Peter referring when he said, "When his glory shall be revealed" (v. 13)?

_____

3. What is there about the resting of God's Spirit upon a believer (v. 14) that brings happiness?

_____

4. For Old Testament background to 4:17-18, where the judgments of believers and unbelievers are compared, read Proverbs 11:31; Jeremiah 25:29; Ezekiel 9:6. In what sense were the Christian exiles already being judged by God?

_____

_____

5. What does 4:19 teach about God's work in us, involving (1) creation, (2) testing, (3) protecting?

_____

_____

_____

Paragraph 5:1-4

1. These verses are addressed especially to leaders of Christian groups (e.g., local churches), to whom is given that task of shepherding the flock. What three attitudes of shepherding are cited in verses 2 and 3?

_____

_____

_____

2. Observe that Christ is identified as the chief Shepherd (5:4). How should these words be of encouragement and inspiration to pastors today?[1]

_____

_____

_____

1. The word *pastor* means "shepherd." For example, the Greek word translated "pastor" in Ephesians 4:11 is translated "shepherd" in John 10:11.

3. In what sense are rewards, such as the crown of glory of 5:4, an incentive to Christian service?

_____

Is it selfish to look forward to receiving such rewards? Justify your answer.

_____

_____

Paragraph 5:5-11
1. List all the truths taught about submission and humility in verses 5-7.

_____

_____

_____

How is verse 7 related to verse 6?

_____

2. What three commands regarding the devil are given the believer in verses 8 and 9? Compare James 4:7.

_____

3. In what ways is the devil identified in the paragraph? (Cf. John 8:44; 12:31; Acts 5:3; 2 Thess. 2:8-10; Rev. 12:9-12).

_____

_____

4. Study carefully the benediction of 5:10-11. What is taught here about God?

_____

_____

What different shades of meaning do you see in the four verbs: make you perfect

_____

stablish

_____

strengthen

_____

Paragraph 5:12-14
This concluding paragraph of personal notes is typical of salutations found at the end of New Testament epistles. One of the interesting things about these salutations is the abundance of doctrinal and practical truths that are interwoven in them. Make a list of those appearing in 5:12-14, and if you are studying in a group, discuss each phrase at length.

III. NOTES

1. *"Elders"* (5:1). The word itself referred to men advanced in years. In both Old and New Testament days those chosen to offices of leadership were often older men. Hence the word *elder* came to designate *office* as well as *age.*
2. *"Filthy lucre"* (5:2). The Greek word means literally "base gain."
3. *"Devil"* (5:8). The English word translates *diabolos,* which means "accuser," "slanderer."
4. *"Silvanus"* (5:12). Silvanus was probably the Silas of Paul's second missionary journey (Acts 15:22).
5. *"Marcus"* (5:13). This no doubt was Mark, the evangelist, writer of the second gospel. Mark was a close associate of Peter and probably received much of the material for his gospel from Peter.

IV. FURTHER ADVANCED STUDY

1. Study the subject "glory of God" as it appears throughout the Bible. An exhaustive concordance or a book on Bible words will be of help.[2]
2. Satan is referred to in many ways and under various titles in the Bible. Make a study of this important subject.[3]

V. APPLICATIONS

1. What good comes from trials that God brings to His children?
2. How has God shown Himself to be a faithful Creator on your behalf?

2. E.g., W. E. Vine, *An Expository Dictionary of New Testament Words.*
3. Cf. Irving L. Jensen, *Acts* (Chicago: Moody, 1969), p. 32-34.

3. How does Christ fulfill Psalm 23 in your life?
4. Why is humility such an important Christian grace?
5. In what ways can a Christian *resist* Satan?
6. What does your life have to do with the glory of God?

VI. WORDS TO PONDER

Casting all your care upon him; for he careth for you (5:7).

A SUMMARY EXERCISE

Before moving on to Peter's second epistle, review the lessons of this manual up to this point. What parts of 1 Peter stand out to you as highlights? Recall at least ten important truths taught in this epistle.

Lesson 9
Background and Survey of 2 Peter

About three years after Peter penned his first letter to saints in exile, he was moved by the Spirit to write again. This message, though different, was equally important. One's study of 2 Peter should be bolstered with the conviction that what was important to those first-century believers is important to twentieth-century believers. So we will approach 2 Peter *as though it were written directly to us.*

Following the order of studies in 1 Peter, we will first consider *backgrounds* and *general survey* of 2 Peter (this lesson). The remainder of the manual will treat *analysis* of the Bible text.

I. BACKGROUND

There are not as many personal references in 2 Peter as there are in 1 Peter. Nevertheless, a fairly accurate picture can be composed concerning the epistle's background, from the materials we do have.

A. Author

The opening verse of the epistle identifies the author as Simon Peter, an apostle of Christ. This Petrine authorship has been challenged by critics, who have maintained, among other things, that internal evidence points to a date later than Peter's lifetime and that the style of the second epistle differs from that of the first.

External evidences of the church's *early* acceptance of 2 Peter as one of the inspired books of the New Testament canon are relatively scanty. For example, the epistle is not quoted directly by any of the church Fathers before Origen (*c.* A.D. 250).[1] By the end of the fourth century, however, the book's rightful place in the canon was recognized by the Christian church. The arguments favoring Petrine authorship are strong. Consider these internal evidences:

1. The name of Simon Peter appears in the text (1:1).[2]
2. The writer is identified as an apostle of Jesus Christ in 1:1.
3. The writer refers to an earlier epistle having been written by him to the same readers (3:1).
4. The writer was a close friend of Paul and had read many if not all of Paul's epistles (3:15-16).[3]
5. Autobiographical references in the epistle are about Peter. Read these:
(a) Mount of Transfiguration experience (1:16-18; cf. Mark 9:2-9).
(b) Christ's foretelling Peter's death (1:13-15; cf. John 21:18-19).

B. Date and Place

Peter wrote this letter from Rome around A.D. 67, when his death was imminent (1:14; cf. 2 Tim. 4:6, concerning Paul).

C. Destination

From 3:1 we conclude that the Christian exiles addressed in 1 Peter also received this letter. Others besides them may have been addressed in the second epistle, however.

D. Occasion and Purpose

In his first epistle Peter had much to say about opposition to Christians originating outside the group in the form of persecution. In this epistle he refers mostly to the more serious danger originating inside the group, namely, apostasy and false teaching. Thus his purpose in writing the epistle was to expose the false teachers and instruct the Christians as to what they should do to combat the ugly threat of apostasy.

1. Merrill C. Tenney in *Zondervan Pictorial Bible Dictionary* (Grand Rapids: Zondervan, 1963), p. 643, gives this reason: "The relative silence could have made it more susceptible to being overlooked or lost."
2. Some of the earliest manuscripts read only the name "Simeon." But this is a reference to the same person. (Cf. Acts 15:14.)
3. Paul was executed by Nero in A.D. 67, probably the same year Peter wrote this second epistle.

II. SURVEY

Follow the procedures of survey study suggested in Lesson 2. Here are reminders of things to do and things to look for:

1. Use pencil and paper in all of your study. Do not hesitate to mark your Bible. Remember, "the pencil is one of the best eyes."

2. Be on the constant lookout for key words and phrases. For example, observe how often the word "know" and its cognates appear in the book. Why would the subject of knowledge be emphasized in a book like 2 Peter, considering the dangers threatening the Christians?

3. Mark these openings of main sections in your Bible: 1:1; 1:3; 1:16; 2:1; 2:4; 2:10*b*; 2:17; 3:1; 3:11. Then read each section and try to determine a theme for each.

4. Observe references to true prophecy and to false prophecy in the epistle.

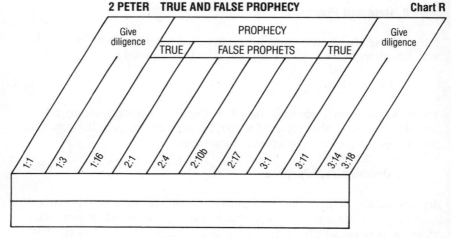

Key verse: "For we have not followed cunningly devised fables, when we made known unto you the power and coming of our Lord Jesus Christ." (1:16)

Key words: Know, remembrance, diligence, prophet, judgment, righteous

5. Observe the various exhortations and commands.

6. What do you think is the main theme of 2 Peter? On this basis, arrive at a title for the book.

7. Try to come up with a simplified survey chart for 2 Peter, on the basis of your studies thus far. For example, if any of the sections identified above (No. 3) treat a common subject, reflect this

on the chart. The survey Chart R may suggest other ways to outline 2 Peter. Study this chart, and keep it in mind as you begin your *analysis* of the Bible text (next lessons).

8. By now you have begun to sense that Peter's purposes in writing 2 Peter were different from those of his first epistle. The following comparison summarizes some of those differences:[4]

1 Peter	2 Peter
1. emphasis: suffering	emphasis: false teaching
2. suffering of Christ	glory to follow
3. redemptive title: Christ	title of dominion: Lord
4. consolation	warning
5. hope to face trial	full knowledge to face error

4. From Merrill F. Unger, *Unger's Bible Handbook* (Chicago: Moody, 1966), p. 809.

Lesson 10

The Man Who Knows God

Peter opens his letter on a high note—extolling the virtues of an intimate knowledge of God. "Learn to know Him better and better!" was Peter's urgent counsel.[1] He was convinced that such knowledge was an antidote to false teaching and apostasy that were threatening the spiritual health of his Christian friends.

Christians today face the same spiritual foes of Peter's day. Not a few have succumbed to the deadening influences of false teachers and have thus brought shame to the name of Jesus. Let us approach this passage with an intense desire to know God better and better in His Son Jesus Christ and so have light for living the Christian life.

I. PREPARATION FOR STUDY

1. Keep in mind as you study this passage what its place is in the whole epistle. Chart S, an excerpt from Chart R, shows this.

EXCERPT FROM CHART R   **Chart S**

1:1	1:16	2:1	3:1	3:11	3:18
GIVE DILIGENCE	TRUE PROPHECY	False Prophets	TRUE PROPHECY	GIVE DILIGENCE	

2. In order to clarify the wording of the King James Version at certain places, make these notations:

---

1. 2 Peter 1:2*b*, *The Living Bible*.

84

verse 3:   read "According as" as "For"
verse 5:   read "And besides this" as "For this very reason"
verse 11: read "ministered" as "supplied"
verse 15: read "Moreover I will endeavor" as "I will endeavor, then"

II. ANALYSIS

Segment to be analyzed: 1:1-15
Paragraph divisions: at verses 1, 3, 12

1. As you read the segment a few times, note words and phrases. What are the important *repeated* words and phrases?

_____

_____

_____

2. Try recording your observations of this segment of three paragraphs on an analytical chart, similar to those shown in previous lessons. Be sure to include a main theme for each paragraph.
3. Starting with the following outline, see how much the Bible text has to say about the subject indicated:[2]

THE MAN WHO KNOWS GOD
I.   Is Blessed for This Knowledge (1:1-2)
II. Acts on This Knowledge (1:3-11)
III. Should Not Forget What He Knows (1:12-15)

4. Let us look briefly at each paragraph. (Let these study suggestions be just starters of other inquiries.)

Paragraph 1:1-2
1. Note the phrase "precious faith." Recall the study made in Lesson 1 on *precious things*.
2. What does verse 1 teach about the righteousness of God and Christ?

_____

_____

_____

2. This procedure is known as the deductive method. Its counterpart, the inductive method, starts with the host of separate facts and arrives at an outline.

85

3. What does verse 2 teach about one's knowledge of God and Christ?

_____

_____

Paragraph 1:3-11
1. The first part of the paragraph (vv. 3-4) records what has been given to a believer. Make a list of these.

_____

_____

What does it mean to be "partakers of the divine nature" (v. 4)?

_____

_____

2. The last part of the paragraph (vv. 5-10) teaches what the believer must do in light of what has been given him. What must he do?

_____

_____

3. What progression do you see in the list of steps toward spiritual maturity given in verses 5-7? Think much about this.
> faith
> virtue
> knowledge
> temperance
> patience
> godliness
> brotherly kindness
> charity (love)

4. What is meant by the command to "give diligence" (1:5, 10)?

_____

_____

In what way is this kind of diligence a preventive against falling spiritually (1:10)?

_____

What does it mean "to make your calling and election sure" (1:10)? (Compare various versions for your answer.)

_____

_____

Paragraph 1:12-15

1. According to this paragraph, what was one big need of Peter's readers at this time?

_____

How could Peter help them?

_____

_____

2. Read John 21:18-19 in connection with verse 14.
3. Make a list of all the truths taught about "knowledge" in 1:1-15.

_____

_____

_____

_____

NOTES

1. *"Partakers of the divine nature"* (1:4). The instrument used of God to make human beings partakers of His nature is the Word ("promises" of v. 4*a*). Of this, George Cramer writes:

> Promises have spiritual substance and meaning only as they lead the believer into a dynamic relationship with the One giving the promises.... Thus maintaining this vital bond, the passions and habits of the old nature slough off and characteristics of the new nature have opportunity to become established in life and character.[3]

2. *"Ye shall never fall"* (1:10). The word translated "fall" means to stumble. The Berkeley Version translates verse 10 thus: "Exert yourselves the more then, brothers, to confirm your calling and election, for if you practice these things you will never stumble." Peter's appeal is essentially: "Walk with care. Accidents (stumblings) don't just happen; they are caused."

IV. FURTHER ADVANCED STUDY

There is a suggestion of rewards in heaven by the words of 1:11: "For so an entrance shall be ministered [supplied] unto you *abundantly* into the everlasting kingdom...." Make a study of this as-

3. George H. Cramer, *First and Second Peter* (Chicago: Moody, 1967), p. 88.

pect of the life hereafter: degrees of reward in heaven, and degrees of punishment in hell.

V. APPLICATIONS

1. Show how the steps of 1:5-7 can be the active experience of a Christian.
2. What does it take to "stir you up" (cf. 1:13) concerning things of God?

VI. WORDS TO PONDER

For as you know Him better, He will give you, through His great power, everything you need for living a truly good life: He even shares His own glory and His own goodness with us! (1:3, *The Living Bible*).

Lesson 11

True and False Prophecy

Peter now comes to the heart of his epistle; his subject is prophets and teachers—the true and the false. The apostle had just written that he wanted to stir up his readers by reminding them of past things (1:12-15). Now he seeks to stir them up concerning things present and things to come. On the bright side, he reminds his Christian readers of the inspiring prophecy of Christ's return. On the dark side are his descriptions of the shocking state and destiny of false teachers and their followers. You will want to linger long over these verses.

This one lesson is devoted to a long section of 2 Peter. Do not attempt to study the entire lesson as one unit. Rather, break up your study into smaller units so that you can spend time with the Bible text as long as necessary. If you are studying with a group, the group leader should determine the length of each study unit.

I. PREPARATION FOR STUDY

Prophets of Bible times were both forthtellers and foretellers. As forthtellers they preached, among other things, the righteous judgments of God—blessing for obedience and condemnation for disobedience. As foretellers they predicted events of the future. Peter uses the words "prophet" and "prophecy" in the large sense, not restricted to foretelling alone (cf. 1:19-21; 2:1). This also is how we will use the words in the manual.

As preparation for analyzing each part, read 1:16–3:10 in one sitting, with the survey outline of Chart T in mind.
Observe in your reading how each of the four sections under False Prophets leads into the next section. For example:

> 2:1-3. *General Statement.*
> "There shall be false teachers"

89

1:16	2:1				3:1 3:10
TRUE PROPHECY	FALSE PROPHETS				TRUE PROPHECY
Christ's Second Coming	General Statement	**2:4** Law of Recompense	**2:10b** Description of Unrighteous	**2:17** Destiny of Unrighteous	Christ's Second Coming

2:4-10*a*.	*Law of Recompense.*
	These unrighteous men will reap judgment (just as the righteous will be rewarded).
2:10*b*-16.	*Description of the Unrighteous.*
	(The one group of 2:4-10*a* is singled out.)
2:17-22.	*Destiny of the Unrighteous.*
	(Their destiny is spelled out in more detail.)

II. ANALYSIS

Section to be analyzed: 1:16–3:10
Paragraph divisions: at verses 1:16; 2:1, 4, 10*b*, 17; 3:1, 8

A. Paragraph 1:16-21: The Surety of Christ's Second Coming

1. In view of the context, the phrase "coming of our Lord Jesus Christ" had reference to Christ's second coming. What main point does Peter establish in verses 16-18?

_____

2. The word "prophecy" appears in each of the last three verses of the paragraph. This is Bible prophecy (cf. v. 20). What do you learn about this subject from these verses?

_____

_____

90

Compare what Peter had written about prophecy in 1 Peter 1:10-12. Verses 19-21 can also be applied to *all* Old Testament writings, not only to the prophetic passages. Study these verses in the light of this larger meaning of the word *prophecy*. For example, what does verse 21 teach about the inspiration "process" by which the Scriptures came into being?

_____

B. Paragraph 2:1-3: General Statement About False Teaching

This paragraph is about false teachers. What descriptions are given of the teachers themselves, their message, and their motives?

_____

_____

_____

_____

C. Paragraph 2:4-10*a*: Law of Recompense

Observe the two opposite destinies illustrated here. According to these examples, what brings punishment and what brings deliverance?

_____

_____

D. Paragraph 2:10*b*-16: Description of the Unrighteous

Make a list of all the descriptions of evil given in these pungent verses.

_____

_____

_____

_____

E. Paragraph 2:17-22: Destiny of the Unrighteous

What is the main emphasis of this paragraph?

_____

What is taught about accountability and apostasy in verses 20-22?

_____

_____

F. Paragraph 3:1-7: The Fact of Christ's Coming Questioned

Study this paragraph carefully, noting the scoffers' challenge concerning Christ's second coming, and Peter's answer.

1. *The challenge* (3:4). How was the challenge based on a supposed status quo situation?

_____

_____

2. *Peter's answer* (3:5-7). Peter cites three supernatural events originating by decree of God (Word of God):

(a) FIRST. The universe was created ("heavens and earth") (3:5).[1]

(b) LATER. The world perished in the Flood (3:6). (The word "whereby" connects the Flood with God's Word. Literally, the Greek is "through which things," i.e., through the Word of God and the flood water.)[2]

(c) YET TO COME. Dissolution of the universe "by the same word of God" (3:7). Peter cited the Flood cataclysm to disprove historically the status quo argument of the scoffers. Having done that, Peter clinched his original point by saying that history can and will repeat itself—another cataclysm will take place, at God's command, in the "day of judgment" (3:7).[3] This will be the dissolution of the universe.

G. Paragraph 3:8-10: The Delay of Christ's Coming Justified

In this paragraph Peter answers another question regarding the Lord's coming, which would sound like this: "If Christ *is* coming again, what delays Him?" What is Peter's answer?

_____

_____

1. *Today's English Version* interprets 3:5*b* thus: "Long ago God spoke, and the heavens and earth were created."
2. Cf. Charles F. Pfeiffer and Everett F. Harrison, eds., *The Wycliffe Bible Commentary*, p. 1461.
3. The "day of judgment" is also called the "day of the Lord" (3:10) and "day of God" (3:12). This is not a twenty-four-hour day but an extended period of time, the dawn of which will be Christ's coming to rapture the church.

What does the statement "The day of the Lord will come as a thief in the night" (v. 10) add to what Peter has said in verse 9 about the Lord's coming? (Note the strength of the word "But.") (On 3:10*a*, cf. Matt. 24:43; Luke 12:39; 1 Thess. 5:2; Rev. 3:3; 16:15.)

Make a list of ten important truths taught by this section of 2 Peter that you have just studied (1:16–3:10).

III. NOTES

1. *"Moved by the Holy Ghost"* (1:21). The word translated "moved" is literally "carried along." *Today's English Version* translates 1:21*b* thus: "Men were carried along by the Holy Spirit as they spoke the message that came from God." This verse of Peter teaches that the *writers* of the Bible were inspired. In 2 Timothy 3:16 is the testimony that the *writings* were inspired.

2. *"Day of the Lord"* (3:10); *"day of God"* (3:12). The context seems to indicate that Peter is using two different phrases to refer to the same time. Cramer writes, "Rather than referring to two different periods, each with its own significance, these terms simply refer to that time when God sets His hand to consummate sin and wickedness, *bringing to an end the day of man*."[4]

3. *"Great noise . . . fervent heat"* (3:10). The cataclysmic dissolution of the physical world, involving this kind of noise and heat, is not a strange picture to this twentieth century nuclear age.

IV. FURTHER ADVANCED STUDY

1. Study the experience of Peter in the presence of the transfigured Christ, as recorded by Mark 9:2-9. How would you have been impressed, had this been your experience?

2. Does the surrounding context of 3:6 (reference to the Noachic flood) lend any support to the position that the flood of Noah's day was of worldwide proportion?

V. APPLICATIONS

Make a list of ten important spiritual applications that may be derived from the passage of this lesson.

---

4. George H. Cramer, *First and Second Peter*, p. 120.

VI. WORDS TO PONDER

And so the Lord knows how to rescue godly men from their trials, and how to keep the wicked under punishment for the Day of Judgment, especially those who follow their filthy bodily lusts and despise God's authority (2:9-10*a*, *Today's English Version.*)

Lesson 12
A Final Exhortation

These last verses naturally conclude a letter to Christians threatened by false teaching and apostasy. Peter had opened the letter by appealing to them to by diligent in their Christian living.
Now he repeats that appeal, based on the serious facts he has recorded in the body of the epistle.

I. PREPARATION FOR STUDY

1. Review the content of the epistle up to this concluding
point. Observe how the appeal of 3:11 follows naturally the
prophecy of 3:10.
2. Read the concluding doxology of the first epistle (5:10-11)
and compare it with the last two verses of 2 Peter (3:17-18).

II. ANALYSIS

Segment to be analyzed: 3:11-18
Paragraph titles: at verses 11, 14, 17

Observe the continuity of Peter's thought from paragraph to paragraph:

3:11-12	"Seeing then . . . looking for"
3:14	"Wherefore . . . seeing that ye look for such things"
3:17	"Therefore . . . seeing ye know these things"

Paragraph 3:11-13
1. What physical cataclysm is inevitable?

---

2. What should be the Christian's attitude in view of this?

95

3. What is the bright suggestion behind the word "new" in 3:13?
Compare Revelation 21:1, 5.

_____

_____

Think much about what the new heavens and new earth will be
like.

Paragraph 3:14-16
1. What is Peter's appeal in verse 14?

_____

_____

2. What was Peter's purpose in referring to Paul at this point?

_____

_____

Paragraph 3:17-18
1. Compare the negative appeal of verse 17 with the positive command of verse 18*a*.

_____

_____

2. What does this final doxology mean to you today: "To him be
glory both now and for ever. Amen" (3:18*b*).

III. A CONCLUDING EXERCISE FOR 2 PETER

Review Lesson 1 and recall what you learned about Peter the man.
With this picture in mind, reread all of 2 Peter in one sitting. What
are some of your reactions?

* * *

A CONCLUDING THOUGHT

Of the many exhortations of Peter's epistles, the most important
must be the appeal to know God and His Son Jesus more intimately. J. C. Macaulay has penned these lines about such a personal
communion:

I read thy Word, O Lord, each passing day,
And in the sacred page find glad employ:
But this I pray—
Save from the killing letter.
Teach my heart, set free from human forms,
    the holy art of reading thee in every line,
    in precept, prophecy, and sign,
Till, all my vision filled with thee,
Thy likeness shall reflect in me.
Not knowledge but thyself my joy!
—For this I pray.

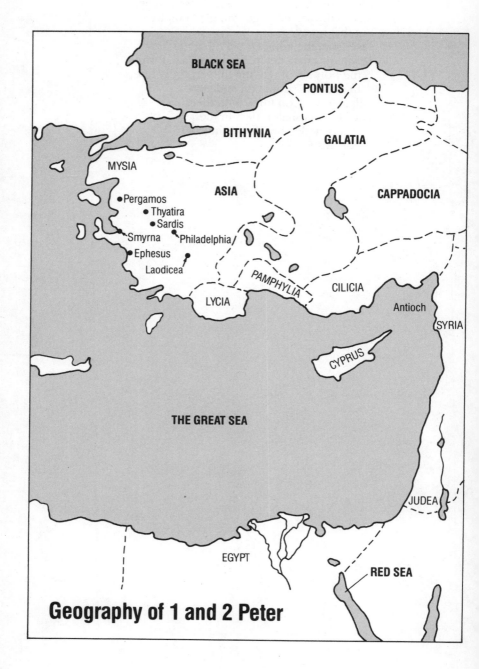

Geography of 1 and 2 Peter

Bibliography

RESOURCES FOR FURTHER STUDY

Everyday Bible. New Testament Study Edition. Minneapolis: World Wide, 1988.

Hallesby, O. *Temperament and the Christian Faith*. Minneapolis: Augsburg, n. d.

Jensen, Irving L. *Jensen's Survey of the New Testament*. Chicago: Moody, 1981.

Manley, G. T. *The New Bible Handbook*. Chicago: InterVarsity, 1950.

New International Version Study Bible. Grand Rapids: Zondervan, 1985.

The Ryrie Study Bible. Chicago: Moody, 1985.

Strong, James. *The Exhaustive Concordance of the Bible*. New York: Abingdon, 1890.

Tenney, Merrill C., ed. *The Zondervan Pictorial Bible Dictionary*. Grand Rapids: Zondervan, 1963.

Unger, Merrill F. *The New Unger's Bible Dictionary*. Rev. ed. Chicago: Moody, 1988.

————. *The New Unger's Bible Handbook*. Chicago: Moody, 1984.

Vincent, Marvin R. *Word Studies in the New Testament*. Grand Rapids: Eerdmans, 1946.

Vine, W. E. *An Expository Dictionary of New Testament Words*. 4 vols. Westwood, N.J.: Revell, 1940.

COMMENTARIES AND TOPICAL STUDIES

Barbieri, Louis A. *First and Second Peter*. Chicago: Moody, 1977.

Cramer, George H. *First and Second Peter*. Chicago: Moody, 1967.

Davidson, F., ed. *The New Bible Commentary*. Grand Rapids: Eerdmans, 1954.

Heibert, D. Edmond. *First Peter*. Chicago: Moody, 1984.

Pfeiffer, Charles F. and Everett F. Harrison, eds. *The Wycliffe Bible Commentary*. Chicago: Moody, 1962.

Robertson, Archibald T. *Word Pictures in the New Testament*. Vol. 6. Nashville: Broadman, 1933.

Selwyn, Edward G. *The First Epistle of St. Peter*. London: Macmillan, 1964.

Stibbs, A. M. *The First Epistle General of Peter*. In *The Tyndale New Testament Commentaries*. Grand Rapids: Eerdmans, 1959.

Thomas, W. H. Griffith. *The Apostle Peter*. Grand Rapids: Eerdmans, 1946.

Wuest, Kenneth S. *First Peter in the Greek New Testament*. Grand Rapids: Eerdmans, 1942.

————. *In These Last Days*. Grand Rapids: Eerdmans, 1954.